LIFELINE
A life of prayer and service

Meherangiz, a portrait

LIFELINE
A life of prayer and service

as experienced by
Meherangiz Munsiff,
Knight of Bahá'u'lláh

Meherangiz and Jyoti Munsiff

in collaboration with Pixie MacCallum

George Ronald
Oxford

George Ronald, Publisher
Oxford
www.grbooks.com

A catalogue record for this book is available
from the British Library

ISBN 978-0-85398-658-4

Cover design Steiner Graphics

Contents

Foreword

My mother, Meherangiz Munsiff, died on 21 June 1999. During her life she accumulated a vast archive of letters and materials related to her travels for the Faith which covered more than 147 countries. I could give you many reasons why I didn't get round to sorting out these papers sooner but suffice it to say that as an only child with no one to assist me, and working full time, the volumes of material languished. Then a guardian angel from my past and with whom I reconnected in Vancouver offered to help me. Pixie MacCallum came to Cape Town where she worked tirelessly to support me in creating some order out of the accumulated documentation and press cuttings. To my amazement, we found a manuscript created by my mother which effectively focused on distilling in book form a course which she had been giving on prayer and meditation around the world to thousands of Bahá'ís. I was quite shocked to discover this as she never mentioned she had embarked on this project, let alone more or less completed it and then abandoned it.

Ever since the demise of my mother, I was constantly being urged to write a book about her life and to publish her course which had deepened so many in the Faith by giving them a greater understanding of the significance and importance of prayer and meditation. I knew that I could never do justice to recounting her life because for seventy-five per cent of it my mother was travelling, as was I for my work, and I was not with her. Furthermore, the details of her travel teaching are contained in hundreds of reports, the only copies of which are in the possession of the Universal House of Justice and the International Teaching Centre. It would literally take volumes and a lifetime to recount. She rarely spoke of her achievements to me and so initially I felt it better to do nothing. With time and encouragement, I concluded that a glimpse into the life of a woman who had no education, and taught herself to read and write, and courageously travelled around the world sharing the teachings of the Bahá'í Faith, and comforting Bahá'ís who were scattered around the world feeling remote and alone, giving them encouragement and as much love as she possibly could, might, even if inadequate in its detail, provide inspiration to others.

As to the manuscript of her course never being published, even though the UK Bahá'í Publishing Trust was eager to print it, and after talking to others close to her at the time, I realized that the reason she brought her endeavour to an abrupt halt was because she didn't believe she was worthy to publish anything. Her lack of formal education scarred her perception of herself and she clearly thought she should forget the whole idea as she never wanted to do anything which might be an embarrassment to the Faith. She overcame her inferiority complex when she was speaking about the Faith because she would pray constantly for guidance and was convinced that, as for any sincere believer, guidance came when asked for. My mother would often tearfully say to me that she wished she had been educated as she could have done so much more for the Faith. As her educated daughter, I truly believed and tried to convince her that her reliance on Bahá'u'lláh, not on her intellect, was what had enabled her to be brave beyond description and overcome obstacles which anyone with any sense (and education) would have concluded were insurmountable.

The first part of this book recounts her life to the extent that I know it and experiences others have shared, but certainly represents only a minuscule insight into her achievements. These achievements were grounded in her unwavering and profound love for Shoghi Effendi, the Beloved Guardian, which was cemented deep in her soul during a unique pilgrimage in 1953 when our family had the bounty of being the only pilgrims in Haifa for eleven magical days. These few days defined the course of Meherangiz's life, not least by her arising to pioneer to Madagascar and the French Cameroons, rewarding her with the station of Knight of Bahá'u'lláh.

In presenting the second part of this book which is the manuscript on prayer and meditation – spiritual transformation – I have tried very hard not to edit it in a way that loses her personal style which in its directness and sincerity is what distinguishes her perspective on this subject, compared to the many erudite and eloquent treatises on this theme. I would ask you to remember that Meherangiz went to school for two years from the age of seven and that her accumulated knowledge of the Faith and its writings came about through painstaking reading, assisted by a dictionary. I can confidently say that by the time she died, she had read everything published in English authored by the Báb, Bahá'u'lláh, 'Abdu'l-Bahá, Shoghi Effendi and the Universal House of Justice.

For those of you who attended her course, I hope this will refresh your recollections, and to those of you who did not, both she and I would like you to understand that even if you have nothing and you think you are nothing, serving this Cause needs only faith bolstered by total reliance on prayer. Here is just one of the countless responses to her course: ". . . These four days provided me with the most transforming experience of my Bahá'í life. By praying, meditating, reading and discussing the Holy Writings Mrs Munsiff created an atmosphere of the Spirit where all of us felt the presence of Bahá'u'lláh. Truly I saw the greatness of this Cause, and the flood gates of my heart were opened to the Divine Power of Bahá'u'lláh. . ."

PART I

MEHRANGIZ'S LIFE STORY

The pioneers who opened this area [South and West Africa] to the Faith were, as the Guardian testified, "a singularly distinguished and devoted group of pioneers" and more than most they need heroic qualities and wisdom to deal with the manifold problems confronting them in this part of the world. One day their story will be told freely, and their glorious deeds will be cherished by generations to come[1]

Introduction

Meherangiz Munsiff was born to Sarwar Rashi Irani and
Bahaman Rashid Irani on 23 November 1923 in Bombay,
as it was then called, India. Her family came from a
Zoroastrian background. At the time of Meherangiz's
birth, her mother Sarwar was a Bahá'í but her father was
not, although he was to declare his faith in Bahá'u'lláh
twenty-three years later in 1951. Meherangiz was given
her name by 'Abdu'l-Bahá's sister, the Greatest Holy Leaf:
it means "the giver of love" and was to prove to be the
template by which she lived her life.

When Meherangiz was only two, her mother died
unexpectedly during a simple medical procedure, leaving Meherangiz and her sister Bahaiya (always known
as Molly) motherless and with a father who, devastated
by the loss of his beloved wife, rejected all belief in God
and was totally opposed to his children having anything to do with religion generally and the Bahá'í Faith
in particular. However, Bahaman had a restaurant to
run and reluctantly had to ask his wife's sister (Dawlat
Mehrban Behjat) who, like his wife, was a devout Bahá'í
to care for his daughters, stipulating that they were not to
be taught the Faith. Neither daughter was deterred and
despite strong objections from her father, Meherangiz
declared her faith at a young age. At 14 years old she

had the great privilege of travelling with Martha Root in Northern India and looked after most of the practical logistics, such as buying train tickets, arranging accommodation, and organizing venues for meetings while Miss Root was in Bombay. In addition to her Bahá'í teaching work, Meherangiz, in her teens, engaged in social work amongst the poor of Ahmedabad which was and remains a textile centre in India. She recalled a life-defining conversation with her aunt at the time of Martha Root's visit to India when Meherangiz was in the middle of the arrangements for Miss Root. "One day when I was a little girl, I ran in to tell my aunt, 'I worked so hard for the Faith' – I was so cocky and proud. My aunt didn't say anything, but continued looking out of the window. She spotted a horse-drawn carriage and there underneath the carriage was a dog, walking along so elegantly under the carriage. She said, 'you see that dog under the carriage? He thinks that he is pulling the carriage, when all that he is doing is walking under the shadow of the carriage and is being protected from the heat.' With that example I realized that I had not yet done anything for the Faith, but was just walking along under its protection."

A lifetime of public speaking started in Meherangiz's early teens and was to be the forum where, at 16, she met Eruch Munsiff who, out of curiosity attended one of her meetings. The romance didn't start well, as Eruch – who was highly educated (unlike Meherangiz who only attended the Roman Catholic school of St Therese in Bombay for two years between the ages of seven and nine) – was thrown out of the meeting by Meherangiz, who said he was "an ass laden with books!" Nevertheless, with great perseverance and sacrifice from Eruch and a love which blossomed over the following five years, the two finally married in February 1945.

Eruch had been adopted at the age of seven following the death of his father. He had two brothers, but his mother was unable to support all three of her children so gave Eruch to his paternal aunt and uncle as they were not married and had no children. They were also very comfortably placed financially and were only too pleased to educate and care for Eruch. In return for their kindness Eruch read agriculture at university with a view to managing the significant tracts of land owned by his aunt and uncle. Sadly, although they were very fond of Meherangiz, they disinherited Eruch as he wanted to marry someone who was not a Zoroastrian. While his inheritance would have been significant, his love for Meherangiz was greater and with his mother's blessing the union was sealed.

Unfortunately for Eruch, the prospect of looking after the family's lands having gone, he was compelled to look for an alternative career. He took and excelled in the Indian Civil Service examinations and on the declaration of India's independence in 1947 he was selected to be part of the first cohort to go to London to work at India House. It was his idea to start the Indian Tourist Board, a concept which was quickly to catch on amongst many of the other Embassies and High Commissions.

November 1947 was not a good time to come to England. It was one of the worst winters ever. Coming to a new country where it was freezing cold with a nine-month-old baby, plus rationing still in place and an environment where wearing a sari made her obviously foreign and not warmly received, Meherangiz was often to reflect that she truly thought she had come to hell. Her father was so worried that he used to send the family food parcels!

Throughout her life Meherangiz had a significant number of dreams of the Central Figures of the Faith and Shoghi Effendi, which were to provide guidance and insights and on which she acted. They will be referred to in the following pages and are important, because in addition to her total reliance on prayers these dreams gave her the strength and confidence to carry on at times of complete desolation and isolation.

Pilgrimage: Eleven Days with Shoghi Effendi

In 1952 Meherangiz and her family had the bounty of going on pilgrimage to the Holy Land. It was a very blessed time for them all, and Amatu'l-Bahá Rúḥíyyih Khánum would later remind Meherangiz on a number of occasions how unique their visit was. Why, you may ask?

We share with you below Meherangiz's own recollections of those precious days. Her recollections are not exhaustive as many of the emotions she experienced were too harrowing to share and nor are they chronologically set out. The accounts which follow were collated from various talks and conversations and at best should be regarded as memories of someone who was almost in a trance-like state for the duration of her pilgrimage.

After being in the presence of Shoghi Effendi in Haifa in 1952 every evening for an hour and a half alone, with Jyoti, sometimes with Khánum present, my love for Bahá'u'lláh greatly intensified. It is the Guardian who said that we must become "intoxicated lovers". I can honestly say that after meeting the Guardian my soul was truly wedded to the Cause of Bahá'u'lláh.

It is almost impossible to put things into words, but I

will try because when I was a teenager and I heard that now, in place of 'Abdu'l-Bahá, Shoghi Effendi had come to guide us and protect us, I became totally reliant on him as my source of guidance and ultimately my destiny for all my future actions. I already loved 'Abdu'l-Bahá because my Aunt Dawlatmai had told me all about Him. She and her husband had visited the Holy Land three times during the life of 'Abdu'l-Bahá and were always sharing stories. (How I wish I had paid closer attention to her stories when I was growing up, but I thought I knew everything at that time and couldn't be bothered!) When I was just a little girl of seven, I dreamt of 'Abdu'l-Bahá. . . And then when I was a teenager I learned Shoghi Effendi was now in charge. I think I must have said to my aunt, "How lucky you are that you were able to meet 'Abdu'l-Bahá, and some people who were even blessed by being in the presence of Bahá'u'lláh, and I have met no one and am unlikely to. Why was I born at such a time . . . that I can't meet 'Abdu'l-Bahá?" "Oh", she said, "but now, you know, 'Abdu'l-Bahá's grandson is in charge. Shoghi Effendi, he's our beloved Guardian. People do go on pilgrimage to meet him and it's wonderful." Somehow I was comforted by these assuring words and my heart was enveloped in a tranquil peace. I wanted to meet Shoghi Effendi. Frequently, I used to weep at night because I so wanted to meet the Guardian but I couldn't believe that I would ever get the chance. You have to understand I came from an extremely poor family in India with a father who was not supportive of me as a Bahá'í.

In 1944 Shoghi Effendi wrote to the National Spiritual

Assembly of India that as much publicity as possible should be given for the celebration of the Centenary of the Declaration of the Báb, 1844 to 1944. From morning to night I worked very hard with Shirin Fozdar who was the daughter of my mother's sister. We hired Cowasji Jehangir Hall which was a very big public hall in Bombay and I was told to put up very large posters. Apparently, I could have gone to prison for putting up these posters as they were 4ft large and during the war there was a restriction on using only A3 size posters. Fortunately, I got away with it. We thought we had done everything in readiness for the meeting including securing the Governor's secretary to take the chair.

All seemed in order and Shirin and I went out early in the morning to do some errands and when we came back it was lunch time and waiting for us was a letter delivered by hand from the Commissioner of Police. Shirin read it and said, "Oh, my God!"

I asked "What's happened?"

She said, "The Police Commissioner has banned our public meeting."

It was about a quarter to one, and Shirin said, "Before we figure out what we should do let's eat, I'm hungry." And as she sat down to eat, I sat on the sofa.

Now, normally in our house, 'Akká would be on my left, and Shoghi Effendi's photograph was on the right. As a child when I talked to 'Abdu'l-Bahá, I had turned to His photograph and said, "Now, what?" But on this occasion I said to myself, "Now, what, Shoghi Effendi?" To think I had done so much, prepared even to go to prison because of these posters, and now this. Very clearly, very clearly in my right ear, I heard a voice: "Go and see the Police Commissioner, immediately! Immediately! Immediately!" The voice repeated the word "Immediately" three times. And suddenly some power came over me, and I said to Shirin, as she was putting food in her mouth, "Stop! We have to go right away."

Shirin said, "For heaven's sake, it's lunch time. There's nobody there now. We'll go after lunch."

I said, "No. We're going now." And I insisted, "We must go now. Immediately."

And she uncharacteristically obeyed and left her lunch to come with me. And then her husband, Dr. Fozdar, who was a very powerful man in our family and whom everybody was scared of, said, "Where are you going?"

I said, "I'm going to the Police Commissioner . . . right now!"

He said, "I'm also coming."

So I agreed, and off we went. The police station was across the road from where we lived, and maybe about a three-minute walk. For some reason on this day, I took a taxi.

Shirin said, "Why are you taking a taxi?"

I replied, "Get in and don't talk." I was twenty-two years younger than Shirin Fozdar and had never in my life dared to have spoken like that to her or her husband Dr. Fozdar. To this day I don't know what came over me but they both got in the taxi and travelled the short distance to the Police Commissioner's.

When we arrived I said, "Now Dr. Fozdar, you will sit

down here in the waiting room." And miraculously he obeyed. It was as if I had a lamb with me, not a lion which was his usual controlling demeanour.

I said to him, "Say the Tablet of Aḥmad." And to Shirin I said, "We'll go, the two of us. I will pray. You will talk to the Commissioner."

We walked in and Shirin said to the Commissioner, "Why have you banned us?"

He said, "Because we had reports that there would be a riot."

She said, "There will be no riot. There may be a few street people but they are unlikely to do anything. We guarantee there will be no riot at all."

He looked at us. Then he said, "Okay." He picked up the phone, called the secretary of the Secretary to the Governor and said, "The meeting is on. You may go." He put down the phone, looked round, and said, "Ladies, do you know how lucky you are? If you had come five minutes later, I would have left for my holidays and nobody would have changed the decision."

That was my first experience with Shoghi Effendi's power. For decades I never told anybody about this incident. Furthermore, at that time I didn't know whose voice it was that had spoken to me. Only much later did I find out that it was Shoghi Effendi's voice. I had heard a voice, and I knew it was help from him, but it never occurred to me that it was his voice.

That was in 1944. From then on my love for him increased on what seemed like a daily basis and I seemed to feel his guidance in a way it is difficult for me to explain.

"Who needs an education?" I said to myself when I felt like the Guardian was by my side. (Many pioneers have felt this personal connection with the Guardian enabling them to achieve things they could never have contemplated without his guidance). But also, there was absolutely no hope of seeing him.

The years passed, and in 1947 my husband was part of the first group of diplomats from India after its independence to be sent to England. Then in 1952, a cable came, saying something to the effect that, "Now the way is open and the friends may apply for pilgrimage. They are welcome." Who do you think was first in line? We sent a cable, and Shoghi Effendi said, "Most welcome." Then suddenly I realized, "Oh my God, you know, we never asked whether Jyoti, who was our five-year-old child, could accompany us." So, we sent another cable and by return came the response saying, "She is most welcome."

By that time, we had travelled to India through Europe and my husband was only a civil servant with not very high wages. We didn't have money. Finally he said, "You know, we have applied but I don't think we can both afford to go, but you should be the one to go on pilgrimage."

I said, "No, you are a new Bahá'í (my husband had eventually become a Bahá'í, in November 1948) and you are the one who is educated with capacity to do much more than I can."

We argued backwards and forwards. Eventually he said, "Okay, let's see what I can do". He went and he got the cheapest return fare, both on the boat and on the train to Marseilles, but this meant that all of us could go to Haifa.

Before leaving for Haifa he said, "Don't tell our daughter where we are going and who she is going to meet."

I said, "Do you think I know how to explain the significance of a pilgrimage and the station of the Guardian to a five-year-old?"

On the last day prior to our departure I went to the Bahá'í Centre and met a Persian lady who had a shining, brilliant face. In those days, I was rather fond of fashion and tried to look as glamorous as I could. Appreciating how lovely she was, I asked her, "How come you are so beautiful? What have you done to your face? Do you eat or do anything special?"

She said, "Nothing."

I said, "Come on now." She was Persian, so I said "No *tarof*, tell me."

She said, "I don't know what you are talking about."

I said, "Your face is just brilliant. It's beautiful."

She said, "Maybe, just maybe, I don't know. . . I've just come back from Haifa, meeting Shoghi Effendi."

I said, "That's it! Come on, you are coming home with me."

I took her home. I said to her, "Sit down. Please tell me everything that happened, and what's the protocol." My husband being in the diplomatic service I was very conscious of protocol, and anyway I didn't know how to behave in the presence of Shoghi Effendi.

"Oh," she said, "It's nothing in particular. There were

twenty pilgrims from Iran and Shoghi Effendi would walk with the men in the garden, go into the Shrine, pray with them, and then come back into the Pilgrim House, and just for ten minutes or so, in general, ask the ladies how we are and what we are doing, and say a few words, and then he would leave."

To me this was a disaster; an utter total disaster. I had always wanted to be alone with Shoghi Effendi. So that night, I started to pray in the bedroom, talking to Shoghi Effendi. "Shoghi Effendi I love you so much. I don't want anybody to be there. I just want to be with you, alone. I don't need you to explain any plans, because I'm not intelligent and not so clever to execute plans. I have no wishes other than to be alone with you. I have no complaints about anybody. All I want is that you just let me sit by your feet. You go on doing what you have to do. And I'll just sit there and look at you and be there. That's all I want. But please let me be alone with you."

My husband, observing these rantings, kept saying, "My dear, I think you've lost your marbles. Shoghi Effendi's not here. He's in Haifa. Who are you talking to like that all the time? Get to bed. We have to get up early and go at 4 o'clock for the train to Marseilles."

Finally I told him, "You go to bed. Shoghi Effendi can hear me. I know he hears me."

"Oh my gosh," he muttered, "She is really crazy." Understandably, my poor husband was quite worried that I had truly lost my mind.

From Marseilles we got the boat and arrived in Haifa after a very difficult passage. When we landed, I don't know why but the captain took us out through the first-class exit. The press was there and when they saw us, Indians, they thought we must be important people and they came for an interview and my husband said, "No comment. We have come here to be on a Bahá'í pilgrimage." But he was grateful not to be coming out with all the refugees from the dungeon. Clearing customs took a very long time with each and everyone's luggage being checked. Then over the loudspeaker there was an announcement that Dr. Lutfu'lláh Hakím and Jessie Revell had come to receive us.

Perhaps some of you have no idea who these people are, but please ask those who might know, as they were very special. Lutfu'lláh Hakím had been serving in Haifa at the time of 'Abdu'l-Bahá. Jessie Revell had a sister, Ethel, and 'Abdu'l-Bahá had gone to their house during His trip to the States. He told both sisters that they would one day come to the Holy Land and serve, which they did. Jessie was the treasurer of Shoghi Effendi.

Anyway, these two distinguished people had been sent to receive us and all of a sudden there came another announcement. "Where are Mr and Mrs Munsiff? Shoghi Effendi is waiting for them." At which point I have to say I lost it: I had my purse in my hand which they still had to examine. I just banged it on the counter and said, "Look, sir, that's all yours. I'm going. Did you hear that announcement? Shoghi Effendi is calling us. He's waiting. I won't make him wait. You can take all you like."

Stunned, he looked at me and said, "Okay, okay, madam, don't get so upset," and he quickly passed us through.

My sense of direction is not good at the best of times and as we were walking up the hill, I didn't really know where we were. As we came through a gate, I saw a lady waiting, and another lady beside her. As I was going up the steps, I knew it was 'Abdu'l-Bahá's house. The other lady was Persian, but I didn't know whether the first lady was American or European. But as I first saw her, I felt compelled to fall at her feet, until something said, "Come on now. Control yourself, you're going crazy. This time your husband is right. You don't just fall at the feet of anybody."

I didn't know who the lady waiting to receive us was. Later I came to know she was Rúḥíyyih Khánum. I had not seen Khánum's photograph. I had no idea who she was, but seeing her had a profound effect on me. I did manage to control myself by telling myself, "My husband will really get mad at me now." Fortunately, I didn't do anything. And she embraced me, "Welcome, welcome, Shoghi Effendi is waiting for you."

It was late at night. My husband was taken in first. And Khánum made me sit down. She realized I was terribly nervous, not nervous in the sense of being afraid, but nervous with excitement. She gave me tea and reassured me, saying, "Calm down. Settle down." Then after a while she said, "Okay, now you and Jyoti can come." I had not prepared Jyoti in any way but when she walked in, without any prompting, she immediately fell at the feet of Shoghi Effendi. He picked her up and said, "It's not allowed. You mustn't do that." Well, I prefer not to share what happened to me, but in any event he welcomed us...

When we were coming out, I was weeping, and my daughter said to me, "Mummy, mummy" very softly so as not to be rude, "Please don't cry. Did you know he's the biggest, the greatest man in the whole world? Did you not hear his voice mummy?" She thought I was crying because I was disappointed. She kept insistently saying to me, "Did you not hear the power in his voice? He is the biggest and the best."

I said, "Yes, I know."

"Then," she asked, "Why are you crying?"

I said, "Because I am happy."

She had very big eyes and long eye lashes, and she just turned her eyes up as though saying, "Well, I don't understand. How can you cry when you're happy?" Children don't cry when they're happy, so this was beyond her comprehension. One thing was clear, my innocent child of five had never been affected by another human being in this way and was completely consumed by the Guardian's unique spiritual force.

At a meeting in the United Kingdom I had promised the Bahá'ís there that I would pray for them. And then I had said, "Why pray only for you? I will pray for the whole world to be able to go to Haifa, but not when I'm there." Of course, they all laughed.

During that first meeting Shoghi Effendi said to me, "You must be tired now. I have given you a room in the Eastern Pilgrim House. From the window you can see the Shrine of the Báb. Don't forget to pray for the friends!"

As we were leaving him he said, "You know, Mrs Munsiff, twenty pilgrims are coming from Iran." I must be honest, I felt as if my heart stopped, and, as I was standing up, I nearly lost my balance with what can only be described as real physical pain. I said to myself, "In my heart I talked to you all night but you didn't hear a word? Not one word? Twenty pilgrims? Twenty? and all I want is to be alone with you." As this thought was just leaving me the Beloved Guardian just looked at me, with those powerful hazel eyes and with a twinkle in his eye, and a twitch in his smile, he said, "But now these pilgrims are stuck in Alexandria for passport reasons." And life came flowing back to me. "Thank you," I said. He bade me goodnight, "Now go and sleep well."

Those twenty pilgrims never did come until the day we were leaving. Their taxis arrived as we were departing. It was truly amazing and I was eternally grateful. We were the only pilgrims for eleven days although two pilgrims from the West, Marion Little and Bahíyyih Ford, left the day after we arrived.

Twenty years later when I was in the Canary Islands, and I was telling this story, one of the men sighed with astonishment, "So you are the cause of our getting stuck in Alexandria! The immigration officer took all twenty of our passports without giving any explanation. I would go every day and he would say, 'No!' And without any reason he refused to give them back till on the eleventh day he released them." But I will always believe the real reason they were stuck in Alexandria was because my prayers had been answered and as a family we enjoyed the immeasurable bounty of being on pilgrimage alone in Haifa for eleven days.

In my humble opinion, I don't think the Baháʼí world really understands and appreciates completely Shoghi Effendi's spiritual powers. Although he was not a tall man his physical, intellectual strength and energy were extraordinary and obvious for all to observe. But his ability to assist spiritually those who loved the Faith and who arose to serve the Cause has often remained hidden from the Baháʼí world at large. With the passage of time, the true station and power of this humble being who worked tirelessly for the Faith and responded unfailingly to the requests of Baháʼís all over the world will become apparent.

Can you imagine what it was like to have the whole of the Eastern Pilgrim House to ourselves? Our bedroom was the room on the left-hand side as you enter. The food would be brought to us from ʻAbduʼl-Baháʼs house by Khánum, or the maids. We could not have been made to feel more special.

Every day at 4 o'clock Shoghi Effendi would come to the Eastern Pilgrim House and my husband would wait for him at the gate. Together they would go into the Shrine and say the Tablet of Visitation. Shoghi Effendi would chant, and my husband would listen. They would come out and walk in the garden. And every day, my husband would prepare about twenty questions for Shoghi Effendi. He would ask one question, and then mystically the rest would be answered without being specifically asked. This would continue until 6 p.m. My husband was meticulous in writing down all the answers even as they were walking . . . I, on the other hand, never wrote anything down. Then from 6 to 8 p.m. or a quarter to 8 my daughter and I would be in his presence. And sometimes <u>Kh</u>ánum would join us.

After we came out, the first night, from meeting Shoghi Effendi, <u>Kh</u>ánum was waiting by the gate outside to receive us. She hugged me and she kissed me, and thinking I knew Persian (whereas I actually understood only a little), said to me, "You were thirsty and you drank the ocean." It seems Shoghi Effendi must have told her how thirsty I was to meet him. And 'Abdu'l-Bahá speaks about that. He says, in effect, "Some people absorb like a sponge. And some are like a stone: they get hot but soon become cold again, and are as much a stone as when they went. No effect." I believe the impact is not about worthiness but in direct proportion to our love for the Cause, for Bahá'u'lláh, the Báb, 'Abdu'l-Bahá, and Shoghi Effendi.

We arrived on 19 November 1952 and in the Pilgrim House there was only one cold tap, together with a single oriental-style toilet. And that was it. We were able to make our own tea and a little bread and butter for breakfast. In those days, just after the war, there was a shortage of everything. It was cold in November in Israel, but even without hot water all three of us religiously would wash our hair daily and cleanse ourselves with exceedingly cold water and put on a daily set of fresh clothing. Once <u>Kh</u>ánum said to me, "I see you bathe every day." I don't know how she knew. And she continued, "One of these days, you know, you'll catch cold or pneumonia." I assured her she should not worry.

She also made the observation: "I see you look very glamorous wearing a new sari every day and are nicely made up. Why do you wear a new sari every day and make an effort to look so nice?"

I said, "Khánum, if I don't dress up for my beloved Shoghi Effendi, who in this world do you think I should dress up for?"

She got up and hugged and kissed me. And she said, "Well done. People come here and the women are all wearing black, no make-up."

I was baffled by this as it was clear that the Beloved Guardian loved beauty. In any event, of all the things we should not be is hypocritical and we should present the best of ourselves. From 3 o'clock until 6 o'clock when Shoghi Effendi would come, Jyoti and I would be with Khánum. Being alone with Khánum and able to have intimate and honest conversations was the start of a friendship which lasted throughout our lives. Khánum also had an opportunity to get to know Jyoti, to whom she gave much love and comfort when I was many miles from my child.

We used to meet the Guardian in a small room on the left as you enter the Master's House. As you go in, there is a large room with the flowers and plants, with bench-type seats where Khánum received people. The room in which we met the Guardian was smaller and a more intimate space, with a settee to one side on which Shoghi Effendi would sit, and we would sit on chairs in front of him.

Every time I would enter, Shoghi Effendi would welcome us, and bid us sit down. He would talk a lot about the progress of the Faith, how it progressed from the time of the Báb, to the time of Bahá'u'lláh, and 'Abdu'l-Bahá, with all the statistics and history. He spoke in a most beautiful voice which I find quite difficult to describe. At times when he was emphasizing something, I used to feel the whole world was shaking despite the fact that he wasn't shouting or even speaking particularly loudly. His voice was unique both when he was speaking and when he was chanting prayers. I believe it was that uniqueness which impressed Jyoti so much even though she was a child who, despite her tender years, had already travelled halfway round the world speaking to many different people, none of whose voices had she ever commented upon.

One day he was explaining in his commanding tone, "Now, you know, we are nearing the completion of the Shrine of the Báb, and so many visitors come." I don't remember the statistics he gave me as numbers and I don't get on too well with them. Then, he said, "And so many thousands visit the Mashriqu'l-Adhkár in the United States, look what the Bahá'ís have achieved. The Bahá'ís have done wonders. Look at all this in Haifa, near the Shrine. And now", he said, "the Bahá'ís are not satisfied. They want to conquer the world." Because it was 1952, and in 1953 the World Crusade was to start.

I said "Beloved Guardian, the Bahá'ís always try their best but it's you who will conquer the world, and get us out, and get us doing something."

And he smiled. I was eternally grateful that during my first meeting with him I was courageous enough to thank him for all he had done for the Bahá'ís. When I first met Rúḥíyyih Khánum that evening, and we were having tea before I went in, Rúḥíyyih Khánum asked me if I had read his Ten Year Crusade cablegram.

I said, "Yes."

She asked, "Did you understand it?"

I said, "No, but I understood one thing, that Shoghi Effendi will lead us to victory."

She said, "You understood well."

So, I thought, "Why should he say that the Bahá'ís would do it? He had such faith in us and such confidence that we would be successful. . ."

He assured me when he said "Yes, from time to time, cablegram guidance will go from here." He never used the word "I". He could have said, "I will send cables". No, he said, "From time to time the guidance will go from here, to the Bahá'í world."

It would be difficult to find a more humble person than Shoghi Effendi. But his humility was not a false modesty, nor was it even that he felt he had to be humble; it was innate in him. It was clear that he also did not forget his obligations representing the Cause of God as the Guardian, at that time on earth, and never permitting others to forget that or to insult the Faith.

In the same way as Bahá'u'lláh and 'Abdu'l-Bahá, Shoghi Effendi would pace back and forth while talking. On this occasion he was lamenting, "See how the Faith will progress and what a wonderful world we will have." Then he said, "I don't understand why the friends will not arise to pioneer. Why don't they arise?"

At this I felt sorry for the friends in England, where I'd lived, and of course for the friends in Bombay, my birthplace. So I pleaded for them, "But beloved Guardian, the friends in India, and the friends in the British Isles are trying very hard. It's very difficult to get visas and permits and go to the pioneering goals. It's very difficult."

He stopped in his tracks and looked at me, and at that moment I just wished the earth would swallow me up. He firmly responded, "Because it is difficult, the Bahá'ís are asked to do it."

I'll never forget that as long as I live. At that time, I felt the whole world shook in such a way that there would be an earthquake. He was not prepared to accept any excuses. Since that evening, I've heard Bahá'ís, many times, around the world say, "It's difficult to teach. It's difficult to pioneer. It's difficult. . ." I've grown to loathe that expression. I've used it myself, but it is not acceptable, so I suggest we stop saying things are difficult. That was the first lesson I learned during my pilgrimage.

Continuing to pace up and down, he said lots of prophetic things like, "Africa", you know, "will be wonderful." And then he would praise somebody. He said, "Did you know Marion Jack?"

I said, "Yes, I've heard about her. What a wonderful pioneer she was."

When Shoghi Effendi was talking, it was often a stream of consciousness referring to a variety of unrelated topics which would surface. Frankly, I didn't mind what he wanted to say; I was blissfully happy just being there and listening to him. Also, frequently he would lapse into Persian which I didn't speak, at the time, so I might be forgiven for not being able to register some of the things he said, although if they were personal comments I somehow was able to understand what he was saying. Later Rúḥíyyih Khánum asked, "Do you understand Persian?"

I said, "No."

She said "What do you mean? Shoghi Effendi talks to you in Persian most of the time. You must tell him to speak to you in English."

I said, "No, I'm not going to tell him anything, I'm very happy."

She said, "That's not the point, Meherangiz. He's talking to you. You must understand."

I said, "Please Khánum, you listen carefully and when we come out, you translate for me."

She said, "No. He's talking to you. And you must understand as he talks to you. I cannot interpret that for you."

I said, "I'm sorry. I'm not going to tell him." I was convinced he knew, so there must be a wisdom in it. In any event, in my prayers before leaving for Haifa all I had asked for was to be able to sit at his feet and that I had no wishes other than to be alone with him. My prayers had been answered, and I wasn't now going to ask for anything else. If you pray for something, you can't then start picking and adding when your original prayer is answered. That's another lesson I learned. We have to be very careful what we ask when we communicate with God.

I felt unable to confide in Rúḥíyyih Khánum what I had prayed for prior to my departure and that in my heart my prayers had been answered and that I neither felt able or wanted to ask for anything more. Sensing my resistance she said, "Okay, I'll come and request Shoghi Effendi to speak to you in English."

I told her, "As you wish."

So Shoghi Effendi would sit on the settee, as I said, and I would sit on the chair, and on my right was another chair for Jyoti to sit on. As Shoghi Effendi entered the room, Khánum would be sitting on the left-hand side. The next time we had an audience with the Beloved Guardian, Rúḥíyyih Khánum very humbly said, "Mrs Munsiff doesn't understand Persian, doesn't know Persian, would Shoghi Effendi be so kind as to speak to her in English?"

He just looked at her, smiled, and continued in Persian. He didn't change. Two days passed, and she asked me again on Monday, when she couldn't come, "Is he still talking to you in Persian?"

I said, "Yes."

She said, "Won't you request him to change?"

I said, "No."

She said, "Okay."

So this time when she came again she once more asked Shoghi Effendi. He looked at her, and continued in Persian. The third time when she made a request, he didn't even look at her. In the middle of his conversation he said in English, "Did you read the Ten Year Crusade cablegram?"

I said, "Yes."

He said, "Did you understand it?"

I said, "No."

He said, "But that was in English." (laughter).

So I got up on the edge of my chair, and half in English and using one or two words of Persian, I tried to explain with my hands and fingers, using my index fingers to demonstrate. I said, "But your sentences are that long, and not even the British can understand what you are trying to say."

He said, "They would understand if they would read it, and read it, and read it, and discuss it among themselves: they would understand."

And this was, I think, to show Rúḥíyyih Khánum that language was irrelevant whether it was English or Persian. He understood that I was under a spell of spiritual wonderment and was absorbing the experience in my soul and not through words and my mind.

Every time I used to come out from meeting with the Guardian, Khánum would say, "Now come and sit down, come and sit down beside me." And she would stroke me and help me to calm down. It is almost impossible to explain my state of being after experiencing the presence of the Beloved Guardian. It was not of this world and his influence was to remain with me for the rest of my life, as was his voice which I remembered hearing long before I even arrived in Haifa.

On one occasion when he was speaking to me in English he said, "You go. You'll be successful," and he repeated this three times. He said, "Teaching, pioneering."

To my eternal regret, I responded: "I would go pioneering, but you can see I have a child, my husband is a diplomat and he needs his wife, and we've spent all our money. I don't have any degree as a nurse, or a teacher, or doctor with which I can be useful, and language might be a problem."

How shameful that I would waste the Guardian's precious time with all these excuses! He patiently and calmly listened to everything and then he said, "To teach the Faith you need only faith, devotion, and sincerity." Clearly, none of my excuses impressed him. And then he referred to Mr Músá Banání. He said, "Did you know Músá Banání?"

I said, "Yes."

And he said, "He didn't know he was a businessman. He didn't have specialized degrees or any skills. And", he continued, "in one year in Africa, he brought in a hundred and sixty-five people." Then Shoghi Effendi said, "Go. Follow in the footsteps of the Apostles of Jesus Christ." Then three times he said, "Rest assured you will be successful. Rest assured you will be successful. Rest assured you will be successful."

When he said that, I remembered the voice, in 1944, telling me, "You go immediately, immediately, immediately." I said to myself, "I know this voice. It *was* Shoghi Effendi."

I came out from that session and I must have looked totally dazed. Khánum said, "What's the matter with you?"

I said, "Khánum, I think I am going crazy."

She said, "No, you're not. What's the matter? What's happened?"

I said, "I knew this voice of Shoghi Effendi's. How can that be possible? I heard it before I came here. Heard it very, very clearly. I know I've heard this voice before."

She said, "You heard it? Then what did you do with that voice? Did you act upon it?"

I said, "Yes, instantly."

She said, "Was it successful?"

I said, "Yes."

She then calmly said, "Then it was his voice. I am sure that anyone who loves him, and wishes to serve, and turns to him for help, he assists. He is aware of the spirit that turns to him, but he doesn't necessarily know what the body looks like." Khánum went on saying that sometimes he would say, "Bring me the photograph. I want to see what the body looks like." You cannot imagine my relief when Khánum clearly didn't think I was going mad.

* * * * *

Since I am on the subject of hearing voices, I would like to take time out from my pilgrimage to share with you another later experience.

During the Ten Year Crusade while I was in the United Kingdom, I recalled Rúḥíyyih Khánum telling me that "if Europe fails, we have failed Shoghi Effendi". With this in mind, I felt the need to be actively working for the Faith constantly. On a trip to Cardiff in Wales where the friends had been working very hard, they had managed to get the television/ radio and mass media to agree to interview me. The television people had already agreed and set a date and time. Prior to the BBC interview, I was travelling with the Newman sisters to a variety of nearby suburbs. On our return from one such trip, we found Barbara Lewis standing at the front door. And as I entered, there was a chair near the steps. She was tired and looked totally despondent; holding a telegram in her hand she said that the television people had postponed my interview.

Just as in 1944, I don't know what possessed me, but I sat down on the chair at the foot of her stairs and I said, "Now what, Shoghi Effendi? Now what?" And his voice came to me, "Ignore the telegram. Ignore. . ." three times. "Go immediately, immediately, immediately."

I said to the Newman sisters, "Come on, we are going to go anyway."

They said, "We've just come. We're tired."

I said, "Come on."

They agreed. So, we went to the BBC Cardiff Studios. The secretary came and said, "Oh, Madame Munsiff, we are very sorry, we did send you a telegram. Did you not receive it?"

I said, "No I didn't see your telegram," which was true. I hadn't "seen" it. I had just heard, but I wasn't about to split hairs.

She continued, saying, "We asked you to postpone the interview."

I said, "Please let the producer know that I'm not just a tourist here."

Fortunately, I was carrying in my bag a newspaper item on me going to Buckingham Palace which I showed her, explaining that my time was precious and that it was a great inconvenience if my interview was to be postponed. She went in and came back and said, "Well, we apologize."

Fairly indignantly, I said, "I am a busy person and I need to have some certainty so that I can organize my diary and be available."

The secretary said, "Madame Munsiff, we promise you we will give you prime time tomorrow evening after the evening news, at 6 o'clock. One of the best spots of the evening."

I said, "You assure me you won't inconvenience me again?"

She responded "No, ma'am."

And it was done. It was the first ever interview about the Faith on television in the United Kingdom (see p. 73 below). In case there is any misunderstanding, at no time did I think I, Meherangiz, was important, but I did think the message of Bahá'u'lláh was important and should be treated as a priority and with respect and this was an opportunity which could not be missed. What was most gratifying to me was that despite the Beloved Guardian having passed away two years earlier, my pleas to him had not gone unanswered. Believe me, it was his voice I had heard clearly in my right ear: no one else's.

When we returned to the home of Barbara Lewis, I decided I would share with all of them what I had experienced and why I was so insistent on going to the studios despite the telegram. I cannot repeat often enough that there is nothing, but nothing, special about me: Shoghi Effendi is there for each and every one of you provided you are sincere, with the sole intention of serving the Faith. That incident gave me the confidence to call on him whenever I was in a predicament, and by God's mercy he never let me down.

It is imperative that when we serve the Faith with sincerity we should not look inwards at our own failings and inadequacies or at our social and economic status. The only thing which is important is that we remember the truth and divinity of God's solution for mankind in this day and age. If you do this, no matter where you are or who you are with, you will find yourself able to converse eloquently and will find that you command the respect of those around you, whoever they might be. Never allow yourselves to be humiliated, for you are the ones who are offering the answer to all the problems which the intellectuals of the world have identified with nothing to offer by way of a remedy.

* * * * *

Going back to my pilgrimage: the Guardian was about to announce his plans to the world for the Ten Year Crusade. He had just completed, in his own hand, a map of the world outlining the goal areas of the Plan in great and beautiful detail. I was in his presence when he asked Rúḥíyyih Khánum to please bring the map to Mrs Munsiff so that she might study it. Rúḥíyyih Khánum acted as if she were stone deaf. Again, the Guardian requested her to show Mrs Munsiff the map, and again she sat resolutely still. Finally, the Guardian spoke a third time, very firmly, and told her to bring the map to Mrs Munsiff "right now", along with several accompanying explanatory booklets. He showed me the map and told me to take it back to the Pilgrim House and study it. Rúḥíyyih Khánum parted with this precious document with great reluctance, telling me that this was the only copy and that the Guardian had put infinite hours and toil into it, and that I must be very careful not to damage it.

I took it back to the Pilgrim House and looked at it. To me, it wasn't a map, it was a beautiful work of art, like a painting by a great master. I hadn't the faintest idea why the beloved Guardian had given it to me or what I was supposed to do.

While I was just gazing at this item of beauty, my husband Eruch started to take an interest in it. That evening he started to study the map in intricate detail together with the accompanying booklets also prepared by the Guardian. In the morning, I asked him what he thought. "It is very interesting," he replied. "However, I have found two mistakes in it."

For me, that was it – I saw red. "As soon as we get back to England, I'm divorcing you!" I told him. "I've had about enough of your arrogant, intellectual attitude. The Guardian of the Faith, the Vice-Regent of God on earth, has prepared this with his own hand – and you dare to say that there are mistakes in it!"

Eruch replied that he was a Bahá'í on his own account

and that his faith had nothing to do with mine, and that I might do or say as I liked – but that there were two mistakes and he believed the Guardian should know about them.

Apparently, my husband did inform the Guardian of his findings – as you can imagine, I certainly wasn't going to. Later Rúḥíyyih Khánum reported to me that the Guardian had told her, "Thank God that we have Bahá'ís like Eruch (Munsiff). If he hadn't noticed those errors, two National Spiritual Assemblies would have fought for ten years over who had the proper jurisdiction over certain locations."

This was a good lesson for me. I learned then never to judge the ability of anyone to serve the Faith according to my own limited standards, and to understand that we each have our own different skills and qualities which are there to be applied for the benefit of the Faith.

One day, Rúḥíyyih Khánum inquired, "Can you cook?"

I said, "I can try. What would you like?"

She said, "Can you make Indian curry?"

I said, "Yes."

She then said, "We have one chicken and we have a few guests."

If there were pilgrims, the Western pilgrims dined with Shoghi Effendi, and the Eastern pilgrims prayed with him. My husband prayed with him as well as walked with him, probably because he was the only male pilgrim. As for me, I had the bounty of being in his presence.

I naturally agreed to cook for the Guardian and his guests. Khánum had been collecting various spices for over six months and little by little I started putting them all in the pot. I have to explain that when I cook I am unable to follow a recipe but rely on my experience and instinct to determine the quantities of the ingredients. To the onlooker this all appears a little bit like hit and miss and I was clearly making <u>Kh</u>ánum very nervous.

"Meherangiz, what are you doing? This had better be good! If it's not I'll kill you because Shoghi Effendi hasn't eaten for 12 hours."

I said, "Okay, <u>Kh</u>ánum, if it's not good, you kill me. But if it is good how will you reward me?"

"Oh," she said, "now you know your laws as well."

I said, "Of course – reward and punishment, remember?"

She replied, "Okay, I will pray that your boat gets stuck for a couple of days delaying your departure."

I said, "Alright, fair enough, I accept. That's wonderful."

While I was still cooking, and the curry was simmering on the stove, Shoghi Effendi sent for me. If anyone thought I was going to remain in the kitchen when the beloved Guardian had sent for me they had better think again. Quickly, I removed my apron, put it round <u>Kh</u>ánum, and said, "You watch that curry of mine."

What could she do but say "Okay"? And I left her to it and hurried to the presence of the Guardian who welcomed me and he was clearly in a good mood. He resumed talking about the progress of the Faith, and how well the British and the Americans were working. I bravely said, "Abdu'l-Bahá visited both America and Britain and also you were in England." I became very emotional: "No one has come to India and all we seemed to have were strong Covenant-breakers." I implored him, saying, "Forgive our shortcomings and help us. What have we done that nothing is happening in India? Nothing!"

He said, "If you stop crying, I'll tell you."

I sniffled and stopped crying. And he instructed me: "Write to the National Spiritual Assembly of India and Pakistan that the members should disperse and teach. The members of the National Assembly should go pioneering. Then as 'Abdu'l-Bahá said" (using his beautiful hands for emphasis) "the community will rise, and new believers will be marching in by troops."

Again, you see, he would avoid using the word "I". When he said "Write", I truly thought it was a joke. Sincerely, to this day, I laugh about it. I said, "Beloved Guardian, they don't listen to you, do you think they will listen to me? You are seriously asking me to write?" as I couldn't imagine anything funnier than me writing to a Bahá'í institution. I still think it's funny but he insisted, "Yes, of course, Write!"

So I did and I never did get a reply, but I can imagine what they must have thought. They knew me as someone with absolutely no education, yet I had the nerve to write to the National Assembly. Clearly, going on pilgrimage has made her too big for her boots and what is more she is telling us what to do in the name of Shoghi Effendi.

To this day I have no understanding of the purpose of that letter or if it had any impact. All I know is that I obeyed the instruction. At that same meeting he explained, "There will be the most beautiful Temple, and the Temple will attract thousands upon thousands, and then the Faith will grow and they will start marching in like troops. People will start marching in." He went on to say, "They will receive the portrait of Bahá'u'lláh for the dedication of the Temple."

As it transpired, we were not shown the portrait because there were too many people and other obstacles, so the House did not send the portrait for the dedication of the Temple. But eventually they did see the portrait in 1992 during the World Congress when India was sent the portrait.

As a postscript to the cooking bargain with Khánum, I can only assume that the Beloved Guardian enjoyed the food and Khánum prayed, because our boat was indeed delayed, giving us two additional days in Haifa.

Not only did the Guardian tell me to write to the National Spiritual Assembly of India and Pakistan, he also told me I must "write to the friends and communicate with the National Assemblies". You must understand that not only could I not spell – I also had developed a phobia about writing. When confronted with a clean piece of paper, my mind would invariably go blank and I would start to shake. Truly, I would rather have walked miles to say "hello" rather than put pen to paper. With that instruction to write, somehow that phobia disappeared, although my ability to spell did not miraculously improve. In my later travels around the world the Universal House of Justice and the International Teaching Centre would expect reports, and although I

knew my grammar and spelling were shameful, Shoghi
Effendi gave me the courage to write and if, I say so
myself, I became a prolific correspondent. Everyone
knew they had to put up with the misspellings and gram-
matical mistakes but generally my messages were quite
clear, even if they had to fill in the blanks.

On one occasion I entered the room where Shoghi
Effendi was waiting and I was absolutely shocked to
see how exhausted he looked. I was devastated to see
Shoghi Effendi in that state. And he said, "Welcome.
Don't worry. Don't worry. Yes, I am exhausted. I am very,
very tired." I could see his shoes were covered with mud,
himself tired, sitting on that settee, totally exhausted. But
he said, "Don't be uncomfortable. I wanted to see you.
That's why I sent for you." In my heart I said, "Oh God,
go and rest." He then very intently said, "Meherangiz,
take it all in because you may not get another chance. It's
only physical exhaustion." That was another lesson. Now,
every time I feel tired, I recall his exhaustion and know I
must keep going.

Once Jyoti was playing outside with the peacocks and
flowers, and Khánum enquired, "Where is Jyoti?"

I said, "Oh, let her be." I was perfectly happy for her to
be entertaining herself in the garden.

At that moment Shoghi Effendi sent for me, and I was
up like a shot. But before I could go in, Khánum said,
"No, no, no. Jyoti must come in. This is her reward." She
said, "We know how much she's suffered since she was a
baby."

I still didn't take any notice. I just walked in and sat.

And then the door opened and my child was pushed in by <u>Kh</u>ánum. I thought, "Oh my God. Now this child will run towards me, and when she runs towards me she will turn her back towards Shoghi Effendi."

In my culture that would have been such a mark of disrespect and I would have been mortified. But it seems Shoghi Effendi somehow froze me. I couldn't control Jyoti with my eyes, or speak, or anything. I couldn't move. I couldn't even blink. And this child stood there at the door. Three times she bowed and said, "Alláh'u'Abhá!" And then Shoghi Effendi said, "Welcome, welcome," all in Persian. It could have been any language, but she understood him. And then she backed towards me all the way and came and sat down on my right-hand side. And then Shoghi Effendi said, "She's a good girl. Give her the best of education in England. She will serve in the East and the West and the whole world." What I found extraordinary was that a child with no priming was able not only to know how to behave respectfully but clearly also able acknowledge the spiritual significance of the meeting. I know that all parents are proud of their children, but both Eruch and I throughout the years have been grateful that our child has always responded to the unique opportunities which arose for her to serve the Faith.

On the last day, when we were leaving and I knew that I wouldn't be able to enter the Shrines again or be with Shoghi Effendi, something happened to let me know that you can come to the Shrines, no matter where you are in the world. When speaking to <u>Kh</u>ánum once I had shared with her that I would always keep my pilgrimage and my experiences with the Guardian in my heart and not share them with anyone including my husband. And she would say, "But you must!"

I am ashamed to say I didn't pay much attention to her admonition. However, when Shoghi Effendi was bidding us goodbye, he said, "Tell the friends to come. Encourage them to come. And tell them that if circumstances do not permit for them to come here, then they should bring their thoughts to the Holy Shrines." Turning to me he said, "When your thoughts are here, you are here." He then looked me straight in the eyes and said, "If you don't talk about your pilgrimage, your pilgrimage will not be accepted."

Consequently, if I have the slightest opportunity I've talked and talked around the world to the friends about my pilgrimage and the bounty of meeting Shoghi Effendi. I have observed how much of an impact sharing these memories has had on those who have not had the blessing of visiting the Shrines or meeting with the Guardian. Believe me, I urge you to allow your spirit to travel to the Shrines of Bahá'u'lláh, the Báb, and 'Abdu'l-Bahá. I know it can be done because that's where I transport my spirit every time I want to speak about the Faith.

When we got back to England in late 1952, we pressured and begged so many British Bahá'ís to go to Haifa. Naturally, they are happy they went. In those days the normal number of Western pilgrims was eight at a time with Shoghi Effendi. Many years later, during a period when I wasn't feeling well, my daughter said, "I know exactly what treatment you need." Her remedy was to take me for a three day visit to Haifa. <u>Kh</u>ánum was still alive and she very kindly and graciously invited us for dinner. She said, "Jyoti, I will hold you responsible. Make your mother put her pilgrimage notes on tape. It was a unique pilgrimage."

While I knew that my pilgrimage was precious, as it is for all pilgrims, it had failed to register with me that because we were the only pilgrims at the time, our individual access to the Guardian and its timing, just before the announcement of the Ten Year Crusade, was both special and unique. Memories of my pilgrimage give me the strength to overcome tests small and large alike; they have helped me to learn the quality of detachment from everyone, including my husband and child. Don't get me wrong; I love them both with every fibre of my being but when I am serving the Faith I am able to sever my emotions so that they don't get in the way of my objectives. Detachment is probably the hardest lesson I have had to learn in my life but it is the one lesson that has enabled me to have the courage and strength to focus my life towards the Faith, and that lesson started in Haifa where my love for Shoghi Effendi was cemented in my soul. I would humbly suggest you pray daily for detachment.

Shoghi Effendi had said: "I hope you are going to the Kampala Conference." I nearly fell off the chair, and so I just pointed to myself, and he said, "Yes, you. I would be very happy if you would go there and your meeting with the friends is sufficient." Again, three times he said he would be happy if I were to go to the Conference. My surprise at his request was born out of a complete sense of my own inadequacies; it would never have occurred to me that I was of any particular relevance particularly at a Conference where there were to be many distinguished Bahá'ís. On the other hand perhaps he wanted me to experience the purity of the African Bahá'ís, which I would be able to hold in my heart as inspiration when I embarked on my pioneering ventures in virgin territories.

I never spoke much in the presence of the Guardian, so I didn't ask any details about where to go pioneering in Africa, or for that matter anything else. I did ask if my husband should go with me but Shoghi Effendi said only if he could get a good job; otherwise he should remain in the United Kingdom.

I thought it would be easy. All I had to do when I came back was talk to the committee and they would make arrangements for me. Then I came back to London and told the secretary of the Africa Committee that I would like to meet with them because I wanted to pioneer to Africa. I asked where they thought I should go and the Committee suggested I should go to Madagascar because nobody had gone there. I said alright and didn't ask any other questions. When I came home, I told my husband that he had to get me a visa for Madagascar because I was going there pioneering. He said that I must be crazy because of the political situation at the time between India and France. But I said Bahá'u'lláh would take care of it. And that's how I went pioneering.

Meherangiz (far left seated) and her sister Bahaiya (far right seated) grew up in this family which influenced their acceptance of the Bahá'í Faith. Dawlat Behjat (second left), Mehrban Behjat (middle), Shirin Fozdar (second right). Back row, left to right: Jamshid Fozdar, Khodabux Fozdar, Behjat and Dr Khodadad Fozdar. Front row, left to right: Mona Fozdar, Zena Fozdar, Mona Irani (Bahaiya's daughter) Minoo Fozdar and Jehangir Fozdar

Farewell party for Martha Root, Bombay, 1937, with "little angels"; Meherangiz at the top, holding the garland of flowers

Bahaman Rashid Irani, Meherangiz's father

Meherangiz with her sister Molly (Bahaiya)

Modelling in Bombay, 1942

Meherangiz playing the sitar

Meherangiz in 1947, shortly after her marriage to Eruch Munsiff

*Eruch and Meherangiz
Munsiff, late 1940s,
in England*

Meherangiz with Jyoti

The Munsiff family on pilgrimage, 1952

The Munsiff family, just before Meherangiz pioneered to Madagascar in 1953

Pioneering to Madagascar during the Ten Year Crusade

On 7 February 1953 Meherangiz left for the Kampala Conference on her way to Madagascar, arriving early on 9 February. Eruch had booked a hotel for her in Kampala, Uganda, but when she was about to register, another person insisted on having the room assigned to her so, not wanting to get into an argument, Meherangiz let her have the room. This was quite fortuitous as Mr Daulat Ram, who was the Assistant Director of Education and had arranged for her transport from the airport, after consulting with his wife, invited Meherangiz to stay in their home. Meherangiz accepted the invitation, having remembered that she had decided to be guided by the words of Bahá'u'lláh: "Be unrestrained as the wind, while carrying the Message of Him Who hath caused the Dawn of divine Guidance to break. . ."[2]

'Alí Nakhjavání, pioneering there at that time, on hearing that she was staying with Daulat Ram, said this was a great bounty because, although there were Bahá'ís in Kampala, the local believers in the villages had recently been having some trouble, and perhaps after Mr Daulat

Ram became more familiar with the Faith through Meherangiz then things might improve for the Bahá'ís. Before she left Uganda she was taken by her Indian friends into some of the villages. In one village she was entertained by the Chief who put on a dinner for her. She also had an opportunity to talk about the Faith.

Meherangiz attended the Conference every day without fail. Nine Hands of the Cause were in attendance, and were extremely kind to Meherangiz even though she didn't know any of them. Mr Furútan told her that she must always treasure the privilege that she had been specifically told by the beloved Guardian to come to the Conference and to engage actively, as this privilege was not given to everyone. Meherangiz recalled:

Then, in the meantime, I met a most beautiful black American lady who said that Rúḥíyyih Khánum sent her love to me and I was overjoyed and tears ran down my cheeks. Mrs Dorothy Baker saw this and told me not to weep, that the Master's arms were around me and she got hold of my hand and told me to think of the beloved Guardian, as she was going to say prayers for me. She also said 'Yá Bahá'u'l-Abhá' nine times and then she said everything will be okay. She felt a good spirit present and told me not to worry about my home and child. I said I didn't worry about them. I could sacrifice being with them for the beloved Guardian. Mrs Baker said that she knew that I would do great service to the Cause here.

While all of these expressions of love were wonderful, they also made Meherangiz acutely aware of what might be expected of her.

Meherangiz had to go through Nairobi on her way to Madagascar in order to extend her one-month visa at the French Consulate. Once again, she was offered hospitality in Nairobi by an Indian family and also taken care of by the local Bahá'ís. Fortuitously, she had an opportunity to speak twice on the radio about the Faith. Her onward journey to Tananarive in Madagascar was not straightforward, requiring her to go through Dar-es-Salaam and then get a boat to Madagascar which stopped at a number of places. An Ismaili, Mr Nathoo, whom she had earlier met and who was a member of the Legislative Assembly in Nairobi, came to Meherangiz one day and offered her a seat on his plane to Dar-es-Salaam. After arriving there, she went to the steamship company to make a boat reservation. She explained:

The agent told me all the first class was booked, because it was the maiden voyage of the vessel "La Bourdonnais". So I enquired about the second class, and he told me it was only first class and the class for the army personnel, and this was also fully booked. Not to be daunted, I asked if one soldier fell ill, could I have his berth. The agent was a patient young Frenchman who politely explained that each cabin was fitted with four berths, and even if one soldier were taken ill there would be three soldiers in the cabin. I then asked if four soldiers fell ill, could I have the whole cabin for the price of one berth. To this the genial agent who, I am sure, was thinking "stupid woman", and just to get rid of me I think, said that in that event I would get the whole cabin for the price of one berth. The boat was leaving the next afternoon, 14 April 1953, but I should go in the morning to see if it would be possible for me to travel.

The next morning I went back, and sure enough four soldiers had been taken ill, and so I got the cabin for the price of one berth and I bought my ticket. I then went on board and was asked for 150 Francs by way of security. In those days this sum was a fortune. I knew the boat still had a few hours before leaving, and I asked Jalál Na<u>kh</u>javání, who had taken me to the boat, if he had the money, and he said no, nor did any of the Bahá'í committees. So . . . I hailed an Indian man, and for the first time in my life I was hitch-hiking! I went to the Mayor's office and asked him to lend me the 150 Francs for security and told him that when I returned I would let him have it back. If not, I would get my husband to send it from London. He said when I got back from Madagascar would be fine. . . He sent me back to the docks in his chauffeur-driven car. . . I had assumed the boat was going straight to Tananarive so I never asked. I soon found out that it was not a direct sailing!

Meherangiz was very sick on the boat and everyone only spoke French. However, at each stop she was met by a member of the Indian community and ultimately arrived after some weeks in Tananarive, where she was met by Mr and Mrs Ismail, neither of whom was a Bahá'í but who invited her to stay with them and asked if they could look after her. Apparently Mr Nathoo from Nairobi had been in touch with them. After Meherangiz had been there for some time, Mr Ismail asked what she was up to, since he had noticed a member of the secret police in front of their house from the time she had arrived. She explained to him that she had come to teach the Bahá'í Faith, and showed him her passport and luggage. He was quite satisfied, and throughout her stay the Ismail family were exceedingly kind to her and remained firm friends throughout the following decades.

In the early days Meherangiz felt very alone and begged Bahá'u'lláh to send someone to whom she could talk about the day's events. According to her: "In retrospect, I have come to realize that those lonely days were valuable experiences which taught me the importance and power of prayers and made me understand the value of inspiration. I also felt that Shoghi Effendi was with me all the way."

Mrs Ismail's parents were suspicious of Meherangiz and thought she was a young person with ulterior motives. To prove them wrong, Mrs Ismail showed Meherangiz where the safe was, where she kept her jewellery, and how the safe could be opened. One day after this she left a whole bunch of keys with Meherangiz while the family went out. Meherangiz did not move from where she was guarding the safe. After this as nothing had been taken Mrs Ismail's mother felt more comfortable. However, one day she heard Mrs Ismail's father still complaining about her to which Mrs Ismail answered: ". . . She is not interested in wealth, she is not interested in my husband. . . We love her. . . She's from God. . ."

After staying with the Ismail family for five months Meherangiz felt she was overstaying her welcome and left their home to stay in a hotel. Mrs Ismail was not happy and after one night asked her to return. Meherangiz told her that as she was not able to repay their kindness financially they should permit her to do some work in appreciation of their hospitality. Mrs Ismail was still not happy about this but as it happened one of their servants fell ill and so Meherangiz took over her duties, much to the chagrin of her host.

Meherangiz often cried and prayed in her room because she did not feel she was reaching the ordinary people of Madagascar. When her visa was running out, she went directly to the Commissioner of Police and got it renewed. After a few days five men came to the house and asked to meet with her and she arranged to see them again the next day. The problem was that Meherangiz did not speak Malagasy (the local language of Madagascar) and they did not speak English.

That night she got down on the floor, putting her head to the ground, crying and praying in desperation. As she finished praying, Mrs Ismail came and told her that there was someone on the phone for her. The person on the other end of the phone said that he had heard she had come from a big conference and that he spoke English and French and offered to help her in any translating she

48

might need. Meherangiz told him that she could not pay him but he said that he did not want money. Apparently, he was Mauritian and a father of thirteen children! So he came to the meeting with the five men and translated. In Meherangiz's mind her prayers had once again been answered.

One day one of these five men, Gilbert Robert, knowing Meherangiz's situation, offered to give her accommodation with his family. Meherangiz felt she had imposed on the Ismails long enough and had no alternative but to accept his kind offer on condition that she could look after their two young sons. The husband and wife both went out to work but only received a meagre income and she felt this was the least she could do to repay them for their hospitality. They lived in a small cottage with no spare bedrooms so Meherangiz slept on a straw mattress on the living room floor and that is how she lived for the remaining four months of her stay in Madagascar. However, while she was in the Roberts' home, their friends would come by every evening to learn about the Faith. If they had difficulty understanding Meherangiz's French, then Gilbert's wife, Daisy, would assist with the translation. This process eventually resulted in not only Daisy but four of the others, of different nationalities, declaring their faith in Bahá'u'lláh. Gilbert shared with Meherangiz a dream he had had. Prior to meeting her, he dreamt that there would be mention of God in his house twenty-four hours a day. Consequently, he had white-washed his house in preparation for this. When his wife had asked why he was doing this, he explained his dream to her. Daisy thought he was crazy, but it turned out of course that after Meherangiz went to stay with them, mention of God was indeed made twenty-four hours a day in their house.

Despite the modest circumstances in which Meherangiz was living, somehow she still managed to make contact with the elite in the city and among other events was invited to the reception given by the British Consul General in honour of the Coronation of Queen Elizabeth II in June 1953. Later that year she also attended a reception hosted by the Governor General of Madagascar on the occasion of the visit of General Charles de Gaulle.

When Meherangiz moved to the Roberts' house, so did her secret police "shadows", which never worried her because she knew she wasn't doing anything illegal. However, their maid, a Malagasy, got quite vexed about them hanging around and chased them away telling them to go and do some proper work. "All she does all day is pray or sing or dance or cry. What do you think she is doing to us?" she told them. Strangely enough, after that things did improve. The maid declared her belief in Bahá'u'lláh a short time later.

After moving to the Roberts' house, Meherangiz began to learn French very quickly. She had arrived in Madagascar with very little luggage and no books, but after a while she was able to arrange for a number of Bahá'í pamphlets, booklets and books to be sent from India and Geneva. The literature was a way of assisting those interested in becoming a Bahá'í to deepen their understanding in their own language.

One of the five new believers, Mr de Jouvancourt, came late one night to the Roberts' house, desperate that his grandson had meningitis and the doctor had said he would die. His Catholic family were blaming him for this because he had become a Bahá'í. He was very upset and said: "Meher, you have to do something." Meherangiz was very worried about this and went into a corner and cried and prayed and begged Bahá'u'lláh to spare these new believers from severe tests. When Mr de Jouvancourt returned home, his daughter (the mother of the child) told him that she knew where he had been and who had prayed because the whole bed shook and the child woke up, opened his eyes, smiled and asked for a drink. The timing of this coincided exactly with the time Meherangiz was praying. Mr de Jouvancourt was ecstatic and the attitude of his daughter towards the Faith changed for the better.

In August she received a message from Shoghi Effendi: ". . . He was very pleased you could go to Africa, and he appreciates the devotion that animates you and your dear husband as well, for without his help and moral support your service there would not have been possible . . . He will pray for your success, and that you may be able to confirm some of those souls you have spoken to already of the Faith."[3]

On one occasion when Meherangiz was invited to the Governor's residence, the invitation slipped her mind because she had heard from Eruch that he and Jyoti were unwell and she did not know what to do. Then she received a message from the Governor's Aide-de-Camp who had been sent to find out what had happened to her. She immediately rushed to the Governor's residence, where she was an hour late and she discovered that the event had been delayed by one hour to wait for her! Usually he would never even wait five minutes for anyone who was late. At the dinner table she was placed on the right of the Governor and the British High Commissioner was on her left. The British High Commissioner knew she was a Bahá'í and did not drink alcohol and whispered to Meherangiz that he would be interested to see how she would avoid insulting the Governor when she replied to his toast without champagne, which would be considered an insult. Meherangiz explained:

> I prayed for guidance as to what I should do as the Governor proposed a toast to me. No sooner had he sat down than I was on my feet with water in my glass. I offered my most sincere thanks to the Governor for his kind and generous words, and stated that I could not possibly respond to his toast in something like champagne which was only for the wealthy, and sometimes had a tendency to "go flat". I had therefore chosen the purity of the water because it was natural, could be used by all and would never lose its sparkle. I wished for the blessings of God for the Governor and his family and said that because of his help and co-operation offered in the promotion of the Bahá'í Message, future generations would remember his name. Fortunately, the entire formality of the toast passed off without any embarrassment for anybody

with humour and warmth. The British Consul General with his typical British humour whispered to me after I sat down, "By God, you've done it again!" After dinner, the Governor told me if I needed any help at all, I should just ask him.

Meherangiz always reminded people that the purpose of telling these stories was to reinforce the power of prayer. She insisted that she was not a clever person to whom these solutions would come naturally. Her inspiration exclusively followed moments of praying to Bahá'u'lláh and relying on the thoughts which then immediately arose.

A young Malagasy, Daniel Randrianarivo, had attended firesides on two or three occasions. He lived on a farm some distance away and would come to study the Faith. Unexpectedly, he stopped coming. When the time for her departure was approaching, Meherangiz was feeling disappointed that there was not one real Malagasy believer. Then the day before she was due to leave, someone knocked on the door and fell into the house. Daniel had run for hours and hours to reach her before she left. When he caught his breath, he said: "Please, I want to be a Bahá'í. Please enrol me before you leave." Thus, he became part of the group of five who enrolled in the Faith while Meherangiz was serving in Madagascar.

After being in Madagascar for nearly nine months, Meherangiz's visa was running out again, and the Police Commissioner hinted that it would not be appropriate for him to keep renewing it. Meherangiz was really ill at this time and apparently Gilbert had written to the Guardian, and the Guardian had replied saying that she should return to England. So she left.

It is interesting to note that the Tananarive Spiritual Assembly was formed in 1955 and the first National Convention of Madagascar took place in 1972. Meherangiz was very grateful to the Universal House of Justice who arranged her travel teaching itinerary that year so that she could attend this National Convention in Madagascar. Meherangiz saw Gilbert Robert and his family again in Paris in 1986.

By way of a postscript: Jyoti was able to attend the commemoration of the 50th anniversary in 2003 of the introduction of the Faith to Madagascar. When she was addressing the hundreds of people in the hall, she knew that all the sacrifices had been worthwhile.

*At the Intercontinental Conference in Kampala, 1953,
on the way to her pioneering post in Madagascar*

. . . with Sipola Atai and Claire Gung

. . . and with Eddie Elliott, the first African-Canadian to become a Bahá'í (in 1929). He worked at the Maxwell home in Montreal

Meherangiz with a tribesman in M'bale, British East Africa, April 1953

Mr and Ismail with their son. The Ismail family offered hospitality to Meherangiz following her arrival in Tananarive

Meherangiz's early days in Madagascar were filled with longing for her family back home in London

First Bahá'í group in Tananarive, Madagascar, October 1953. Left to right: Daisy Robert with her younger child, Daniel Randrianarivo, Arsène de Jouvancourt, Meherangiz Munsiff, Gilbert Robert, with the Roberts' elder son standing in front

Daniel Randrianarivo with Meherangiz

Bahá'ís and friends visiting the ancient royal residence of Ambohimanga, October 1953 . . .

. . . and photographed on the stairs

1972: first National Spiritual Assembly of the Bahá'ís of Madagascar, at the national Ḥaẓíratu'l-Quds in Tananarive

Pioneering to the French Cameroons during the Ten Year Crusade

It so happened that when Meherangiz left Madagascar in January 1954, she already had secured a visa for the French Cameroons but for a number of reasons at that time she was advised against going. On her return to the United Kingdom, Meherangiz felt that, given she had a visa, she should go to the Cameroons but Eruch, her husband, was reluctant to agree due to the state of her health. The National Spiritual Assembly of the British Isles was also opposed to her pioneering as they sincerely believed she should spend some time with her family and regain her health. Despite the fact that the beloved Guardian had sent a cable that he wished someone to go to the French Cameroons before Riḍván (April) 1954, there was a continuing resistance from the National Assembly to her returning to Africa. While at all times being respectful of the administrative institutions of the Faith, Meherangiz was desperate that the wishes of the Guardian be fulfilled. She knew she was the only one at that time who had a visa for the French Cameroons and there was very little time left before April 1954. Given the brick wall she was facing, she wrote to Hand of the Cause Leroy Ioas, explaining the situation. Almost by return, she received a cable saying that the Guardian was delighted and that the Indian National Spiritual Assembly had been instructed to send funds for the airfare. She also received a reply to her letter from Leroy Ioas saying the beloved Guardian "greatly appreciates your offer to undertake this important teaching service. He assures you of his prayers in your behalf." [4]

This was all Meherangiz needed, and with the support of her husband, on 15 April 1954 she left London for Douala via Paris and Tunis, arriving in the French Cameroons on 16 April 1954, five days before Riḍván, as desired by Shoghi Effendi. Coincidentally, at exactly the same time in the previous year she had embarked on her trip to Tananarive, Madagascar.

At the request of Mr 'Alí Nakhjavání, Samuel Njiki, a Bahá'í from the British Cameroons, had been asked to meet Meherangiz on her arrival in Douala. The only address which Samuel had was a Poste Restante and so their rendezvous was arranged at the Post Office. Meherangiz had received instructions that she would recognize Samuel on a prearranged date and time by a red Bahá'í prayer book which he would be holding. She approached Samuel cautiously and in a very soft voice, she whispered the Bahá'í greeting "Alláh-u-Abhá". At that time Meherangiz, although Indian, was considered white and although the racial situation was not as bad as in East Africa, there was an understanding that the races should not mix. Meherangiz had also received a letter from the Guardian, cautioning her not to react or show any expression on her face, irrespective of what she saw and however upsetting it might be.

After making contact with Samuel, Meherangiz installed herself in the Akwa Palace which was the only hotel in Douala where an unaccompanied woman could stay. Unfortunately, the situation was such that she was unable to meet Samuel easily because of the risk of arousing suspicion. In addition to the cost of remaining in the hotel where she couldn't afford to eat and her money was rapidly running out, she felt she must have a place of her own where meeting others would not come under constant scrutiny. During this time she was surviving solely on a continental breakfast of bread and a banana.

Having become friendly with the receptionist at the hotel, Meherangiz was able to find out who the Manager was and approached him to ask if he knew of any place which was not very expensive and where she might stay for three months. He said he had a hut which was his servants' quarters and which had two rooms, one of which was occupied but she could have the second room. Meherangiz was most anxious to have her independence and be somewhere she could teach black Africans, and, as she had so little money, she thanked him and took it sight unseen. She concluded that if she economized on food she would just about be able to manage the rent. Her quarters consisted of a bed, a table and two chairs with another little space where there was a table, a toilet, a tap, but no sink, and a bare cement floor. The walls were made of wood and she pinned up a photo of 'Abdu'l-Bahá.

She had with her also the Greatest Name and a picture of her daughter, Jyoti. The roof of the hut was thatched and when it rained, it would leak and also allow an abundance of insects to come in from the rain. Although the bed, for which she had one set of linen from the hotel, was a double bed, all the springs were broken, so finding a comfortable spot to rest was difficult. Unfortunately, she remained constantly fearful as the other room was occupied by a young Greek man who had the habit of getting drunk, bringing young African girls back to his quarters; when they asked for money in the morning he would beat them up, so, shouting for their money, they would then go outside the hut where they felt safer. Despite the insects, her life was a little more peaceful when it rained but she was always fearful that he might break down her door and force his way in when he was in a drunken stupor. Then one day, when he was not working and he was sober, Meherangiz decided to explain to him why she was in Douala and share with him the teachings of the Faith and the station of Bahá'u'lláh. She remained convinced that once he heard the name of the Manifestation of God, Bahá'u'lláh, he would not attack her. From then on, he treated her most respectfully and Meherangiz at least felt safe from him.

There were very few white people in Douala which, situated on the Equator, had the reputation amongst foreigners of being a hell-hole to be avoided at all costs. It was certainly the case that no women ever travelled there alone and this raised suspicion about Meherangiz with the authorities. They concluded she was either a spy or a prostitute. Visits by Samuel complicated matters as any men who were observing thought they too could visit Meherangiz. She had been advised not to talk about the Faith to any white people. At first when some black men came to her hut, she thought Samuel had sent them to talk about the Faith, but fortunately, her antennae were fairly keen and she quickly realized this was not the case, and was able to send away those who came at night, saying, "If you want to learn about religion you must come in the daytime."

Meherangiz was required to report to the Police Commissioner, Monsieur Jean Richard, every morning when he would repeatedly ask her why she was there. It was difficult to get him to understand that she had come to "teach the religion of God, the Bahá'í Faith", as she was a woman and he was only accustomed to men or ministers talking about religion. He agreed to accept her explanation as long as she provided him with the name and whereabouts of anyone she shared the teachings with. At least this had the effect of the authorities no longer thinking she was a prostitute, but her status as a spy was still under consideration. After a few weeks of intense interrogation, the daily interviews transformed into relatively informal chats which would go on for quite a long time, leaving those wishing to see the Commissioner waiting past their appointment times. They would talk about her time in Madagascar where he knew the Police Commissioner, and she went to great lengths to explain how much she had enjoyed the nine months in Madagascar and how helpful the authorities had been, giving him the assurance that the French Colonial Government was against neither her nor the Bahá'í Faith. During one of these chats, she mentioned her desire to go to Rio de Oro in Spanish Africa and he offered to take her in his plane on condition that he wasn't responsible once she got there!

In addition to the constant scrutiny, the practicalities of living, effectively in great poverty, were not easy. When it rained it rained a great deal and the area around the hut flooded, preventing Meherangiz from emerging outside. She was obliged to come to terms with the mice and the snakes which would slide through into her living space with the flood waters. While observing a large black widow spider on her ceiling catching insects, she became despondent, comparing the insect's success in life with her failure to find seeking souls. The pain of her separation from her young daughter was growing ever more acute and painful. She also found that, although her time in Madagascar had been difficult and had left her seriously unwell, this time in Douala was becoming painful beyond endurance. To make matters worse, one night in May of 1954 a note was put under her door to say that Samuel had suffered a heart attack. The effect on Meherangiz was monumental: she passed out, possibly from shock, and then was unable to muster the physical strength to move from her bed for days. Finally, the Manager of the hotel alerted a doctor to her condition, which had deteriorated significantly, and he counselled her firmly to return to her family as she was at risk of malnutrition and worse. But Meherangiz felt unable to leave because she believed that as yet she had not accomplished anything and must find at least one believer to justify her journey to the Cameroons.

The cost of living in Douala was also becoming an issue. One day she received a letter from the Guardian pointedly asking her if she was eating well. That day she ate lunch at the Akwa Palace which cost her £5, which was the equivalent of the cost of being able to live in the United Kingdom for more than a week. It did, however, enable her to reply on that day affirmatively to the beloved Guardian without telling a lie. She felt completely unable to respond in any fashion that might indicate that she needed funds, as she was already receiving some money from the Indian National Assembly which troubled her greatly, but for which there was no alternative.

Her personal safety was also becoming an additional problem and through an acquaintance who had a shop frequented by influential people, a police officer approached her and said she was far too vulnerable to continue to live on her own without a gun. He tried to emphasize that when the men got drunk in Douala, they were motivated to attack white women and if she refused their attentions, they would kill her. He kindly showed her how the gun worked and handed it to her. After holding it in her hand for a few seconds, she explained she would be unable to shoot anyone. He reacted angrily and with total disbelief about why she was being so "stupid" as to remain in this dreadful place on her own. In an effort to pacify him, she said, "God will protect me". To which he retorted "God protects those who protect themselves".

In her time in Douala up to then, she had not come across any Indians. Eventually, she met a couple from southern India but unfortunately she did not speak the same language and so they were obliged to communicate in French which none of them spoke well. They kindly invited her to lunch where they introduced their infant daughter, of approximately one year old. The wife wanted to have some dresses made for her child so Meherangiz offered to sew in return for the occasional meal. There was no sewing machine and Meherangiz had never sewn a lot, let alone by hand. Try as hard as she could, it was impossible for Meherangiz to work in the exhausting heat with insufficient lighting and mostly on a diet of bread and tea, which left her totally weak. She recalled a dream where she was eating so much food that it was actually coming out of her eyes, which awakened her only to find she was crying instead.

In order to pass the time of day, she would sit outside watching the people going by, or walk along the riverside, praying that someday the British and French Cameroons would become one country, and Mr Olinga who lived on the British side would then be able to freely help with attracting some pure souls.

By chance, Meherangiz struck up a friendship with an Englishman, Peter Price. They would chat generally but she was careful not to talk about the Faith. One day he said to her, "Meher, I see you have absolutely nothing, yet you are serene and even able to have a sense of humour. I want to know what gives you this contentment." He then disclosed that he had really come to Douala to die. He had a job and a home but, as he put it, "I am neither dying or living and I look at you and can't believe it." As it happened, that day she had been reading *Bahá'u'lláh and the New Era* which she had put aside when he approached. After a while he asked what she was reading, to which at first she remained silent. Then thinking he might get suspicious about what she was reading and, as she couldn't afford to be surrounded by any intrigue, she lent it to him. They parted and clearly he had read non-stop until the early hours of the morning when he banged on her window, saying he wanted to talk to her. She protested that this was not the time to talk and to return the next day, but he continued to bang on her door. In frustration, she asked him what was the matter that he could not wait, or was he drunk, either way he had to go home. He started to cry and said he wasn't drunk but wanted to know how he could become a Bahá'í. She insisted he leave but was not anxious that he become a Bahá'í, having been told to concentrate on the African population and not to teach the whites. But God clearly works in mysterious ways, for the first person to declare as a Bahá'í in French Cameroons was an Englishman!

Shortly after Peter's acceptance of the Faith, Samuel Njiki brought a young woman with an 18-month-old baby. He had introduced the woman to the Faith but was anxious that she meet Meherangiz. After talking for some time, Meherangiz held out her hands to the baby who literally flew out of her mother's arms. The mother in some astonishment said, "Now I know that you have a true Faith." Curious, Meherangiz enquired why she had come to that conclusion and she responded by saying that Meherangiz was the first white person her child wanted to be with; normally she would never go to anyone who was not black. Apparently, in her mind this meant that Meherangiz had genuine love for the people of Cameroons.

During her time in Douala Meherangiz's resolve and spirit were sustained by the thoughts and prayers from Shoghi Effendi conveyed in letters written either by Leroy Ioas or Rúḥíyyih Khánum. Rouhangiz Bolles was another regular correspondent whose letters were like a breath of fresh air and so helpful, as they often contained quotations from the Writings and included pamphlets which were very useful. Meherangiz never forgot how much letters meant, and throughout her life, although she hated writing because she was dyslexic and with a lack of education could not spell, she would religiously correspond with all the lonely pioneers and friends she met on her travels.

When Meherangiz returned to London, she confided that during her time in Douala she had missed her daughter and husband so much that they would appear as mirages at her door and she would go to hug them. For some significant periods of time she would cry and was desperately lonely, praying to Bahá'u'lláh night and day to give her strength as she didn't think she could go on for much longer. Her despair was compounded by total physical weakness from a diet devoid of nutrition. She didn't know what she was doing wrong and, with her visa and money due to run out, she begged in her prayers to know how she could attract more pure souls to the Faith. On one such occasion when she was severely despondent in her supplications, she heard a voice which she believed was 'Abdu'l-Bahá's, very clearly saying, "You have others in your heart. There is no room for me." Immediately, she knew that in constantly missing her family she had excluded spiritual guidance. In an instant, she resolved to cut out these thoughts of her husband and child and rely entirely on Bahá'u'lláh.

Coincidentally, that same evening or the next day, Samuel came to visit her and said, "I am so dejected, Meherangiz; the French coloured population only want to drink cheap wine and nothing seems to happen and I don't think anything will happen." Her response was swift; "Samuel, in that case why did Shoghi Effendi ask the Bahá'ís to come and form an Assembly!" She shared with him her recent experience and immediately Samuel was on his knees, asking for forgiveness for his negative thoughts. They then both prayed together, supplicating to have only the love of Bahá'u'lláh in their hearts and the thoughts of service in their minds. Almost immediately thereafter, they started to find people who were interested in the Faith.

Providentially, a friend from Madagascar had asked Meherangiz's husband, Eruch, to purchase some vinyl records in the United Kingdom, and send them to him. When it came to reimbursing Eruch for the purchases, Eruch requested the money be sent to Meherangiz in the French Cameroons. Finally, Meherangiz had a little money to sustain her. As a treat, she recalled purchasing some butter to put on her bread. After she washed her hands before eating, she returned to the saucer where she had placed the butter, which had melted and was covered in ants. That day she ate bread, butter and some protein... ants!

During the time Meherangiz was in Douala, John Robarts, his wife Audrey, and daughter Nina were pioneering in Mafeking and he had been appointed an Auxiliary Board Member by the Hands of the Cause. In the course of his duties as a Board Member, he would correspond regularly with Meherangiz to find out what was happening and how she was managing. She replied honestly that she was only able to eat once a day. In response he kindly sent her $20, saying it was his daughter's birthday, and they would be happy if she would celebrate it with them by treating herself. He also indicated he would come to visit her soon. Sadly, the money was drawn on a South African Bank so she was never able to access the funds. Nevertheless, years later at the second International Teaching Conference in 1958, she gratefully repaid him the money and thanked him for his kindness.

Meherangiz was beginning to become seriously unwell, passing out several times a day. On one occasion, as she was regaining consciousness, she heard an American voice next to her saying, "Oh honey . . ." Thinking it was John Robarts, she replied "Alláh-u-Abhá". On opening her eyes she was startled to find that the man was profusely apologizing, saying he thought she was "Rosie". It appeared he was a ship's captain and he offered his card and any assistance she might need. Observing her condition, he felt he should send the ship's doctor to attend to her. Meherangiz, however, was so shocked that all she could do was to order him out of the room. The next morning she received a card of apology with a beautiful bouquet of pink carnations and an invitation to call on him if she was ever in New York. Apparently, Rosie had given him a key to her room and then moved without advising him of her whereabouts!

Walking down the road wearing her usual attire of a sari, she realized that a crowd of men, women and children was silently following her in a procession. Eventually, she became aware of their presence and enquired why they were following her. It transpired that because she was wearing a blue sari with her head covered, they thought she was "Our Lady, the Mother of Christ". One of the men said everyone knew she lived a pious life and the association of the blue colour with the depictions of Mary had inspired them to follow her. Meherangiz immediately took the sari off from her head and told them she was not Mary and they should not follow her. The last thing she needed was to attract the attention of the officials, however innocently.

Samuel Njiki's life in Douala was also not easy. He lived with an uncle who was against the Faith and really didn't want to have anything to do with him. One day in August 1954, Samuel was in an accident with his bicycle and was promptly put in jail. This was the usual practice: incarceration of a foreigner first, questions later. The uncle, not wanting to do anything himself, sent a message to

Meherangiz explaining what had happened and asking her to get Samuel out of jail. Meherangiz was not sure how successful a foreign woman, barely able to speak French, was going to be, but, relying on Bahá'u'lláh, she went and miraculously was able to get him released without charges. The effect on the uncle was to convince him that at least the Bahá'ís practised what they preached about the oneness of mankind, which he was sure was a myth. After all, what white person was going to do anything to help a black man? Going forward, the uncle was kinder to Samuel and showed more respect for the Faith.

One of the waiters at the Akwa Palace was a Spanish gentleman, Ramiro Hijano, and Meherangiz, who was already planning her next pioneering assignment to Rio de Oro in the Spanish Sahara, was taking Spanish lessons from him. Ramiro told Meherangiz that he had never met a "missionary" like her and he wanted to know more about the Faith. Meherangiz acquired a copy of *Bahá'u'lláh and the New Era* in Spanish and gave it to him. Shortly after Meherangiz left the country, Ramiro registered as a Bahá'í and continued to write to her frequently in England. After Meherangiz's departure, Ramiro and Peter Price were a source of financial support to Samuel, who found it almost impossible to find a job as he did not speak French.

Samuel and the other Bahá'í friends were becoming increasingly concerned at Meherangiz's health, which was deteriorating even more rapidly. Without telling her, they sent a telegram to the Guardian saying they felt she should leave Douala. It appears that at that time Shoghi

Effendi was in Switzerland and a reply came through Mr Banání in Uganda that Meherangiz should leave Douala and return to England. Air France, however, was only prepared to fly her out provided she signed a form discharging them of all responsibility if she were to die before reaching England, and authorizing them to bury her at any point of the return journey if that happened.

During the early days after her arrival, the Police Commissioner had instructed Meherangiz to give him all the names of any contacts who became interested in the Faith. When she consulted with Leroy Ioas about what she should do regarding this obligation, he counselled that unless she felt committed it would be wiser if it could be avoided. Now that her time to leave had come she felt worried about this promise and felt uneasy about not giving the names to the Commissioner. In the days leading up to her departure, she prayed long and hard, seeking guidance as to her best course of action. Eventually, she concluded she should be true to her word and would go and see the Commissioner as she was leaving.

A friend offered to drive Meherangiz to the airport but was very perturbed when Meherangiz was insistent on stopping at the Commissioner's office to report in, as she had promised. The friend was, however, very concerned at how weak Meherangiz was and wouldn't let her get out of the taxi but went up to see the Commissioner herself. She berated him, saying how inconsiderate it was to expect Mrs Munsiff, who was so ill, to stop and make a report. In the event, the Commissioner came down to the car and wished her well and a safe journey home and didn't ask her any questions at all. Bahá'u'lláh had once again answered her prayers and protected His own.

By the time Meherangiz returned home after some months away, she was in a truly desperate state and the effect on both her husband and daughter was devastating. Eruch was a relatively new Bahá'í and somehow in his mind he could barely believe that she had gone to serve God and returned a broken woman. Rúḥíyyih Khánum wrote a consoling letter at the time saying how much she knew Meherangiz had suffered but that Eruch had suffered the most. The doctors were appalled at her condition and she was hospitalized for three months in the beginning, being fed every hour on milk beaten with a raw egg and honey. Her nervous system had almost collapsed and she was kept at the National Neurological Institute, with a view to erasing all her memories of the last months. Fortunately, not all her recollections were lost.

Fairly soon after she was discharged from hospital, Leroy Ioas came to visit her on the instructions of the Guardian with the sole purpose of telling her that Shoghi Effendi was pleased with what she had accomplished, and he knew how much she had suffered. He went on to say that she had given the equivalent of twenty years of her life in the time that she had pioneered to Madagascar and the French Cameroons. There were no less than three cables received from the Guardian, asking her to look after her health and to obey the doctors. In one particular letter, he explained it was necessary for her to be careful of her health as she had many years of service in the Faith ahead of her.

In April 1955, Meherangiz received the most joyous news of all from Samuel Njiki: the first Local Spiritual Assembly of Douala had been formed at Riḍván. His letter of 30 April read:

> This goal has been achieved. The Assembly has been formed and our beloved Guardian is very pleased. Here below find the wordings of a cable received from Mr Banani quoting the beloved Guardian's cable:
> "Delighted loving remembrance Shrines".

Meherangiz returned to the French Cameroons twenty years after she had left in 1954. By coincidence, on the plane she sat with the officials who were going to Yaounde to finalize the details for the amalgamation of the two Cameroon territories into one country with Yaounde as the capital. Never one to lose an opportunity, Meherangiz gave both government officials she was sitting next to Bahá'í books, telling them that twenty years ago she had prayed hard for the unification of these two countries and here she was sitting next to the people who were going to make this possible.

Meherangiz and Samuel Njiki were both named Knights of Bahá'u'lláh. In a letter dated 7 June 1954 to the pioneers in the virgin territories, the British Isles National Spiritual Assembly wrote:

> The Guardian feels there is "no service in the entire Bahá'í world as important as their pioneering work" and that they have "achieved a great station of service"...

> You are the Knights of Bahá'u'lláh, a title accorded to
> no other servants of the Faith since its foundation,
> and you have gone forth to conquer the world for Him
> under the guidance of the beloved Guardian. . . He
> relies on you to live up to your proud title.

In 1984, Meherangiz received an encouraging letter from
a friend in Cameroon: ". . . at least you could see that
the sufferings you endured in Douala, as a Knight of
Bahá'u'lláh, have borne such good fruit – an active community and a beautiful Ḥazíratu'l-Quds. . . Two of the
friends, young men, stayed behind to help clean up – so
you see that Cameroon is progressing!" And later another
letter from a Cameroon Bahá'í during a return visit to
Portland, Oregon in 1998, the year before Meherangiz's
death:

> The words and wisdom of Bahá'u'lláh, which you very
> generously shared with us, continue to bear fruit as my
> love for Bahá'u'lláh increases day by day and I am able
> to liberate myself from the chains of this earthly life
> and its possessions. The specific things you said about
> praying for the healing of one's soul and the souls of
> others, writing to one another, accompanying thought
> and meditation with actions of service, obedience to
> the wishes of the divine institutions – have all made a
> tremendous impact on my life for the better. I feel that
> my life is full of meaning now that I have dedicated it
> to the service of Bahá'u'lláh. . .

The Years 1955–1999

Not only did Meherangiz visit about 147 countries throughout the world (see Appendix 2) many of them more than once, but she also travelled to town after town and village after village in each country. Wherever she went, she attracted a great deal of publicity through newspaper and magazine articles and radio and television interviews. In 1959, after a television interview, the British National Spiritual Assembly, in appreciation of her efforts, stated: "This is the first time the Bahá'í Faith has been mentioned on television in this country and we regard it as a great victory for the Faith and a great achievement for all concerned. . ."[5]

Meherangiz was always mindful that she was personally unimportant in any publicity which she might generate but she was determined to promote the Faith and was fiercely protective of its reputation. After one occasion when Meherangiz was interviewed on Cardiff (Wales) television in 1962, the Bishop of St. Davids had called the station and spoken against the Faith on the radio. Meherangiz called the producer and insisted he give her the right of reply. He duly invited her to come and face the Bishop on television, which she did. The Bishop kept referring in a dismissive tone to "Eastern religions". Eventually, when this had happened once too often, Meherangiz interjected, asking, "Excuse me, where do you think Christ was born, in Cardiff?" At this point, even the cameramen laughed.

Meherangiz was fluent in seven Indian languages but mostly gave lectures/talks in English, Persian, Hindustani and, if there was no alternative, in French which was very poor, having been acquired in Madagascar and French Cameroons. For many years she was a radio and television broadcaster on the Hindi programmes for the BBC. One of her broadcasts which is of some interest is from when she was visiting Mauritius in the late 1970s. It was during a time when the Navidi family were pioneering there and were well known throughout the island, both as Bahá'ís and prominent residents in Mauritius.

It appears that an interview had been arranged for Meherangiz. The day before the interview, however, Shamsi Navidi came to Meherangiz and said the interview would have to be cancelled as she had just discovered that it was to be conducted in French. Shamsi made it clear to Meherangiz in no uncertain terms that her French was so dreadful that it would be an embarrassment to the Faith and to Shamsi herself if Meherangiz were to try to give the interview. Meherangiz listened to Shamsi and said she needed to pray about it. Shamsi said there was nothing to pray about. Meherangiz respectfully disagreed and secluded herself for a couple of hours, after which she said, to Shamsi's reasonable dismay, that she was proposing to proceed with the interview. Shamsi, gracious as ever, took Meherangiz to the radio station and on arrival Meherangiz told Shamsi to quietly go somewhere and pray. The interview went ahead and when Meherangiz emerged from the recording booth, she was confronted by Shamsi whose blood appeared to have drained from her face. Meherangiz asked, "What is the matter with you? You look like you have seen a ghost." Shamsi replied, "It is not possible but your French was word perfect during the interview." Meherangiz smiled, taking Shamsi by the arm, saying, "It appears our prayers were answered."

Wherever she went, she was involved in public meetings, firesides, discussion groups, panels and institutes as well as coffee meetings and informal gatherings with the Bahá'ís and their friends. She gave presentations in schools, women's clubs, colleges, universities, art galleries, Rotary clubs, guilds, exhibitions and Girl Guide meetings. She was regularly asked to be part of United Nations Day panels, speak at World Religion Day events on the Bahá'í Faith and give presentations on the Universal House of Justice's statement *The Promise of World Peace*. There could be up to 700 people or more at any one meeting or only a handful.

In America she attended receptions, luncheons and Girl Scout dinners, and she organized fashion shows depicting women of India. She was also involved in Theosophical meetings, and accepted invitations to the Methodist and Presbyterian churches and the YWCA. In Belfast, Northern Ireland, she compered an International Festival in aid of a Freedom from Hunger Campaign. She was invited to participate in tree planting ceremonies, Salvation Army meetings, events in the Hindu Culture Centre and at a prison in Norway, as well as events in

Westminster Abbey, dinners in the House of Lords, tea at Lancaster House, a gala in the President's palace in the Central African Republic, and the Bahá'í Asian Women's Conference. For some years she served on the Executive Committee of the Royal Society of India, Pakistan and Ceylon, whose Patron was Queen Elizabeth, the Queen Mother; the Executive Committee of the Women's India Association of the British Isles; Girl Guides Association and Associated Member of the World Association of Girl Guides and Girl Scouts; and on the Board of the Advisory Committee to the BBC programmes for immigrants on television and radio.

Her philosophy was simple: participate in any gathering, because there would always be the opportunity to make mention of the Faith directly or its teachings, and more importantly to come across sincere souls who were searching for spiritual guidance.

Despite living in a very modest home in London, she constantly held dinners for prominent people. The remarkable thing was that they often returned when hospitality was extended again, despite the Munsiffs' humble circumstances.

Meherangiz gave talks on a variety of subjects, such as Zoroaster; Women and Youth in India; East and West Shall Meet; Dawn of a New Age; Peoples and Customs; The Mysterious East; Religions of the World; Educating a Multi-Racial Society; Rights and Responsibilities of Man; A Stranger in our Midst; The World is My Country; A New Charter For Women; Living the Bahá'í Life; the Generation Gap; The Execution of the Bahá'ís in Iran

(1979); The Role of Women and the Faith; Táhirih; My Travels and Experiences; A Pattern for Future Society; The Role of Women in Present Day Society; The Sufferings of Bahá'u'lláh; Unity in Diversity; Pilgrimage; Religion for Mankind; the World's Greatest Prisoner; Unity; the Recurring Heritage of Humanity; and How to Unite the East and West. It didn't matter to Meherangiz what the subject was. If she was invited to speak, she would do so because she was confident that somehow she would be able to introduce an aspect of the Faith which was germane to her subject.

She was also mindful of Bahá'í activities and was happy to share her knowledge and experiences which she felt would inspire and deepen the Bahá'í friends, whether it was in connection with the Fund, Bahá'í marriage, obligatory prayers or any other subject. She was thrilled to meet Bahá'í communities in different countries when she attended Nineteen Day Feasts and gave talks at Holy Day commemorations.

During Meherangiz's life she served on three different Local Spiritual Assemblies and served as a delegate to both the United Kingdom and United States National Conventions, although she always felt that she was better at being out in the trenches, rather than sitting in a room contributing to administrative matters.

Wherever Meherangiz went, she mixed and mingled with people from diverse races and social backgrounds – from the Queen of Thailand to the Gypsy people of Europe, from Presidents to the First Nations people of America, from Prime Ministers to the Ainu people of

Japan, from Governor Generals to local Mayors as well as Ambassadors and Members of Parliament. In addition, Eruch and Meherangiz could count the United States Supreme Court Justices Warren and Douglas as personal friends during their time in Washington D.C.

Countless people of all ages were attracted to the Faith through Meherangiz's sacrificial efforts, and hundreds, if not thousands, embraced the Cause of Bahá'u'lláh throughout the world. This is evidenced by literally hundreds of letters from seekers embracing the Faith and expressing their gratitude for her interventions, even when they were quite direct.

Meherangiz suffered ill-health most of her life, some times more acutely than others when she required hospital treatment, but, despite constant fatigue and migraines, she would arise again and again to attend the meetings, reach out to the friends and respond to the needs of those with whom she came in contact. As soon as she felt relatively healthy again, she would be on the road, travelling to one country after another for months at a time.

Throughout her life of service, Meherangiz constantly received guidance, encouragement and motivation from the Holy Land, whether from Shoghi Effendi, and the Hands in the Holy Land after his passing, the Universal House of Justice or the International Teaching Centre. Repeatedly they shared their concerns regarding her ill-health, imploring her to take it easy, but generally these concerns were unheeded. The one task she dreaded arising out of her travels were the requests to send in reports of her teaching trips and pioneer experiences to the Holy

Land, which she did, but due to her minimal education she found this duty to be excruciatingly challenging.

Meherangiz cherished the encouraging and loving letters she received from 'Amatu'l-Bahá Rúḥíyyih Khánum and other Hands of the Cause or individual members of the sacred institutions in Haifa. Here is an extract from a letter Meherangiz received in 1994 from 'Alí Nakhjavání referring to her special relationship with the Guardian:

> The days of the Guardianship have passed away, but those pure souls, like you, who were touched by the rays of his light, and awakened by the breeze of his divine grace, can, thank God, transmit the charm and magic of his presence. His spirit lives on in his immortal writings, his superhuman efforts and his stupendous achievements, but, in addition to these, the dynamic transformation which he produced in such hearts as became enamoured of the celestial splendour which emanated from him, will be handed down from generation to generation, as long as God's Holy Cause will abide amongst man. You are one of those hearts that beats and throbs with love for him, and servitude at his door . . .

In 1955 Eruch was promoted into the diplomatic service and posted to the Indian Embassy in Washington D.C., where the family remained until 1958. In December 1955 Meherangiz received an encouraging message from Shoghi Effendi:

He wishes you to know, however, that the services you
and your dear husband are rendering the Faith, are
very deeply appreciated. He feels sure that in America
you are able to do a great deal of good in stimulating
interest in the Cause amongst non-Baháʼís; as well as
firing the believers themselves with a greater spirit of
dedication, and thirst to pioneer.[6]

During the years in America, Meherangiz continued to
travel, and during her time there she travelled extensively
throughout the United States and Canada, and whenever
possible taking Jyoti with her. They visited over thirty
states, usually by Greyhound bus, which was the only
mode of transport they could reasonably afford. During
one of the rest stops in a southern state, Meherangiz and
Jyoti were thirsty and saw a water fountain, but when they
approached it, they saw a sign saying "Whites Only". Next
to it was a tap over which the sign read "Blacks and Dogs".
This was the first time Jyoti, as an eight-year-old child,
had come face to face with such overt racism. Not knowing what to do, her mother explained that they were not
white so they would take the water from the tap, but that
she (Jyoti) should always remember that in the sight of
God everyone was the same and that was why they were
on this long trip, to bring the message of Baháʼuʼlláh.

Meherangiz particularly cherished her visits in
October 1956 to the Zuni, Navajo and Hopi reservations where they stayed for a while, often sleeping on the
ground in the open desert air. It should be noted that
in 1978, Mary Gibson in a letter from Haifa wrote that,

National Teaching Conference in the British Isles, January 1952, held at the Grand Hotel, Sheffield. Meherangiz Munsiff is in the front row, third from left

A meeting in London in the 1950s.
Meherangiz is seated centre back, with Jyoti on her lap

Fashion commentator: looking over her script for a television commentary on fashion in South-east Asian countries

Cookery demonstrations

Meherangiz and Jyoti meeting Jawaharlal Nehru, the first Prime Minister of India after Independence during his visit to Washington, D.C. in December 1956

At a meeting of Soroptimist International, Baltimore, 1957

Meherangiz as a guest of honour at a dinner hosted by Mrs Theodore McKeldin (right) wife of the Governor of Maryland during a visit to the State Legislative Assembly where she was introduced to the House by the Speaker Mrs Norman Polk, standing in the picture with Mrs Jesse Price, seated left

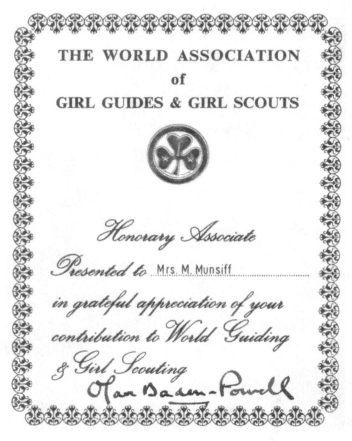

THE WORLD ASSOCIATION
of
GIRL GUIDES & GIRL SCOUTS

Honorary Associate

Presented to Mrs. M. Munsiff

in grateful appreciation of your contribution to World Guiding & Girl Scouting

Olav Baden-Powell

Certificate of contribution to the work of the World Association of Girl Guides and Girl Scouts signed by the World Chief Guide, Olave, Lady Baden Powell

Some of the many Lions Clubs Meherangiz spoke at in the United States

On tour teaching the Zuni Indians in New Mexico

*Receiving an award from the American Red Cross for
"exceptional service on behalf of humanity"*

Red Cross project in Beleghata, Calcutta, India

Photograph taken to commemorate the first mention of Bahá'u'lláh on British television, Lyme Hall, Stockport, 23 May 1959. Pauline Senior at the far left, next to Margery Parker (?), and Ronald Bates standing behind, with the Mayor in the front row

Looking at a bust of Rabrindanath Tagore by Jacob Epstein, at Foyle's Gallery, London, 6 January 1962, with the Earl of Listowel who opened the exhibition of work by members of the Royal India, Pakistan and Ceylon Society

Speaking at Kensington Central Library, London, on World Religion Day, 26 January 1962

while she and her family were on a camping trip on the Navajo reservation, "it was most natural that we should think of the Munsiffs as Jyoti and Meherangiz, with the assistance and blessing of Eruch, were the first visitors to launch a teaching campaign on the Navajo reservation during the Ten Year Crusade. Now there are 10 Assemblies on the Navajo lands. Praise be to God!"

In 1957, the Maryland State Legislature presented Meherangiz with a replica of the State Seal and an address of appreciation for her services to Maryland State citizens – the full gathering of the House gave her the high honour of a standing ovation. In Washington she was made an honorary member of the Capitol Hill Lion's Club for her contributions through lectures promoting better international understanding. At the time she was the only woman to have received this honour. And in August 1958 she was awarded a certificate of appreciation by the Red Cross for exceptional humanitarian services. Meherangiz would be the first to tell you that these accolades were only achieved through the guidance and bounty of Bahá'u'lláh, without which, none of these things could have conceivably happened. Her constant encouragement to the friends was to get involved with the wider community and that when they did this in the spirit of service, the Bahá'ís always excelled and were appreciated.

After a trip to Louisville, Kentucky in January 1958 taken solely by her mother, Jyoti received the following message: ". . . very much appreciate the recent visit of your beautiful, brilliant, eloquent and devoted mother.

We wish you could have been here too – to hear how magnificently she spoke on every occasion and how happy she made us all!"

Throughout her stay in America, Meherangiz gave many interviews to the press as well as radio and television. Here are a very few excerpts from the hundreds of newspapers publicizing her activities, which give a glimpse into the media's impression of her. In addition, within the following pages are sample extracts from the thousands of letters received by Meherangiz which reflect the influence she had on a wide-ranging spectrum of people and the multiple facets of her teaching endeavours, as well as her course on prayer and meditation which resonated with so many of them. These excerpts are included in the hope that whatever your perspective on teaching the Bahá'í Faith or praying might be, you will see how a wide variety of individuals were impacted and inspired after understanding more deeply the importance and effect of adhering to our obligation to disseminate the message of the Cause and to pray daily.

Since coming to the United States she has been invited by community groups, including many service organizations, to speak in some 55 cities covering more than 8,000 miles in cross-country tours . . .

The interest of this distinguished Indian woman in various humanitarian activities began at the age of 15 when she associated herself with the welfare of the uneducated and poverty-ridden labourers of

Ahmedabad, a leading textile manufacturing centre in India.

Her desire for the removal of poverty, eradication of illiteracy and other similar social evils confronting the peoples of the East has attracted her to the study of many welfare centres of varied types in India, Great Britain, United States, and some African territories. . .

Mrs Munsiff has spoken to groups ranging from thousands of people in many American and Canadian cities to small groups in other countries.

A beautiful gracious lady, she spoke with wit and charm, interspersing interesting information. . .

An East Indian woman who recently visited Indian reservations and a sheep ranch in northern Arizona is broadcasting, in three languages, for the Voice of America in Washington, D.C.

Mrs Munsiff wears Indian dress but has the effusive, almost back-slapping friendliness of a typical American. She does not script her talks but gives them in a chatty way making points of essentially human interest.

In 1960, after Meherangiz had visited Arnhem in Holland, one of the friends wrote to her saying:

. . . since you left, it is as if a bright star, two in fact, had risen, shone for an instant and passed out of sight. But the illumination is still with us and the joy of the moments spent with you will buoy us up for a long time. The only trouble is – it has whetted our appetites to hear more from you and experience more of the spirit that surrounds you and flows out to us. . .

After Meherangiz gave a talk in Edinburgh, a young man recalled:

In June 1961, in the midst of my exams, I met a visitor, Meherangiz Munsiff, an Indian lady who believed almost fanatically in prayer. I listened to an inspiring talk and then asked my questions. She refused to answer them, saying only God could. She then asked me to open a prayer book and read a prayer aloud. "Which prayer?" "Any prayer. Open the book at random." I did so and started to read. The prayer was over five pages long. During that prayer, the months of my search, in feelings but not in logic, cascaded through the words. I cried quite a lot (me, an English man!). I ploughed on and by the end it was easier. The words carried me. I rode the torrent rather than fought it. Meherangiz said nothing except, "Have you had your answer?" I replied that I had and left the meeting.

Meherangiz could fill a room with laughter, as noted in a letter from a friend in Winchester, England in November 1961: ". . . what an unexpected joy it was to me to see your lovely face after so long and to hear your voice with its ripple of laughter in it. It seemed to refresh my soul and start me off with fresh hope and happiness . . ."

In 1962, Meherangiz's family moved to Wimbledon in England. By now Eruch was a senior officer in India House. They were the only Indians living in that area at that time.

Meherangiz kept up a lifetime correspondence with hundreds of people throughout the world, many of them sharing the effect she had had on their lives. A friend from Florence in Italy wrote:

I want you to know what your visit to Florence meant to me. It is hard to put it into words, but that afternoon with you was like a refreshing rain to a parched and desolate land. That sounds exaggerated but it expresses my state of mind before and after being with you! I know you can read between the lines!

And another from Winchester in England wrote:

Three years ago . . . I was having lunch with you in our home and enjoying your loving kindness and it ended with me making my declaration. . . I always remember seeing and hearing you for the first time at Rutland Gate. You wore a pure white sari, and you gave me hope that even I might be able to be of use to the Faith.

A letter from London in 1965 read:

How on earth (or in heaven) do you manage to do it? How on earth do you manage to shower so much love and kindness on all the people you must meet on your travels so that each one feels that he holds a special place in your heart? How fortunate I count myself to have the acquaintanceship of someone who sets such an inspiring example to me! It is a wonder to me that you even have to utter one word about the Faith. It seems to me that any reasonable person who has the privilege of knowing you for even a short time would say "this is for me", and rush off immediately to make his declaration.

It is also important to recognize that there were times when Meherangiz could be blunt and, occasionally without meaning to, cause offence. There were moments when the Bahá'ís could hardly believe their ears. One such occasion was when she was asked to speak at a fireside and she was advised that one of the attendees had been coming for twenty-five years. At the end of the meeting Meherangiz approached the lady and asked, "What is your problem, are you just coming for the social benefits or is there an issue in the Faith you disagree with and, if not, why have you not become a Bahá'í?" The poor Bahá'í hostess was mortified but before she could say anything the lady said "No one has ever asked me if I want to be a Bahá'í but I do." The evening ended with a celebration and much joy and many hugs. Meherangiz often tried to explain to the Bahá'ís that not only was it important to share the Faith but it was equally important to attune one's antennae to pick up when it was timely to invite someone to come into the Faith, to help with the enormous task facing the Bahá'ís and for which every additional willing soul was essential.

Institutions of the Faith also wrote to her after her visits. For example, the Italian National Spiritual Assembly wrote on 19 March 1963: "Your teaching trip to Italy brought us a real wave of joy . . . we are sure that all those who had the privilege to attend your talks, both Bahá'ís and non-Bahá'ís, will remember this happy occasion as the one in which they met the best and true example of a Bahá'í lady of the New Era of Bahá'u'lláh . . ."

Youth all over the world were also positively affected by Meherangiz's talks. In 1969 she received a letter from a friend in Brighton, England saying:

Yesterday . . . told us with great joy and in detail that you had greatly encouraged them and that you had kindly asked them to lunch as well. . . That is exactly what the youth need, otherwise they will soon be discouraged and will not continue with their activities. Because of your encouragement they have decided to continue with their meetings even if no one attends . . .

And from a Youth Conference in May in Manchester, England the youth committee wrote:

. . . we would like to send you our sincere love and thanks for your wonderful contribution to our conference. We are still living in the wake of your inspiration, and the wave of enthusiasm has already resulted in a declaration.

In the Solomon Islands in December 1977:

She gave a talk on the Fund and stories about the sacrifices of pioneers and martyrs. The youth were strongly encouraged to ensure the proper use of Bahá'í Funds, with the youth seeming to respond well to Mrs Munsiff's firm manner in discussing this with them . . . The youth treated Mrs Munsiff most respectfully by rising when she entered. This is a marked change and was a good example of how the youth responded to her.

After the United States Louhelen Summer Regional Youth Conference in 1989 attended by 80 youth the following reactions were shared:

The presence and classes of Mrs Munsiff had an astounding effect on the entire conference, including the declarations by eleven youth and one adult, including a student from South Africa . . . coupled with personal recollections by Mrs Munsiff, produced appreciation for the Guardian and commitment by the youth to continue to study his writings.

One of these things is the symbol of the Greatest Name. It is important to me now. Before I used to think of it as just another symbol, but now it is like a priceless painting, worth more than the world

88

Photograph from the Sunday Times Magazine, 6 April 1969, in an article on women who give lectures at "ladies' luncheon parties': 'I started yapping in India at 14 and I haven't stopped since.'

Eruch and Meherangiz with friends at a Ball organized by the Bahá'ís of Wandsworth, London in 1968. Left to right: Rowshan Knox, Dermod Knox, Riaz Khadem, Robert Lewis, Linda Khadem, David Lewis, Barbara Lewis, Meherangiz Munsiff, Brian Giddings, Joan Giddings, with Eruch Munsiff in front

The last Local Spiritual Assembly of London before dividing up into boroughs

Travel teaching in Switzerland: in Bienne/Biel,
with the mayor and his daughter

Meherangiz, Eruch and Joyti Munsiff,
guests at a wedding in England in July 1970

It was as if I was a new Bahá'í again and the words
of Bahá'u'lláh and His Power were unknown to me
. . . You became our spiritual mother and we became
your spiritual children . . .

This is the first class I've never been late for! I love it . . .

I now realize that praying to Bahá'u'lláh with my mind
instead of my heart was stunting my spiritual growth.
Learning this one lesson is enough to change my life . . .

You have revived and healed my soul. Now I must
protect and nourish it as you have taught me . . .

. . . and the stories that you told, they just lift me up . . .

The Station of Bahá'u'lláh, His Majesty and Kingship,
the Glory of God, The Prince of Peace. This station
is made more poignant because we know of His sufferings, saw the silken satin scarf replaced by the
weightiest chain . . .

To the Blessed Beauty's Knight in shining armor
whom he led me to in time of need. You have helped
me to reignite the fire of His love in my heart that I
never thought would return . . .

In 1990 after her second visit to Chile that year
Meherangiz received a letter regarding their youth. There
were lots of youth present and she reminded them to say

the Tablet of Aḥmad and their obligatory prayers.

> Parental reaction – so far all favourable . . . one of the
> youth . . . said that now you had attracted him back to
> the Faith and reawakened his soul . . . He had known
> you were coming but had forgotten when. At 5:00 p.m.
> Friday, he was on the bus going home. Looking out
> the window he saw you walking down the street in the
> same sari you wore on Saturday. He quickly got off the
> bus at the next stop a few blocks away and called the
> Centre asking when you were going to speak. The Bahá'í
> that answered said that you had started speaking just 5
> minutes before! No wonder you are tired after a talk –
> apparently you are in more than one place at a time!

In May 1972 Meherangiz received another encouraging
letter from the Universal House of Justice in response to
one of her reports:

> As your report clearly reveals, your visits wherever
> you go bring inspiration to the hearts of the friends,
> stimulate and enhance their efforts to proclaim and
> publicize the Faith and attract the hearts of the true
> seekers to the divine Message. We will once again offer
> prayers on your behalf at the Holy Shrines, and sup-
> plicate the Blessed Beauty to enable you, as you desire,
> to witness the entry by troops into the Faith of God . . .

And again in October of 1975:

Your valiant efforts to attract new adherents to the Cause of Bahá'u'lláh, to re-teach and deepen the believers in the countries you are visiting, to guide, inspire and enthuse these friends with a new spirit of devotion are all invaluable. Those friends who are deepened and inspired will no doubt be so uplifted that they will carry on the teaching work after you have left them. Your success with the use of radio and television has also demonstrated to the friends the possibility of the use of these media for the proclamation of the Faith . . .

And also in March of 1978:

The Universal House of Justice has followed with keen interest the reports of your fruitful visits in that area [South Pacific] . . . It is hoped that the work you have done will be reinforced by other efforts; meanwhile you are encouraged to keep in touch by correspondence with the friends, both Bahá'í and non-Bahá'í, with whom you established a special rapport, to further develop your friendship and keep them stimulated in the Faith . . .

Meherangiz took this encouragement to heart and never ceased in her correspondence with "both Bahá'í and non-Bahá'í", which, as mentioned earlier, was no easy task for her. She sublimated her embarrassment at not being able to spell correctly or write grammatically correct statements with the consolation that she was being obedient to the Beloved Guardian and the House of Justice and nothing else mattered. In her final days she was visited by someone who was not a Bahá'í but because of his prominent position had been able to assist the Bahá'ís in overcoming obstacles in securing land for the Bahá'í House of Worship in India. He told Jyoti that although he had a large family she was the only person who for the last thirty-five years had always remembered his birthday and never failed to send him a card. Meherangiz would tell you that this man helped the Faith and to her last breath she would be grateful to him and wanted him to know it.

In November 1974 Meherangiz gave the first of her talks focusing on prayer and meditation. These talks ultimately led to a comprehensive four-day course on this subject, the essence of which you will find in Part 2. During this first talk in London one of the participants who attended but who was not a Bahá'í relates:

A point she made was: "If you pray for guidance but don't meditate, it is like knocking at a door and then not waiting for an answer." Quoting the Guardian's "Dynamics of Prayer" as cited in *Principles of Bahá'í Administration*, Meherangiz stressed that having received what one felt could be guidance, one then had to act. Despite there being much in the Faith that I could accept wholeheartedly – especially the concept of progressive revelation, as I had already reached this conclusion – there were two major barriers: a firm belief in reincarnation, and the decision not to be "labelled". However, the more I read about the Faith, the more I fell in love with the teachings and the Central Figures. Having been particularly moved by Gloria Faizi's *The Bahá'í Faith*, I reached the stage where I had to resort to prayer to resolve perplexity. Following Meherangiz's advice and praying: "dear Lord, how best can I serve thee", meditated, and found the most persistent thought was: "become a Bahá'í". Recalling her words that one must then act, got straight into the car and drove the 18 miles to the nearest Bahá'ís in Canterbury [England)], . . . and "declared" on their doorstep. . .

In January 1977 one of the friends from Haifa captured some of Meherangiz's spiritual qualities in a letter to her:

You are often in our thoughts. Your radiance, your frankness, your wisdom, your perseverance, your charm, your perspicacity, and your love and ardour for the Cause are qualities which penetrate the hearts, inspire the souls, deepen the faith and understanding of the believers, and ignite the spirit of the friends . . .

While in South Africa, in December 1979, a minister of the Methodist Church declared his faith in Bahá'u'lláh. The National Spiritual Assembly wrote: "Mrs Munsiff taught, entertained, inspired, encouraged, pleaded with, threatened, 'thumped' and delighted with her course on 'Prayer and Meditation.'"

Meherangiz was encouraged by the Universal House of Justice to reach the East Indians in the Caribbean countries. In 1982 she was able to meet with the First Lady of Surinam and the President. She connected with the Indian Association and gave two one-hour live radio interviews. Despite being unwell in Surinam, Meherangiz as always rose from her sick bed to talk to a group of women on a "Bahá'í View of Women in Society Today". "Sick or well, Mrs Munsiff is informative, humorous and impressive."

While revisiting an island in the Caribbean she was told that the Bahá'í Centre could not be used because, after losing his voting rights, the Secretary of the Assembly had padlocked the building and told the Bahá'ís that if they tried to enter he would put a spell on them. Meherangiz was mindful of the fact that the believers had come from a culture that practised voodoo, so rather than telling them not to be ridiculous she ascertained that the building belonged to the Bahá'ís and they had every right to enter. She then told them to get bolt cutters and unlock the Centre and instructed them to tell the ex-Secretary this had happened. She then proceeded to place herself on a chair with the door open and spend the night there, telling the Bahá'ís that if no spell had been cast by the morning they had to understand that no power was greater than the protection of Bahá'u'lláh and that they should not allow themselves to be intimidated by threats of voodoo. The community regained control of the Centre and once again Meherangiz had demonstrated an ability to seek a solution to a problem which was enduring and unique.

After this latest trip she received a letter from the Universal House of Justice dated 13 September 1982:

As you return to your home in England after the long
months of travel teaching, the Universal House of
Justice expresses its warm commendation for your
stalwart efforts in proclamation and teaching, and
in deepening the friends. The numerous mass media
opportunities which you have created, the public
information contacts you have made, the new believers you have been instrumental in attracting and
enrolling, and your classes for the believers themselves, have all been of great service to our beloved
Cause . . . praise for your labours, which you carried
on despite your recurrent illness.

In July 1984 Meherangiz's skill in public relations
and media activities attracted the attention of the
International Teaching Centre:

What we need are details of the practical planning
and step by step preparation of avenues, openings,
activities, methods of gaining cooperation, points of
protocol etc. in the field of public relations, contact
with prominent people and organizations with similar
aims to the Faith, and all branches of the media so that
the time, talents, energy, experience and resources of
travelling teachers may be properly and fully utilized
. . .

Meherangiz faithfully and humbly submitted her sugges-
tions to the International Teaching Centre calling upon
her various experiences during her extensive travels.

In August 1984 Meherangiz visited Iceland where she stayed in a tiny home with no privacy and no shower. But Meherangiz was by now accustomed to personal inconvenience and hardships and her visit was very successful, as witnessed in a letter she received a month later from that National Spiritual Assembly:

The new surge and excitement you brought with you has not subsided. New souls are still finding their way into the Faith of Bahá'u'lláh in a good, healthy, steady stream. Also, nearly 10 of our "former" or "inactive" Bahá'ís have come crawling out of the walls ready and eager to serve and be part of the business of building God's promised Kingdom here on this earth . . .

Later in 1984 her travels took her to Sweden:

Local Spiritual Assemblies have been in contact with the Secretariat asking us to convey their love and appreciation to you . . . The proclamation you have done has already given result in the form of two newspaper articles . . . (The National Spiritual Assembly of Sweden)

It was a spiritual journey for all of us; a spiritual journey through the spheres of love and light. Our hearts were so tenderly touched, our minds refreshed and our souls uplifted. We felt being drawn closer and closer to the love of Bahá'u'lláh and the knowledge that He has so graciously imparted to the world of man and creation... (The Local Spiritual Assembly of Gothenburg)

And another letter, from an individual believer:

Your beautiful words from Malta brought joy sweeter than the purest honey, and bestowed delight more wholesome than the delicately scented spring blossoms ... We all truly cherish the historical memories of your unforgettable visit of enlightenment to these regions, and wish that such valuable and invaluable occasions may be repeated with short intervals ... You are one of those unique human beings who is endowed with the gift of ability to convey that "conscious knowledge". Very few people in history can be found who possess a personality with sterling qualities of courage, knowledge, humility, spiritual maturity and articulation, is hard working, humorous, warm, kind, serious, as well as the host of other qualities. You are one of those who serves with indomitable spirit and startling indefatigability without the least expectation of appreciation and gratitude from the surroundings. The true traits of a most exemplary lover, who only loves the Well-Beloved with ever increasing ardour. May many a person learn such traits from you. May they really learn it! May we all learn!

Before heading out for another long teaching trip in the Caribbean Islands and South America she received a cautionary letter from the International Teaching Centre dated 9 October 1984:

> While we thank Bahá'u'lláh for your boundless energy, we lovingly caution you to rest before you become exhausted . . . Perhaps two or three days in each of the island communities would be sufficient, depending, of course upon their energy and resourcefulness. Most of these are relatively new and they are slowly developing their organizational skills. . . In all of these places, the officials and leaders of thought and prominent persons need to be reached and nurtured to the extent possible. Much more concentrated attention could be paid to this stratum of society for both the growth and protection of the Faith . . .

And then at the end of this trip the International Teaching Centre followed up with another letter in May 1985 summing up her recent activities:

> Your journeys on behalf of the Faith give great upliftment to the believers. The friendships you have made with officials, the goodwill you have created with local and government authorities, the assistance you have given to individuals and Assemblies with their various problems, and the successful publicity you have so often achieved attest the effectiveness of your dedicated efforts . . .

It is interesting to note that prior to the erection of the House of Worship in India Meherangiz shared her own thoughts on what form the design should take. This letter was from a Bahá'í architect friend who had submitted his own designs for consideration of the Universal House of Justice:

A few years ago when the Universal House of Justice asked Bahá'í architects to prepare a design for the Temple in India, I was very eager to participate in this majestic work and I started to note down ideas of drawings, forms and technical data. One day I had the pleasure to have as a guest for dinner in my home Mrs Meherangiz Munsiff who was travelling to teach in this country. Obviously the "in" talk at that time was the magnificent plan launched by the Universal House of Justice – the Mother Temple of India and, since India is the country of origin of Mrs Munsiff, I showed her my preliminary designs and asked for her opinion. She immediately noticed that my work was inspired by Islamic Art and Architecture and she told me: "Put these drawings away; I will tell you what design to produce that emanates the spirituality of the whole of India." She stopped in meditation for a few minutes and then, radiantly and firmly she told me: "You should design a Temple in the form of the Lotus Flower: that is the spirit of India!" When I got down to work I started to draw some sort of lotus flower, but couldn't visualize how this form could be adapted to a Temple . . . I put this idea aside. Later on I completed

my previous designs and sent them to the Universal
House of Justice . . .

In 1988 Meherangiz continued to offer her courses on
prayer and meditation. Two such places were the Louis
Gregory Institute in the United States and the Bahá'í
Summer School in Iceland:

> These four days provided me with the most trans-
> forming experience of my Bahá'í life. By praying,
> meditating, reading and discussing the Holy Writings
> Mrs Munsiff created an atmosphere of the Spirit where
> all of us felt the presence of Bahá'u'lláh. Truly I saw
> the greatness of this Cause, and the flood gates of my
> heart were opened to the Divine Power of Bahá'u'lláh
> . . .

The National Spiritual Assembly of Iceland wrote:

> . . . since your visit 12 new Bahá'ís. Thank you, from
> the bottom of my heart, for the strength that held
> . . . so we could receive your precious gift. The whole
> community is now lit up with teaching . . .

> Many of the friends remark daily how these courses
> have so positively affected their lives . . . your truly
> inspirational classes have contributed immeasurably
> to the renewed courage of the believers in the teach-
> ing field . . .

In 1989 in Korea Meherangiz once again demonstrated her straightforward approach to teaching. She shared this story:

> Before leaving the meeting three seekers were given cards and told to sign them and put them under their pillow and if they felt good then to give the cards in the next day. The American and Korean girl signed their cards but the Korean young man said, "I put the card under my pillow. I used to suffer from insomnia, but last night I slept well. But I am not decided as yet. Jokingly I said, 'I will give you another one and a half hours to decide (up to noon) and after that you are a Bahá'í or you get your insomnia back!'" . . . he decided to be a Bahá'í and feels great relief.

This quality was further demonstrated in a letter from a local Assembly in Oregon, United States:

> She was very effective at attracting new seekers for the Faith and demonstrated this by her direct and thoughtful illustrations of the basic Bahá'í beliefs. She thoroughly inspired the friends and her direct manner challenged the Bahá'ís to re-evaluate their expressions of commitment and service to the Faith. She is superb and undoubtedly the most effective travel teacher we have had in Oregon!

And from someone who completed the course at Bosch Bahá'í School:

You don't try to put on the "face" of a righteous person. You don't try to hide your personality and overly accommodate your students' sensitivities. You are yourself and this allows your students to be comfortable with themselves. This point is of tremendous value to me in my life . . .

During the first months of 1990 she conducted her course on prayer and meditation in many cities in California. We share some of the reactions of those who had the joy of participating in these gatherings:

. . . they put themselves under military style training during a four-day period recently . . . the Sergeant-Major who gave us our marching orders was a smiling grandmother from India, wearing a lovely sari, who would not tolerate wasting of time! They, together with a hundred or hundred and fifty Bahá'ís from the San Diego region attended a course concerning 'Spiritual Transformation'. . . If you ever find the chance to attend a course led by Mrs Meherangiz Munsiff, Knight of Bahá'u'lláh don't hesitate a minute. Order your affairs so that you can find the needed time, because you will certainly profit greatly from going. Don't expect to take notes; that is not permitted. Don't expect to ask questions; she does not permit the students to question her. She sat at the Guardian's feet. That, and her association with Martha Root in India when she was only 14, formed her character as a Bahá'í, and, believe me, ladies and gentlemen, when

I tell you that her words are exceedingly interesting, valuable and, well, transforming!

While you were speaking, recounting the story of your pilgrimage and your meeting with the Guardian, I was entirely moved. Half the time I cried and the other half I laughed but these two behaviours that are normally known as opposites felt not so different from each other that night. I was happy and spiritually uplifted . . . because that night I met the Guardian.

I made up my mind to dislike you . . . and with this visit came the audacious directive that we were to attend every meeting and not miss any. How dare you make such a policy? If I wish to go for just one meeting – and then perhaps get up and walk out – who can tell ME not to do that. So with this attitude, I came to challenge you to keep me interested for at least 15 minutes . . . Come to JUST five sessions???? If you were going to be here for one year or more, I would bestir myself to sit in the glow of this wondrous example of a person allowing Bahá'u'lláh to use her to capture the hearts of men. After hearing a few descriptions of the power of your talks, I imagined this gigantic, overbearing, loud, forceful lady – totally devoid of loving kindness. Instead, I first gazed upon the face of my own dear mother . . . Then I saw the essence of love that I have always imagined SHOULD flow through all of us who love Bahá'u'lláh . . . What you have taught me in these few brief visits with you is that it is unimportant who we are, that we can become blessed instruments of God through losing ourselves and really becoming the hollow reed through which His love may flow to all humanity . . . You have taught me more in these days than I had learned all my life, and that is over half a century . . . I have always loved Baháʼuʼlláh, but did not know how much He loved me until recently . . . I thank you from the bottom of my heart for retaining that spark of naughtiness and your dear sense of humor which enchanted me and attracted my soul to your sweetness and brilliance . . . I love you very deeply . . .

As a Baháʼí who has lived in other States, I have been feeling the disunity and strangeness among the friends here in . . . I spent many tearful nights . . . By watching your love and dedication for Baháʼuʼlláh I am moved again to do something for the Faith . . . I have travelled throughout the world with you during the last three days . . .

My heart is full with the love for Baháʼuʼlláh – my husband and I are requesting a pioneer post anywhere in the world . . . joy, fear, excitement, ecstasy are all mingling in my being . . .

I'm a Fijian . . . I was very ill . . . I knew that coming to the meeting was my last hope for recovery . . . I was also very grateful to the extra push you gave my way to help me make up my mind to either stay idle or go home and teach . . . My husband now wholeheartedly wants to go to Fiji with me to teach . . . we are all of us, as a family, going to teach for the whole month of July . . .

As I mentioned to you . . . I have always wanted to arise to the call to pioneer and now, due to your presentation, my wife and I will go to any area to share Bahá'u'lláh's healing message.

You seemed to have attuned your ears to hear the soft cries of the bird in our hearts struggling to break the tough egg of our material existence. Each one of us has a unique place where that egg is weakest, and you have helped us to find that place so we can chip away at it and finally break through to our own personal spiritual destiny . . .

These last days have been a time of turmoil, wrestling between self and spirit. I have felt so challenged, so resistant, so prideful, so humble . . . so grateful. What else could have shaken me deeply enough to raise me from my slumber? I have wept cleansing tears of relief that the struggle is won – the victory realized, and I give thanks to God!!

I have been uplifted by Bahá'í speakers many times in the 50 years in the Faith, but you are the first to touch the core of me, to reignite the fire that burns within and to inspire me to be a much better Bahá'í . . .

I am so thankful that you have made a way for me to teach my three daughters how significant and supreme this Cause is . . .

The most significant part of the deepenings for me was the insights you provided into the obligatory prayers, the Tablet of Aḥmad and into the Writings in general . . . a gift from God which was delivered to me at the most opportune time . . .

My new appreciation for the power of prayer and the benefit and obligation of meditation, has renewed my commitment toward obedience to the Covenant and tireless service . . .

I won't worry about what "they" are doing, I will focus my energy on what I am doing for my Best Beloved . . .

I have faith now whereas before this conference I did not . . .

. . . but the most significant for me was the emphasis that was placed on approaching our seekers from the heart and avoiding complexities with them.

Driving home today, I was thinking about the Fast. Then I realized that I am already looking forward to it. What a difference this Fast is going to be for me. I am sure I will be thinking about you every dawn . . .

. . . my bonds to Bahá'u'lláh are totally reinforced; my determination to labour in His vineyard consolidated; my understanding of the spiritual nature of the Cause strengthened; and my reliance on prayer, study and meditation on the sacred texts edified . . .

I now know that the luminous building in my vision was the San Diego Bahá'í Center. I see the culmination of this year of growth in the message you brought. It was as if the whole meeting was just for me . . .

Already I have experienced the power of prayer. My ex mother-in-law just left my home with two books written by William Sears. She was open to all I told her tonight . . . she (had) lost interest but tonight she saw the light in my face and the transformation I had gone through this weekend . . .

Later that year Meherangiz offered her course on prayer and meditation in Edinburgh, Scotland. On her way to Edinburgh she met Commander John More-Nisbet on the train. He subsequently attended firesides and became a stalwart follower of Bahá'u'lláh. One of the friends wrote of her course:

. . . it has been to me, personally, a spiritual oasis where time has stopped and I have been able to gather my scattered thoughts and feelings. But, more than that, something has happened to my soul . . . I just know that it is healthier than it was on Friday afternoon!

And the yeast is still at work . . . Of course it is the Words of Bahá'u'lláh and 'Abdu'l-Bahá which have caused this transformation and heightened awareness, but it is also the way familiar passages have been brought together to throw light on their meaning. This brings freshness and lightness. Also, it is so powerful to do something in a group. The unity of souls released an energy, and truly attracted the Concourse on high – the room was always vibrating.

Once again in 1990 Meherangiz continued to offer her course in both London and Los Angeles. Here again we include a selection from the written responses to this course:

Meherangiz has a very special gift in being able to present these sessions with love and authority from the Holy Writings, interspersed with a very special humour on her part. For us, personally there was also a miracle – in that we were guided to meet a waiting soul, a young man from Nepal whom we invited to meet with the Bahá'ís during the weekend, and who not only came along but became a Bahá'í as well.

I've been a Bahá'í for two years now but it's been "head" stuff so far. I'm a G.P. and it was the logic of the Bahá'í principles that attracted me to it. I've never felt love for Bahá'u'lláh and find it difficult to remember to pray let alone do it. Last night for the first time I did the long obligatory prayer. I hadn't even read it.

It is beautiful, humbling and inspiring. I will never be afraid to do it again . . .

I thank you, I bless you for bringing my Beloved to my husband and to me again. The feeling to pioneer, to teach, to pray, to study is strong again – to be the Bahá'í that I yearn to be – the feeling is with me again and I pray it will never fade . . .

For a pioneer (Chile) it is especially vital to maintain a clear vision and an ignited heart, and after being with you for these past few days, both of these things have again come to the forefront of my life . . .

Your life is such an inspiration: the way you show your humanity openly, and teach by example by being so careful that no one has been hurt. I want to give my life in the way you have. I know now what "deepening and consolidation" mean: encouraging and inspiring the friends . . .

In 1991 one of her trips took her to the Isle of Skye in Scotland. We share with you part of a letter Meherangiz received after this visit.

After you had gone we all felt very "high and uplifted", and for the last two weeks we have been teaching non-stop. Opportunity after opportunity has presented itself. . . A young man has suddenly become very, very interested. He comes from a Hindu/

Buddhist background and was not pleased at your attitude towards meditation, and even less pleased at the Bahá'í teachings on reincarnation. I thought these things would put him completely off the Bahá'í Faith, but instead he is confronting these difficulties with a strange sort of enthusiasm, and hardly stops talking about them. We have hardly been to bed before 3:00 a.m. since your visit!

There was one declaration during this visit.

In 1992 she received a letter from a believer who had declared in Meherangiz's home in London: ". . . to let you know that my 25th anniversary in the Faith occurred last month and I wanted to acknowledge this by thanking you for bringing me to the recognition of Bahá'u'lláh all those 25 years ago. I don't know what I would have done without the Faith . . ." This young lady recounted her story:

In 1967, after I had been back in London for some time after a spell of working in France, and while I was employed at the French school where I had originally been trained, I found out that a Mrs Munsiff, a social worker, was going to give a talk about the Bahá'í Faith. A friend of mine at the time encouraged me to go and find out about the Bahá'í Faith as it was "not a religion but a way of life". This was the turning point of my life. Mrs Meherangiz Munsiff gave a very clear, concise talk about the history, teachings and principles of the Faith, and I was hanging on to every word she said. She told me later on that she felt she was speaking exclusively to me, the rest of the audience were simply not there. I subsequently attended the weekly public meetings at the Bahá'í National Centre in London and spent hours reading the books which I bought there . . . Nine weeks after attending this initial lecture on the Faith, I was invited, in fact commanded, by Mrs Munsiff to go to her home for Sunday lunch when she announced to those present, namely her husband Eruch, her daughter Jyoti and another Bahá'í, Miss Mabel Joseph, the news that I was going to join the Faith.[7]

Maybe we can recount at this point a similar story shared by another believer in London, Earl Cameron, who was an established actor:

One night, Meherangiz Munsiff wanted us to come to her place on a Sunday. On the way there, I said to my wife Audrey: "You do know why she is inviting us, don't you?" She said: "Of course I do." At this stage, we were almost ready to become Bahá'ís. After a marvellous evening at Meherangiz's home, and after a lovely dinner, she produced the *Will and Testament of 'Abdu'l-Bahá* and we read it right to the end. Wonderful Meherangiz said: "How do you feel?" as she put two declaration cards down in front of us. My wife signed her card immediately. I was about to sign mine when I suddenly turned to Meherangiz and said: "By the way, I should mention that I am a member of the Rosicrucian Order" and straight away she said: "Well, you will have to give that up, won't you?" I asked why.

She explained that it was a secret society. I didn't know
that; I knew that the Masons were a secret society and
they couldn't be Bahá'ís. I looked up, thinking "What
should I do?" and there was a picture of 'Abdu'l-Bahá
on the mantelpiece and He looked at me as if to say:
"Are you going to let this stand in your way?" Perhaps
it was an illusion? Anyway, I signed the card and I
gave up the Rosicrucians. That night, my wife and I
became Bahá'ís.[8]

Meherangiz visited the Holy Land a number of times,
sometimes inviting friends to accompany her, and in
1991 she accompanied nineteen Bahá'ís from Japan on
pilgrimage. In 1992 she had the bounty of attending
the commemoration for the Centenary of Bahá'u'lláh's
Ascension. Then in 1993 after accompanying a group of
twenty Japanese Bahá'ís on a three-day visit to the Holy
Land, she received a warm letter from a member of the
Universal House of Justice (Douglas Martin) saying:

> . . . it brought back warm memories of those happy
> days in the 1950s when you brought the very spirit of
> Bahá'u'lláh's world to our remote corner of Canada. It is
> a joy to know that you exist and are continuing to bring
> others the sense of Bahá'u'lláh's love and limitless power
> that you have always brought to my all too infrequent
> chance encounters with you over the years . . .

While on yet another trip to Japan in 1993 Meherangiz
renewed her friendship with the Mayor of Kurume who

Presenting Bahá'í literature to H.E: Sourou Migan Apithy, President of Dahomey, in 1972. Meherangiz Munsiff visited fourteen African countries that year

Speaking at a public meeting in Guyana, 1974, during her first visit to Guyana

Bahá'ís of the Central African Republic participating in the parade commemorating Independence Day, 1 December 1975. Carrying the placard are Mr Sabone Pierre, chairman of the National Spiritual Assembly and Meherangiz Munsiff

Portrait, visiting Holland, 1977

Publicity photographs for the BBC-1 'Parosi' series of programmes; 15-minute programmes encouraging Asian adults to learn to speak English. Meherangiz Munsiff was the presenter for the five information programmes on housing and education

Travels,
1978–79: Zaire

Travels, 1978–79: Mauritius

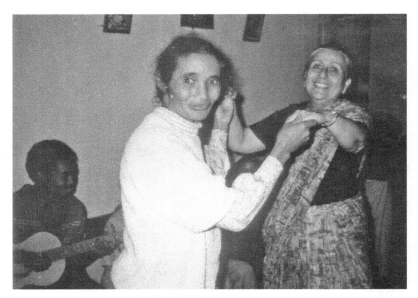

Madagascar, 1978–79. Taking a lesson in Malagasy dancing in a village near Tananarivo. The lady in white enrolled as a Bahá'í the following day, enabling a Spiritual Assembly to be formed in the village

With H.M. the Malietoa (King) of Samoa, Apia, 1980. On the right is Mrs Gol Aidun from Canada

Another visit to Guyana, 1980;
addressing a meeting at the Town Hall, Georgetown . . .

. . . and at a gathering in the Georgetown Bahá'í Centre

Presentation of a book to Prime Minister Ptolemy Reid of Guyana, 1980.
Left to right: Agnes Sheffey, Jennifer Dewar, Meherangiz Munsiff,
Prime Minister Reid, Sonny Griffith, Sydney Friday

Presenting the book A Crown of Beauty *to*
the First Lady of Ghana Viola Burnham

St Lucia, 1981: Patricia Paccassi, Secretary of the National Spiritual Assembly and long-time pioneer in St Lucia, second from left; H. E. Mrs Boswell Williams, wife of the Governor

Nikkeri, Surinam, 1981, giving a talk in the Hindu Temple

Meeting the President of Surinam in 1985

Dominica, 1985, presenting A Crown of Beauty *to Mr Jenner Armour, the attorney who assisted the National Spiritual Assembly with its incorporation*

Iceland, 1988, at the Bahá'í Summer School

Participants at a weekend on prayer and meditation
in High Wycombe, 1990s
(photo courtesy Katharine Hadfield)

With the National Spiritual Assembly of the Bahá'ís of Japan, 1990s

With a group of Bahá'ís from Japan,
on a three-day pilgrimage to the Holy Land, 1993

shared his intention to become a Bahá'í after the completion of his term of office and his disengagement from all political activities. After yet another visit to Japan the following year one of the friends wrote:

> . . . the fruits of the miracles you performed every day you were here are seen by me constantly, I see confirmed believers working and teaching. What a joy! Indeed, what is elementary to you in teaching the Faith is slowly becoming clear to the rest of us – and this working in unity is producing the promised results . . .

Jyoti likes to share an exchange she had with her mother prior to her first visit to Japan which was to follow an extremely successful teaching trip to South America. She cautioned her mother that the Japanese were not too fond of Indians and they certainly would not take too kindly to her more than direct form of communication. Jyoti went on to emphasize that her mother should appreciate that she shouldn't expect the sort of success that she had experienced in South America and in fact perhaps it would be a good idea if she cancelled the trip altogether. Meherangiz's response was simple: "The Universal House of Justice has asked me to go and I must obey. I will just rely on Bahá'u'lláh and pray even more AND you do the same." By any testimony, Meherangiz's visits to Japan were among the most successful ever, with local Japanese accepting the Faith in unprecedented numbers. They loved her and for several years she returned to Japan to help the Bahá'ís deepen and attract others.

During this period Meherangiz also visited Sakhalin and Vladivostok, and she was present to assist with the formation of the first Spiritual Assembly of Sakhalin (Yuzhno Sakhalinsk). She was interviewed on the radio there on the occasion of Women's Day, among other accomplishments.

In July 1994 Meherangiz was giving a public talk at the National Theatre of Bucharest in Romania. As usual she was suffering from an acute migraine and was anxious to get to her bed as soon as she finished her commitment to speak. The Bahá'ís however begged her not to leave and to meet a famous Romanian choreographer who wanted to talk to her after the formal part of her lecture. Meherangiz was reluctant because she felt really unwell, but when it came to the Faith somehow she always managed to overcome her own discomfort. The choreographer and Meherangiz were alone and after a short while Meherangiz asked the Bahá'ís for a prayer book and returned to the choreographer. One of the Bahá'ís present said that those who remained behind had their ears to the door trying to hear what was going on, but it was absolute silence. After a brief interlude Meherangiz emerged and the Bahá'ís insisted on knowing what had transpired. Meherangiz said that the gentleman enquired about movement in the Faith and she had given him the long obligatory prayer to read. He was apparently inspired and satisfied by the prayer and the attendant genuflections and went on to be an enduring friend to the Bahá'ís, using his influence to often speak up for Bahá'ís. The interesting aspect of this story is Meherangiz's response to an enquiry about movement in the Faith. To most, the obvious and normal response would be to talk about music and dancing, but true to her convictions Meherangiz felt that the answer to everything was to be found within the Writings and prayers.

After her course on prayer and meditation was offered in Wales it was reported that "remarks were made as to why the Faith had never been presented to them in this way before". "Having been inspired to go and teach, one of the friends came to the Sunday morning course having enrolled someone the previous night." Four people enrolled in the Faith during this visit and four more took cards to think about it. As a result of her trip one group planned to go on a three-day visit to Haifa and others planned a visit to Shoghi Effendi's Resting Place.

In 1995 Meherangiz had an opportunity to go to Dubai where the Faith is not openly talked about. During her stay there the *Gulf News* reported on her visit and her life. There was no mention of the Faith but it was reported that she had spoken to women all over the world about issues like the empowerment of women and "believes that women united make a force to be reckoned with". Meherangiz attended a meeting of the Kuwaiti Women's Society and met with wives of Ambassadors from several countries. In countries where women were less prominent in public life Meherangiz liked to emphasize the role of women and that they are peacemakers in our troubled world, expanding on the principles of the Faith. The women of Dubai were exhilarated by the experience, as usually their get-togethers tended to revolve around fashion and jewellery.

Meherangiz was renowned for her sense of humour

and while addressing the staff at a particular school everyone laughed so much that they immediately contacted another school insisting they invite Mrs Munsiff so she could make them laugh too. Mindful of her Indian connections, when possible she would keep in touch with the Indians in the countries she visited and was delighted when she accepted an invitation from an Indian believer to find there were seven non-Bahá'ís present. The joy was even greater as this was an environment where the Bahá'ís had to exercise great discretion introducing their friends to the Faith. A banquet was held in her honour on the last night with prominent guests including the Ambassador of the Kingdom of Bhutan and his family, who expressed his happy surprise that she shared so much about the Faith, as previously Bahá'í friends had been fairly reticent. While always exercising discretion and wisdom when talking about the Faith in certain countries she used the opportunity to open up in a way that she knew would be difficult for the local Bahá'ís to do and to continue living there. In keeping with her mission to uphold the reputation of the Faith amongst prominent people around the world, on her last day Meherangiz met various Ambassadors to India, Kuwait and Switzerland.

Later in 1995, amongst her many activities in Spain during a two-week period seven gypsies enrolled in the Faith in a women's meeting in Alicante, sixteen others declared in La Union and two in Elche. She was invited to participate in a teaching conference in Liria where she had an opportunity to talk about prayer and meditation, obligatory prayers, the use of Yá-Bahá'u'l-Abhá, the

Tablet of Aḥmad, the *Hidden Words* and her experiences in the presence of the beloved Guardian – 59 people arose to offer to pioneer, travel teach or give a year of service.

There had been opposition during her second visit to La Union from an evangelist minister, and he had managed to influence the townspeople sufficiently to shun the Bahá'ís whenever they approached. Knight of Bahá'u'lláh Sean Hinton relates a story that on the occasion of approaching the town square in La Union the people there started to turn their backs on the Bahá'ís and to walk away, emptying the square. The Bahá'ís suggested to Mrs Munsiff that perhaps they should leave so as not to draw too much attention to themselves. To their horror, Meherangiz not only refused to leave, she started to read the Fire Tablet in a very loud voice. Sean said he wished the ground could have swallowed him up and the Bahá'ís were mortified, but when they opened their eyes they found that people had come back into the square and were starting to ask questions and exchange details with the Bahá'ís. Curiously, reciting prayers loudly was not a practice Meherangiz had indulged in before, but clearly for reasons that even she would be unable to explain felt inspired to do something out of the ordinary, with extraordinary results.

Meherangiz had always expressed the desire to die with her "boots on" i.e. while teaching the Faith, but was also anxious to be buried next to her husband in a plot purchased in the early 1960s facing the Resting Place of her beloved Guardian. After a trip to Bermuda in 1999 Meherangiz headed to Italy on what was to be her last teaching trip. On the morning that Meherangiz was due to give a public talk in Mantova she started to experience excruciating pains and the Bahá'ís were anxious that they take her to hospital and cancel the meeting. Meherangiz was adamant that the meeting proceed, and after giving her talk, as she walked out of the hall she collapsed and was hospitalized. The Bahá'ís of Mantova were extraordinarily caring, never leaving Meherangiz for a moment in the hospital until Jyoti flew out to take her mother back to London.

The doctors had quickly been able to diagnose inoperable cancer. On returning back to her home the decision was taken by Jyoti and her mother that chemotherapy was unlikely to improve matters and it would be preferable for her pain to be managed, and that she be cared for at home. Jyoti took a leave of absence from her work specifically so that she could care for her mother. While waiting to die Meherangiz was insistent that everyone remain joyous and that all visitors had to come armed with a joke and a happy disposition. During her last weeks Meherangiz trawled her address book to reach out to anyone who might have evinced an interest in the Faith, with the hope that she might be able to assist them or at least say goodbye and give them her love. Her endeavours bore fruit by her accepting five declarations of faith in Bahá'u'lláh including one of her carers. People came from every continent to say their goodbyes to their friend. Young and old, men and women, Bahá'ís and those who were not Bahá'ís. Many were incapable of suppressing their grief and fearful that they would not be able to cope without a friend in whom

they had always been able to confide and who had always
been there for them irrespective of their problems. With
medical interventions Meherangiz's pain had been managed successfully until the morning of 21 June 1999 when
she was unable to speak. Jyoti explained to her mother that
she shouldn't worry about her, it was time and she was
going to ask Bahá'u'lláh to take her. In the instant she did
so Meherangiz looked lovingly at her daughter and passed
away peacefully in her arms. Jyoti recalls that the very first
thought she had when her mother took her last breath was
"hers was a life worth living".

* * * * *

The Universal House of Justice wrote:

> DEEPLY GRIEVED PASSING CONSECRATED, INDEFATIGA-
> BLE, STAUNCH KNIGHT OF BAHA'U'LLAH MEHERANGIZ
> MUNSIFF. HER INTERCONTINENTAL SERVICES TEACH-
> ING FIELD AND AMONG PEOPLES OF DIVERSE SOCIAL
> BACKGROUNDS HAVE ENRICHED ANNALS FAITH IN
> COUNTRIES VISITED IN COURSE HER HIGHLY MERITO-
> RIOUS TRAVELS. CONVEY BELOVED DAUGHTER, OTHER
> RELATIVES, DEEP SYMPATHY AND ASSURANCE FER-
> VENT PRAYERS HOLY SHRINES PROGRESS HER RADIANT
> SOUL ABHA KINGDOM.
>
> UNIVERSAL HOUSE OF JUSTICE

From the National Spiritual Assembly of the Bahá'ís of
the United Kingdom, 23 June 1999:

Dear Jyoti,

With the joyful tidings of light I hail thee: rejoice! To the court of holiness I summon thee; abide therein that thou mayest live in peace for evermore.

It is a cliché to say that no words can adequately convey what we would like to say in celebration of the life and sacrificial service of a dear friend who has forsaken this plane of existence. Of Mrs Meherangiz Munsiff the cliché is true!

Meherangiz, Knight of Bahá'u'lláh, fearless teacher of the Cause, servant always ready to help her fellow servants gain a deeper understanding of the Revelation of Bahá'u'lláh, traveller in the Cause of God, soul of unquestioned and unquestioning loyalty to the Covenant, we salute you and consider how your early contact with Martha Root, that Lioness of the Cause, must have left its traces on you who have left your traces on this century of light. The Universal House of Justice has offered us all the chance to make an enduring mark in this century; you made your enduring mark in every continent and in the midmost heart of the ocean; your traces are left in the hearts of many thousands throughout the world – those whom you taught, those whom you deepened, those whom you launched upon a life of service – your spiritual children. You surely, have made your mark "in deeds that will ensure for you celestial blessings".

All those of us whose lives were touched in some

way by you, will remember to the ends of our own lives your presence, your clear vision of what was right and what was wrong, of what each of us needed and did not need. We will always remember your way of cutting instantly to the very heart of every matter and your sometimes brusque dismissal of what you saw as unnecessary or a prevarication – particularly in those whom you knew to be finding excuses not to recognise Bahá'u'lláh or to serve Him as you did, to the very fullness of your life. Above all we will always remember your voice, full of love for God, for Bahá'u'lláh and for your fellow humans.

As we hold you in our minds and hearts, we also remember Eruch and we think with great love of your dear daughter, Jyoti, knowing that not only has she lost a mother, she has also lost a friend. But it seems that you only allowed her one day to cry (and that unwillingly), not wanting your progress into the next world to be hampered by the attachment of those who have yet to join you, in that glorious realm.

We know that you will have prayed that your service to the Cause – service which you will have thought could never be enough – would be acceptable to your Lord. We join in that prayer, knowing that we can emulate but never equal your heart's surrender to the will of the One you loved most, the Blessed Beauty, Bahá'u'lláh.

With loving Bahá'í greetings,
National Spiritual Assembly

From the National Spiritual Assembly of the Baháʼís of Ghana to the National Spiritual Assembly of the Baháʼís of the United Kingdom, 28 July 1999:

> . . . We remember her visit to Ghana and other West African countries. Her love was all embracing. Even when she was sick she continued with her service to the Cause during her travels.
>
> A fireside of hers was the first talk on the Faith that one member of this Assembly attended, instilling in her heart a love for the Cause and a realization of the oneness of religion . . .

From the National Spiritual Assembly of the Baháʼís of South Africa to the National Spiritual Assembly of the Baháʼís of the United Kingdom, 25 June 1999:

> . . . We recall with pride and awe her endeavours in our region (South-West Africa) which bestowed upon her the "Knight of Baháʼuʼlláh". She left behind her dear husband Iraj and precious four year old Jyoti to open the island of Madagascar. During her nine months residence, the French citizens, Daisy and Gilbert Robert and the first Malagas citizen Daniel Randrainarivo were brought into the Faith. Mr Gilbert Robert was later appointed as a Counsellor for the Indian Ocean Islands. Her two subsequent visits to South Africa to give Summer School courses will long be remembered.
>
> Please convey to dear Jyoti and other family and friends our deepest love and assurance of prayers for

this brilliant teacher of the Cause. May her life be an example of service to the Baha'is of the world.

From the National Spiritual Assembly of the Bahá'ís of Portugal to the National Spiritual Assembly of the Bahá'ís of the United Kingdom, 23 June 1999:

. . . please convey our condolences to her daughter, and assure her that Mrs Munsiff will be remembered in Portugal for her services to the community in the teaching field, both in the south of the country and in the island of Madeira.

From the National Spiritual Assembly of the Bahá'ís of Mauritius to the National Spiritual Assembly of the Bahá'ís of the United Kingdom, 25 June 1999:

The Bahá'í community of Mauritius greatly deplores the grievous loss befalling the entire Bahá'í community of the United Kingdom with the passing of our beloved Knight of Bahá'u'lláh, Mrs Meherangiz Munsiff to the Abhá Kingdom on 21 June 1999.

We treasure sweet memories of her during her several teaching trips in Mauritius. Her indefatigable courage and stamina in carrying the Message of Bahá'u'lláh has left indelible imprints in the islands of the Indian Ocean . . .

Message to Jyoti Munsiff signed Rúḥíyyih, Violette, Ali:

SHARE YOUR GRIEF OVER LOSS BELOVED MOTHER.
SOULS OF YOUR DISTINGUISHED PARENTS NOW BOTH
GATHERED IN THE ABHA KINGDOM ARE CLOSER TO
YOU THAN EVER BEFORE. MOTHER'S OUTSTANDING
RECORD OF DEVOTED SERVICE IS UNFORGETTABLE AND
HER REWARDS IN HEAVENLY REALMS UNDOUBTEDLY
BOUNTIFUL. WE OFFER HEARTFELT CONDOLENCES
AND ASSURE YOU OF MOST LOVING PRAYERS FOR CON-
TINUED PROGRESS HER STEADFAST SOUL IN KINGDOM
ON HIGH.

From The Gambia, 25 June 1999:

. . . We had the bounty of having Meherangiz with us
both times she visited the Gambia. She was devoted
and energetic as well as knowledgeable and a champion
of women's progress and emancipation in all areas . . .

From Nadia and Franco Cucé in Italy, 22 June 1999:

With a heart overflowing with tears, we commu-
nicate the notice of the passing of our dearest Mrs
Meherangiz Munsiff which took place in London on
the 21st June around 1:00 p.m. Those of the Italian
Bahá'í community who know her cannot but suffer for
this most great loss. Mrs Munsiff was in Mantova last
April where she held one of her marvellous Courses.
On the 12th of April we had to accompany her to

the Emergency Room of the hospital where she was diagnosed with an incurable illness. Some days afterwards her daughter transferred her to London, where unfortunately the doctors confirmed the diagnosis. We communicated by telephone with her during this period and she remembered the names of all the friends and had affectionate words for each of us.

With her we lose one of the most indomitable heroines of our beloved Cause. No one knew how to recount the episodes of the life of Martha Root, who she had met personally and accompanied on a trip, as she did, or the many anecdotes of so very many Bahá'ís throughout the world whom she had encountered in her indefatigable and innumerial [numerous] trips. Little stories full of humanity, which painted the interpreters with strokes of love and affection.

She was 75 and her health was not the best, but 3 years ago she even visited Siberia and because of this voyage she contacted pulmonary emphysema because of the pungent cold. She had the great capacity to create an immediate bridge between our soul and the great love of Bahá'u'lláh. At the hospital in Mantova she knew how to create an atmosphere of great respect and spirituality. The doctors and nurses were deeply touched to see such a steady and continual stream of young people surrounding this Indian lady. These youth with the utmost discipline and order, coming and going and bring their loving greetings. And she who so graciously exchanged their affection with her loving smiles. Her daughter had immediately told her of the illness which she had and after only a moment of pause, she was as enthusiastic as a child and began her preparations for her passing.

We all remember the last words of her Course on Prayer. "Do you understand of Whom we are followers? Of Bahá'u'lláh, of the Omnipotent, of the Omniscient! And the followers of the Omnipotent must never be afraid or uncertain!!" "In the Bahá'í Faith there is a Power, a Power . . . Oh if you could only know!"

From Lori Gilbert in Paraguay, 24 June 1999:

. . . I remember when we first met. I had heard so much about you from my oldest brother. I had been invited to tag along with you, Mr Munsiff, Jyoti, Gary and a group of Japanese Bahá'ís that you were taking to Haifa to visit the shrines. What blessings and bounties God showered upon that trip! The things you taught me in those three days, I shall never, ever forget. Remember when we were in London and had gone to see the resting place of the Guardian? I was overcome and began to weep. I turned around to walk away. Suddenly you were at my elbow with your arm around me and a knowing, loving look sparkling from your eyes. "Isn't she sweet!" I thought to myself, "She is trying to comfort me". Then just as suddenly, you turned me back around and indicated that I must never turn my back to the Guardian. You were teaching me about true reverence, respect and humility!

You smiled knowingly and gave me a gentle squeeze. You were to teach me this lesson time and time again on this trip until I finally got it right. You reminded me without a word, just a gesture, to let my Japanese brothers and sisters enter the shrines before me as our special guests, to make sure that both my feet were on the floor and that my posture was one of utter reverence to God when I prayed, to always select what I wore at the holy shrines, with the realization that I would never, ever be in the presence of a Greater King than Bahá'u'lláh. Oh Mrs Munsiff! You knew exactly what I needed to learn. You taught me without a word. You taught me with a loving touch and a gentle nod. Oh how I shall miss you!

Some weeks before God's Messenger of Joy came to take you away from us, you told me over the phone not to forget you in my prayers. Mrs Munsiff! How could anyone who has ever come in contact with you forget you!!! Maybe you will finally see that I have learned my lessons well. I understand reverence, respect and humility. It will be my face, my heart and my soul that will be turned to yours, not my back. Mrs Munsiff, I haven't the words to adequately express how I feel. I only have these few left and they seem so terribly small on this white page. But perhaps God can make you hear them in the way that they sing out from my heart. You were God's bounty to this tired world, like a fresh sprinkle of rain in the early spring: I love you Mrs Munsiff.

From Zia and Jaydev Mody to Jyoti, Mumbai, 23 June 1999:

> ... When I was looking back at her life and her continuingly telling us that she was uneducated and could not read or write and about all the trials she went through, one can only marvel at the miracle of Bahá'u'lláh that He can create such a wonderful teacher from such a simple soul and give her the blessings of the Knight of Bahá'u'lláh and so many other spiritual bounties that many of us with all our education and wealth know we would never achieve ...

From John Fozdar, cousin of Meherangiz, to Jyoti, 27 June 1999:

> ... It is nice to know that she was confident in her last days and was awaiting a transition to another life. We shall all meet up somehow in the other world, though I do not know if we will be able to laugh and joke as we did here.
>
> The memories of her frequent help to my mother both in Baha'i work and also in family care are so fresh in my mind. I remember how she would frequently come to look after us when my mother was travelling and we would often turn to her for "care" and "sympathy" when we most needed it.
>
> Even during her travels, if she met up with us, she was most helpful. When she was here last time, when

I was a continental counsellor, I benefitted from her guidance, help and information . . .

From Anita Ioas to Jyoti, 28 December 1999:

> . . . I remember when I met her in '52 – back from Haifa, astonishingly beautiful in form and spirit. I learned a valuable lesson when she told me she had taken her most beautiful saris to Haifa – this when I remarked on the lemon yellow sari she wore that night in Paris, bordered in silver. Then their time at the Embassy in Washington. For years I met people in the diplomatic circles who knew of Bahá'u'lláh through her. Then the years in Paris later on when Gilbert would tell us how she reached people in Madagascar. And then nine wonderful days when I had her at home – my, what long talks we had.
>
> She left her mark everywhere and I still hear the enchanting sound of her voice and the beauty of her presence. You have a most wonderful heritage, dear Jyoti . . .

At home in London

Knights of
Bahá'u'lláh
gathered in the
Holy Land,
May 1992

Haifa, 1992, with the scroll commemorating the Knights of Bahá'u'lláh

Enjoying the festivities in Haifa, 1992

*. . . and with
Rúḥíyyih Khánum*

PART II

SPIRITUAL TRANSFORMATION:
PRAYER AND MEDITATION

by Meherangiz Munsiff

PREFACE

The prime mover in encouraging me to write this guide or book or whatever you want to call it was Gordon Kerr, a British Bahá'í who attended my class twice: once on his own and then a second time with his family. He would keep pestering me that I prepare something in writing and I would not agree, and he said, no, you must agree because it will be helping so many. Gordon badgered me and was very insistent but in the beginning I was too fearful to contemplate writing anything. Eventually he sold me on the idea, stating that we would work together. Also, I thought if my dear friend Janet Alexander from Chile could come and help too we might just be able to do something useful. The National Spiritual Assembly of Chile gave her permission to come and she said: "This book will be for the friends that have come to your class and will be a review for them, a reminder for them." So that was the idea that sold it for me and I decided we would do it. Gordon was so kind, very kind. He bent over backwards to make this possible. He has faith so God bless him!

Meherangiz

Man is the supreme Talisman. Lack of a proper education hath, however, deprived him of that which he doth inherently possess. Through a word proceeding out of the mouth of God he was called into being; by one word more he was guided to recognize the Source of his education; by yet another word his station and destiny were safeguarded. The Great Being saith: Regard man as a mine rich in gems of inestimable value.

Bahá'u'lláh[1]

INTRODUCTION

O MY SERVANT! Free thyself from the fetters of this world, and loose thy soul from the prison of self. Seize thy chance, for it will come to thee no more.[2]

How on earth can we do this? If we want to free ourselves from the prison of self then first we need faith that Bahá'u'lláh will make this possible. Far too often we don't even have that and we allow our own complicated thoughts and doubts to intervene. If only we could have faith like a child. That doesn't mean we should have blind faith, but once you believe in Bahá'u'lláh as a Manifestation of God, then you have only to follow and do what He says. Bahá'u'lláh says that if we do not follow the laws and ordinances, then, no matter how hard we work, all of our work is as of nothing.

> . . . it is the duty of all besides Him to strictly observe whatever laws and ordinances have been enjoined upon them, and should anyone deviate therefrom, even to the extent of a hair's breadth, his work would be brought to naught.[3]

That's why when I go to many countries, particularly to so-called civilized countries in the western world, people

often say, "Oh, we are so tired. Nothing is going right!"
I suspect that if they were really following the laws and
ordinances of Bahá'u'lláh, with a sincere degree of commitment, then they would experience success. On the
other hand, when we don't follow Bahá'u'lláh's guide-
lines, or when we make compromises with them, no
matter how hard we work, we have zero results.

This is why we need to learn how the Faith works. It's
not entirely our fault that we fail to comprehend how
the spiritual dynamics of the Faith work because, among
other things, we rarely stop to focus on the depth of our
own commitment and faith. The quality of our own personal faith is considered so private that nobody speaks
about it or honestly examines it and therefore we fail to
understand the impact of faith on our actions. Added to
which if we are honest many of us don't really believe
that faith and prayer can produce results which seem
intellectually impossible. On the other hand, reflect for a
moment: does it really make sense that Bahá'u'lláh would
ask us to do something that was not possible?

One who is imprisoned by desires is always unhappy.
The children of the Kingdom have unchained themselves from their desires. Break all fetters and seek for
spiritual joy and enlightenment; then, though you walk
on this earth, you will perceive yourselves to be within
the divine horizon. To man alone is this possible.[4]

Sincerely, I don't know how to share my thoughts with all
of you. The first step in this process was to collect as many

of the writings specifically on prayer and meditation and reflect upon their potency. With enormous difficulty and great trepidation I then decided to create a course which had as its objective a path to encourage anyone who cared to listen that we as human beings are exclusively able to call on the power of prayer with a view to protecting and serving mankind. Obviously, I am no example. There is only one example, and that is the Master, 'Abdu'l-Bahá! But through personal experience and despite my personal inadequacies, I have learned what works and what doesn't. Bahá'u'lláh has given us a simple, practical way to lose our attachments, free ourselves and rely on Him. The only way I can impart a little of my understanding is to share with you some of my experiences.

In response to the Ten Year Crusade in 1953 I volunteered to go to Madagascar with the agreement of my husband who said he would care for our five-year-old daughter, and most importantly with the blessings of the Guardian. Frankly, I didn't know where Madagascar was, I didn't know the language, I didn't know anybody there, and I could only take £50 out of the United Kingdom at that time. Most frightening of all I had no idea where I would live or lay my head on arrival. It was all done by invoking, "Yá-Bahá'u'l-Abhá" and supplicating the Concourse on high!

In the past, when I used to tell this to the friends, they'd say "Oh, yes – that's nice, and then what?", as if it was all a walk in the park and as if I was talking nonsense. For decades, I thought it better to keep quiet on this subject.

Then one day, many years later in London, two of my

friends had gone to Yoga classes. They told me, "We've never had such a wonderful time! What a shame we don't have something like this in the Faith." Quite agitated, I answered: "We don't have what? – You're doing something that we Indians have been doing for thousands of years but what has it done to change the miseries of the world? We have to understand there is so much more in the Bahá'í Faith than philosophy and physical exercises, but only if you want to know and if you want to listen!" That night I wept, heartbroken that the spiritual potency of the Faith was not being understood or accessed by so many of us.

I concluded that no matter how much we believe in Bahá'u'lláh we have failed to absorb the significance of the importance of praying and the force it can be within our lives. Literally, my course has been brought about, not as an intellectual exercise but with buckets of tears. It's not an academic treatise: it's very simple and very practical. After all, Bahá'u'lláh came for every human being, not just those with university degrees. That's why this is written very simply on my personal experiences when I was trying to establish the Faith all alone in Africa and the challenges faced teaching the Faith in the years to follow.

I left Madagascar after five wonderful souls accepted Bahá'u'lláh and returned home to my family. After only three weeks back home in London I felt compelled to venture into the unknown again and left for the French Cameroons, another country in Africa, all alone, with no outward or material help. Once again my only assistance was the Greatest Name, reliance on the prayers and focusing only on establishing the Faith where there were no Bahá'ís. This took every ounce of my being as every breath was accompanied by the image of my young daughter and how much I loved and missed her.

Many decades later I cried a lot and begged Bahá'u'lláh to give me something, to show me some way, how I could meaningfully help the friends to realize that, without any other help or guidance, or by spending a lot of money, but just by depending upon the Greatest Name impossible hurdles can be overcome and victories achieved in the service of the Cause. Slowly I started to collect references from the books. I would stand in front of the bookshelves and say "which one, Bahá'u'lláh?" select the book and open it to whatever page, read, and say – "This sounds good!"

I would copy the chosen passages by hand, and after I collected a reasonable selection, I would talk to the friends, because now there seemed a desire to learn about faith and prayer. Initially we had one-day schools, and then we would have weekend schools, and, as attendance grew, there were visible successes prompting the friends to encourage me to expand and focus on this theme. I copied more and more relevant quotes, plus my insights were increasing having at this stage travelled to about 55 countries of the world. The course developed into a ten-day workshop. Naturally this is a commitment many people can't give so I condensed it to a long weekend.

After giving this course for twenty years, the pressure was increasing to put it on paper. I was constantly being badgered to write it down but little did everyone understand that with my limited education I couldn't even write a proper letter. I would try to dodge the issue by saying: "Why don't you read the Holy Writings?" They'd answer that we read the Holy Writings, but we can't always understand them. Then I realized that even if one has faith, to know how to access and rely on it might need some guidance, explanation and encouragement. 'Abdu'l-Bahá says that you can't read a medical book and just become a medical doctor, or an engineering book and become an engineer. You need a teacher. I don't claim to be a good teacher, but I did have first-hand experience, and I did travel with the star teacher, Martha Root, when she was in India and carefully watched how she taught the Cause and relied on the Writings. In addition, I had been blessed like so many of us by the support and encouragement of Shoghi Effendi.

My offering here is a banquet. When you go to a banquet you don't eat every one of the many dishes laid out on a huge table. You pick and choose what you feel like at the moment. You look at the other things and say this looks delicious, but I don't feel like eating this now. So, take what you want, consume what you can and at the next banquet, perhaps you'll say: "No, I've tried that, maybe I'll try something else. That was nice. Let's see what other things there are." This way, each time you go, you pick up what you want at that time and you enjoy it. And when you enjoy something, you are more open to understanding it, and then you can act. It's as simple as that. One, two, three! But when we try to do something we don't even enjoy, is it a wonder that we don't

understand it. But if we want to do something to understand or serve the Cause, then, as 'Abdu'l-Bahá says, all
we have to do is go step by step, little by little.

TITLES OF BAHÁ'U'LLÁH

Why should I believe? Why should I really believe? Although while we Bahá'ís say we believe, at times do we truly believe? I haven't included all this in detail, but I have taken these titles of Bahá'u'lláh from *God Passes By*, pages 94 to 97, where it shows the origin of each one, so that you can trace it for yourself. No one has so many titles – big leaders, big dictators, not even the past Manifestations of God. They all came and promised us that another Manifestation of God, the Divine, Supreme Manifestation of God, would come and that these would be His titles. These are the titles given to Bahá'u'lláh by the previous Manifestations of God:

THE EVERLASTING FATHER
THE LORD OF HOSTS
THE SPIRIT OF GOD
THE LORD OF LORDS
THE MOST GREAT NAME

Now, what is this Most Great Name? It is Bahá'u'lláh. His name is Mírzá Ḥusayn-'Alí, but Bahá'u'lláh is His title, the Most Great Name of God. When you address God, there is nothing greater, to address Him with, than Bahá'u'lláh.

THE ANCIENT BEAUTY

THE PEN OF THE MOST HIGH

THE HIDDEN NAME

THE PRESERVED TREASURE

HIM WHOM GOD WILL MAKE MANIFEST

THE MOST GREAT LIGHT

THE ALL-HIGHEST HORIZON

THE MOST GREAT OCEAN

THE SUPREME HEAVEN

THE PRE-EXISTENT ROOT

THE SELF-SUBSISTENT

THE DAY-STAR OF THE UNIVERSE

THE GREAT ANNOUNCEMENT

THE SPEAKER ON SINAI

THE SIFTER OF MEN

THE WRONGED ONE OF THE WORLD

THE DESIRE OF ALL THE NATIONS

THE LORD OF THE COVENANT

THE TREE BEYOND WHICH THERE IS NO PASSING

THE GLORY OF THE LORD

THE EVERLASTING FATHER

THE PRINCE OF PEACE

THE WONDERFUL

THE COUNSELLOR

THE ROD COME FORTH OUT OF THE STEM OF JESSE

THE KING OF GLORY

THE MOST GREAT SPIRIT

THE TENTH AVATAR

THE IMMACULATE MANIFESTATION OF KRISHNA

THE DESIRE OF ALL NATIONS

THE PRINCE OF THIS WORLD

THE COMFORTER

THE SPIRIT OF TRUTH

THE LORD OF THE VINEYARD

THE SON OF MAN

THE GLORY OF GOD

THE ALPHA AND OMEGA

THE BEGINNING AND THE END

THE FIRST AND THE LAST GREAT ANNOUNCE-MENT

HIM WHO CONVERSED WITH MOSES FROM THE BURNING
    BUSH ON SINAI

THE ESSENCE OF BEING

THE REMNANT OF GOD

THE OMNIPOTENT MASTER

THE CRIMSON, ALL-ENCOMPASSING LIGHT

THE LORD OF THE VISIBLE AND INVISIBLE

THE SOLE OBJECT OF ALL PREVIOUS REVELATIONS, IN-
    CLUDING THE REVELATION OF THE QÁ'IM HIMSELF.

HE WHOM GOD SHALL MAKE MANIFEST

THE 'ABHÁ HORIZON

Friends, if we look and study these titles, we will understand the enormity of the significance of the coming
of Bahá'u'lláh – for example Christ said that He would
return in the GLORY OF THE FATHER, THE EVERLASTING
FATHER, THE LORD OF HOSTS, THE SPIRIT OF GOD, THE
LORD OF LORDS.

The prophetic cycle is over. Mankind is moving
towards a state of spiritual maturity. However, we all
know that just because we reach the age of 21 we don't

become wise instantly, and know our place in the world. But it means that we begin to take responsibility for ourselves and begin to understand there is a greater life in front of us, rather than looking backwards and clinging on to our childhood and relying on our parents.

THE MOST GREAT LIGHT: This name interests me very much. In every Dispensation we have had Light. In every Dispensation and throughout different ages, God gave us Light (i.e. a spiritual revelation) according to mankind's understanding and capacity to handle and work with that Light. Humanity was never given more than it could handle. Once we had candle light, oil light, gas light. Today there is electricity. Now while electricity provides light, it also does a thousand and one other things for you. This is why this Revelation is the Most Great Light. None of the older forms of lights could do all of the things that we can do now with electricity. First it gives a focused light, but in addition it is able to provide illumination to a much greater degree.

Now, if you're trying to understand electricity completely, that is difficult. Nobody knows precisely what electricity is. Scientists know that it is energy and they can identify different sources and what it can do but they find it difficult to say precisely what it is. This is true of praying as well. We need to practise praying and then find out for ourselves if it works or not. Why is it that we have not stopped using electricity when we don't know what it is? We will never be able to know the precise nature of the energy we create when we teach. We only come to see how it works when we put it into practice. No one is excluded from teaching and sharing the remedy for the ills of mankind. . .

Give your soul a chance, no one else can do it except yourself. It is only through your own efforts that you have any hope of ultimately seeing any results. Others may be able to encourage and help you, but they cannot do that which you are obliged to do. It's like when you need to eat food to provide you with sustenance with a view to feeling well. No one can eat or drink for anybody else: you have to do it for yourself.

Just remember, when dealing with electricity it requires electrical engineers to install it, it requires electricians to fix it. If it is a small problem, you can fix it yourself or ask friends to help you, but if you fiddle with it on your own, when you don't know much about it, you can get electrocuted. And that's why Bahá'u'lláh has created divine institutions, like the local Assemblies, national Assemblies, the Universal House of Justice. All of the divine institutions are there to make sure that the community functions within the laws of Bahá'u'lláh and that it is united. It is the institutions which will find a solution when it is beyond our capacity to resolve the problem.

This is the Most Great Light – you cannot fool around with it.

THE ALL-HIGHEST HORIZON means that we cannot go beyond this horizon. It's the highest we've ever gone or furthest we can ever reach.

THE DAY-STAR OF THE UNIVERSE: What is this star that guides the universe? It is Bahá'u'lláh who guides the whole world with love and justice to bring about the Most Great Peace. And in whatever darkness we may be the Day-Star of this Faith shines through to guide us. Remember, this Revelation is universal. It is for every single man and woman on this planet. Within this Faith there is formulated a plan for peace. If you haven't already, I suggest that you please read *The Promise of World Peace*, the statement of the Universal House of Justice.

THE SPEAKER ON SINAI

Call thou to mind the days when He who conversed with God tended, in the wilderness, the sheep of Jethro, His father-in-law. He hearkened unto the Voice of the Lord of mankind coming from the Burning Bush which had been raised above the Holy Land, exclaiming, "O Moses! Verily I am God, thy Lord, and Lord of thy forefathers, Abraham, Isaac and Jacob." He was so carried away by the captivating accent of the Voice that He detached Himself from the world and set out in the direction of Pharaoh and his people, invested with the power of thy Lord who exerciseth sovereignty over all that hath been and shall be. The people of the world are now hearing that which Moses did hear, but they understand not.[5]

By comparison look at the enormity of how much was revealed to Bahá'u'lláh and what has been committed to writing by the Manifestation of God. Through the instruments of prayer and consultation we can access the meanings of this life and the next, many of which may be hidden in the Writings.

THE SIFTER OF MEN: We are so privileged to live at a time when the Revelation of Bahá'u'lláh has come for the whole of mankind. For the sake of our spiritual development we need to learn how to pray and meditate. Bahá'u'lláh says that if a man does not meditate, he is an animal, nay he is worse than an animal, because animals do not have the faculties to pray and meditate in the way humans can engage in what is essentially a spiritual conversation with God.

Every living thing turns to God, but they do not have the faculty to meditate. This faculty exists in all of us humans but since it is not as obvious a power as our ability to see or hear it is a faculty we need to make ourselves and others aware of. Unlike seeing or breathing we are free to take it or leave it according to our free will and choice. As human beings we are granted the privilege of free will to decide how we want to live our lives and to what degree we want to spiritually develop ourselves during this life. However, for those of us who are Bahá'ís we are required to share the significance of Bahá'u'lláh and His Revelation. Millions of us endeavour to share this Faith not only for our own benefit but so that we can contribute to fulfilling the prophecies of all the former Manifestations of God culminating in the Revelation of Bahá'u'lláh. What is perhaps difficult for us to comprehend is that this is the Day of God.

The Sifter of Men means that Bahá'u'lláh will keep the receptive ones and leave those that are not ready. The sun shines on both barren land and gardens. The garden flowers, the fruit ripens, but what may seem like barren land sometimes comes to life or simply stays barren, enjoying the sun but to no good purpose. It is not our responsibility as individuals to presume to judge who will make a good Bahá'í and who won't. It's God's house and we have to welcome anyone who comes into it. And eventually, God will sort it all out. He is the Sifter of Men, so why should we get ourselves agitated or interfere. The Universal House of Justice says that this is the harvest time – when you harvest a crop – you take in everything, but then Bahá'u'lláh Himself will sift it.

The paramount goal of the teaching work at the present time is to carry the message of Bahá'u'lláh to every stratum of human society and every walk of life. An eager response to the teachings will often be found in the most unexpected quarters, and any such response should be quickly followed up, for success in a fertile area awakens a response in those who were at first uninterested. The same presentation of the teachings will not appeal to everybody; the method of expression and the approach must be varied in accordance with the outlook and interests of the hearer. An approach which is designed to appeal to everybody will usually result in attracting the middle section, leaving both extremes untouched. No effort must be spared to ensure that the healing Word of God reaches the rich and the poor, the learned and the illiterate, the old and the young, the devout and the atheist, and the dweller in the remote hills and islands, the inhabitant of the teeming cities, the suburban businessman, the labourer in the slums, the nomadic tribesman, the farmer, the university student; all must be brought consciously within the teaching plans of the Bahá'í Community.[6]

THE LORD OF THE COVENANT: God has made a covenant with mankind that He will never leave humanity alone without guidance. He has always sent His Messengers, to guide mankind. A covenant means a contract. This contract is that He (the Manifestation) has power from God to guide us and protect us, if we obey His laws and are faithful to our covenant with Him. Previously when a Manifestation of God came to mankind we were not so potentially spiritually mature nor spiritually responsible for ourselves, so nothing was written down as to who would continue to guide the faithful after Him. It is interesting to note the Covenant of Bahá'u'lláh has not been successfully broken. It is the existence of the first written Covenant of its kind which has prevented the division of the Faith into sects. It is the Covenant which has provided the protection for the essential unity of the Faith and will continue to do so as it progresses and grows throughout the world. There are Bahá'ís living in over 400 countries, islands, protectorates all over the world, of every conceivable tradition and background. Of their own free will, they are held together by the Covenant of Bahá'u'lláh.

THE PRINCE OF PEACE: At no time in the past has mankind been given such a clear promise together with a blueprint of how to establish peace. War affects the whole of mankind and never more so than today. All of mankind must be involved in creating global peace. Ironically, when we are affected by war we become united; and in our sharing of purpose or fear, we come together in our communities. But why not, said 'Abdu'l-Bahá, the son of Bahá'u'lláh, become united for a change and work for peace. If you don't like it, you can always go back to war. We've never given universal peace a chance. In fairness, it is arguable that the world has never focused on a global peace because until now we have not had access to a solid plan which has the potential to work.

Why is it important to know about peace, if this book is just concentrating on prayer and meditation? Well, what are you developing yourself for, preparing yourself for? You must have a goal, and peace through unity is the goal for mankind today. If we cannot establish peace in our own souls, it is impossible to establish peace for all mankind. We must first put ourselves in order. Someone wrote to 'Abdu'l-Bahá and said: "I don't have the capacity or ability to do anything." 'Abdu'l-Bahá answered that if you didn't have the capacity or the ability, you wouldn't be a Bahá'í. Many are called, but few are chosen, and you are chosen to do this. Even though we are few, each individual must know that he/she can do something. We must arise, but we can only arise and achieve results when we have prayed and meditated, followed by action.

THE WRONGED ONE OF THE WORLD: Bahá'u'lláh endured prolonged suffering like no Manifestation of God has suffered in all of human history. What had Bahá'u'lláh done to deserve this? He had everything. He didn't need anything. He didn't need position, nor fame, nor wealth. Young, healthy, happy, He had everything.

Bahá'u'lláh himself has written:

The Ancient Beauty hath consented to be bound with chains that mankind may be released from its bondage, and hath accepted to be made a prisoner within this most mighty Stronghold that the whole world may attain unto true liberty. He hath drained to its dregs the cup of sorrow, that all the peoples of the earth may attain unto abiding joy, and be filled with gladness. This is of the mercy of your Lord, the Compassionate, the Most Merciful. We have accepted to be abased, O believers in the Unity of God, that ye may be exalted, and have suffered manifold afflictions, that ye might prosper and flourish.[7]

By My life! Couldst thou but know the things sent down by My Pen, and discover the treasures of My Cause, and the pearls of My mysteries which lie hid in the seas of My names and in goblets of My words, thou wouldst for longing after His glorious and sublime Kingdom, lay down thy life in the path of God.[8]

And 'Abdu'l-Bahá said:

The Manifestations of God have come into the world to free man from these bonds and chains of the world of Nature. Although they walked upon the earth they lived in heaven. They were not concerned about material sustenance and the prosperity of this world. Their bodies were subjected to inconceivable distress but their Spirits ever soared in the highest realms of ecstasy. The purpose of their coming, their teaching and suffering was freedom of man from himself. Shall we, therefore, follow in their footsteps, escape from this cage of the body or continue subject to its tyranny? Shall we pursue the phantom of a mortal happiness which does not exist or turn toward the tree of life and the joys of its eternal fruits?[9]

For each of these titles, one could write a book, but there is not time here.

INDEPENDENT OF ALL SAVE HIM

I understand that all of us, even a child or a toddler, at times feel the need to be independent. Indeed, we all desire independence. But if we are honest, none of us is completely independent. From birth to death, someone is generally doing something for us, and yet we yearn for independence. On the other hand, we all wish that someone would just take over all our problems, hold our hands and lead us through this life. This is a natural feeling experienced by all of us at some stage, so is it not possible that there must be a way to satisfy that universal need? The Báb's answer is: "Make me independent of aught else but Thee."[10] Bahá'u'lláh gives us this prayer that says:

I implore Thee, therefore, by Thy Self, the Exalted, the Most High, not to abandon me unto mine own self and unto the desires of a corrupt inclination. Hold Thou my hand with the hand of Thy power, and deliver me from the depths of my fancies and idle imaginings, and cleanse me of all that is abhorrent unto Thee.

Cause me, then, to turn wholly unto Thee, to put my whole trust in Thee, to seek Thee as my Refuge, and to flee unto Thy Face. Thou art, verily, He Who, through the power of His might, doeth whatsoever He desireth, and commandeth, through the potency of His Will, whatsoever He chooseth. None can withstand the operation of Thy decree; none can divert the course of Thine appointment. Thou art, in truth, the Almighty, the All-Glorious, the Most Bountiful.[11]

When we learn to abide by the laws and ordinances of Bahá'u'lláh, by fully trusting in the Will of God, that is when we become truly independent. That doesn't mean we should be careless and neglect how we are supposed to conduct our daily lives. We should learn to consult with those who may be wiser than us in the family or in the community, or consult with the Assembly, to arrive at decisions which give rise to constructive action. After that, we should leave it to God and Bahá'u'lláh. This is where the test of faith and trust comes in, and assists in making us independent of all else save Him. I appreciate this is easier said than done. Most human beings by nature tend to worry and feel the need to be in control. I suppose that animals, while they might experience fear or stress, don't worry. Provided there is a solution to the anxiety, I consider that to be contemplation, or thinking and planning, but worrying for the sake of worrying serves no purpose and denies us the possibility of relying on spiritual guidance.

A material man lets himself be worried and harassed by little things, but a spiritual man is always calm and serene under all circumstances.[12]

'Abdu'l-Bahá says that even the plants pray for rain and food, because everything which is living turns to God. But not all have the innate ability to meditate. I think we owe it to ourselves and to others to be more aware of the power of meditation, should we wish to access it. We are all free to make the choice to take it or leave it. That's the unique advantage of human beings having free will. How you want to live your life and what you make of it is your choice. I have certainly found this power of meditation as a Bahá'í, as have millions of others, and we should try to share this power with our fellow humans. After all, it is not just for ourselves but for the benefit of all in order to establish heaven on earth, or as Krishna says: Ramarajya, or the Kingdom of God on earth, the Golden Age, the Millennium. All the Prophets of God have mentioned these words promising that this is the Day of God.

It is open to the whole of humankind to come into this Faith. No one is excluded. It doesn't matter how they have lived, where they have come from or if they are seeking a remedy for their problems; the Faith embraces everyone. It is easy to resort to alcohol or drugs or cling to someone's love or devotion as a lifeline, but is it not better to cling to the Divine Lifeline which has always been available to mankind? By relying on the prayers and meditations of Bahá'u'lláh, you slowly wash away your shortcomings, making you into a new person. If your motives are pure and you truly believe in Bahá'u'lláh, then the prayers and meditations are like taking a shower – the dirt and impurities are washed away, as your previous problems, failings, and misguided inclinations fall away. It is entirely up to you if you want to access and apply this divine remedy.

When I asked one lovely young child, Elena, how she felt, halfway through the course, she answered with a glowing face that "I feel as though I were a bird and I have been released from my cage!" My prayer is that if you connect with the spirit within these pages, it will enable you to access the power from God so that you too will feel release and freedom.

WHAT IS SPIRITUALITY?

Animals are not required to understand spirituality or the mysteries of the Holy Writings. Human beings, on the other hand, are capable of understanding spiritual concepts. However, to be able to really comprehend the mystery of life and of death, we have to pray:

> For the core of religious faith is that mystical feeling which unites man with God. This state of spiritual communion can be brought about and maintained by means of meditation and prayer. And this is the reason why Bahá'u'lláh has so much stressed the importance of worship. It is not sufficient for a believer merely to accept and observe the teachings. He should, in addition, cultivate the sense of spirituality which he can acquire chiefly by means of prayer.[13]

No one will nor does anyone have the right to force you into the Bahá'í Faith or for that matter to remain in the Faith. However, once you accept Bahá'u'lláh, it only makes sense that you abide by His Will. It's like selecting your destination and getting onto a plane; you buy the ticket; you choose the airline; you choose your seat. But once you are in the plane, you sit down, the captain welcomes you and tells you, fasten your seat belts, no smoking, switch off your devices. You trust in his orders and obey them, and the airplane takes off. We don't question why we should fasten our seat belts nor do we argue with the captain about how to fly the plane. In the same way, we need to learn to submit to the Will of God with a view to protecting and enhancing our spiritual development. There is no denying that it is not easy and that it takes a long time, but having acknowledged Bahá'u'lláh, there is little point in not relying on His ordinances and God's guidance.

In 1956 I met an old man in Cincinnati, Ohio, while I was travelling in America. He said to me, "I am a Bahá'í at heart." "This is all nonsense," I responded. "Either you are or you are not." He then agreed, saying "You're absolutely right, Mrs Munsiff. You're absolutely right! Either you're pregnant or you aren't. You can't be a little bit pregnant." I've never forgotten that!

The fields and flowers of the Spiritual Realm are pointed out to us by the Manifestations who walk amid their glories. It remains for the soul of man to follow Them in these paths of eternal life through the exercise of its own human will.[14]

Likewise, man, no matter how much he may advance in worldly affairs and make progress in material civilization, is imperfect unless he is quickened by the bounties of the Holy Spirit; for it is evident that until he receives that divine impetus he is ignorant and deprived. For this reason, Jesus Christ said "Except

159

a man be born of water and of the Spirit, he cannot enter into the Kingdom of God." By this Christ meant that unless man is released from the material world, freed from the captivity of materialism and receiving a portion of the bounties of the spiritual world, he shall be deprived of the bestowals and favors of the Kingdom of God, and the utmost we can say of him is that he is a perfect animal.[15]

Reality on this earth consists in the remembrance of the Almighty, whereas in the Realms above, the soul progresses through the bounty and under the shelter of the All-Merciful. Therefore, let your earthly life become a mighty Sign of God, that thou mayest prepare the way for Eternal Life. Shouldst thou fail in this endeavour thy life in this world and the next shall surely come to naught. Verily, true mention of God lies above all else in the teaching of His Cause.[16]

It is neither necessary nor productive to feel guilty about your failures. If you dwell too much on feeling guilty, you risk becoming depressed, and if you are depressed, Bahá'u'lláh says, God will not be able to inspire you. So why let your guilt get in the way of your inspiration? Guilt, forget it! We must learn to depend upon His forgiveness and submit to His justice and His wrath. Forgiveness in the Bahá'í Faith is a totally different concept of forgiveness compared to how we know it as mortals.

Our concept of forgiveness, our concept of justice, our concept of God's wrath, has hitherto been fashioned by stories and images generated by priests, clergy and mullahs. In the absence of a priesthood in the Faith, we don't have confession and, in addition, our relationship with God is much more intimate, with the assistance of prayers and writings revealed by the Manifestation of God, rather than created by human beings. We must ask forgiveness only from Bahá'u'lláh and God, not from man. We must try to turn to God; learn to converse with Bahá'u'lláh. Bahá'u'lláh will know how sincere we are. If we are truly sincere, He will in His Mercy forgive us. Even Covenant-breakers have been forgiven despite the treacherous nature of their actions.

How do we get guidance? First, we can search the Holy Writings, but if we don't understand them, or don't know them, then find a friend who is wise, it might be someone in the family, or the local Assembly. But remember in the end, it will be you and only you who will be praying to Bahá'u'lláh for help and guidance from God.

We are never condemned for eternity for anything, provided we truly yearn to correct ourselves and get back on the right track again. This is the beauty of the Bahá'í Faith. However, repentance in itself is not enough. We must repent and act. We have to change our ways and use every endeavour to secure that change. If the obstacle in our life is attachment to the love of a man or a woman or even the love of a child, we have to direct ourselves towards the love for Bahá'u'lláh. Then we can march forward, confident that our love for Bahá'u'lláh will intensify our love for all those around us.

There is a special bounty when someone becomes a

new believer. When you first become a Bahá'í you start anew; completely fresh. The past is completely forgotten. As a Bahá'í, it's a clean slate, a new everything. But you have two responsibilities: one is to remain firm in the Faith, obey all of the laws and to have no doubt whatsoever, and the second is to teach the Faith and help others to be attracted to the Faith. These are two responsibilities we must all work on continuously. When we start doing this in all sincerity, then we will be astonished at how many opportunities arise and so much falls naturally into place.

If we don't continuously keep cutting the grass, weeds will grow. We have to continuously keep ourselves in trim and spiritually maintain ourselves by doing exactly what Bahá'u'lláh has asked of us.

> O servant! Warn thou the servants of God not to reject that which they do not comprehend. Say, implore God to open to your hearts the portals of true understanding that ye may be apprised of that of which no one is apprised. Verily, He is the Giver, the Forgiving, the Compassionate.[17]

When we come into the Bahá'í Faith, we commit ourselves through our own free will. There is no coercion: it is a voluntary, conscious act for which we are individually responsible. We accept that Bahá'u'lláh is the Manifestation of God for this day and age and that by virtue of His station everything that He has revealed is for our collective and individual benefit. This Revelation is to last for at least one thousand years and the teachings have to provide remedies not only for the world as we know it now but also for the future, into which we as mere mortals have no insight. If there is something that we do not understand, it does not mean that it is not true; it means, simply that we don't necessarily have either the vision or capacity to understand. By definition, everything that the Manifestation of God says is true, otherwise He would be a mere mortal, however wise.

We are ourselves the means of our degradation and exaltation. 'Abdu'l-Bahá once addressed a young man who was about to leave Haifa in this way:

> Now that thou hast decided to live in Aleppo, thou must act, speak and conduct thyself with such holiness, sanctity, purity and chastity as to attract to the Cause everyone who comes in contact with thee, that everyone may testify that here lives in our midst an upright and virtuous man, that has turned his face towards God, that he is spiritual, celestial and divine. A person through his own action and deeds makes himself loved or disliked by the people; or through his own unselfish conduct and behavior, refined morality and selfless intention, trustworthiness and rectitude he suffers himself to become favored and beloved at the threshold of God.

There is a young man of Jewish origin in the College of Beirut by the name of Mírzá Habíbulláh Khodabaksh, who has fulfilled these requirements. Formerly he was not known, but now everyone knows him through his sanctity, purity of life, sincerity of aim and the beauty of his holiness, and he is favored and near the court of the Almighty, and loved and respected by all. From whomsoever you enquire of him the utmost satisfaction and pleasure is expressed concerning him.

Therefore, it is now proven that we are ourselves the means of our degradation and exaltation; that people are attracted to us or repelled by us according to the attributes and deeds emanating from us. In short, I hope that thou mayst live in such wise in Aleppo that all the inhabitants may exclaim: "This man is not a Bahá'í in a nominal way, but in a real manner; he is a Bahá'í in deeds and not in words alone." For this reason His Holiness Bahá'u'lláh hath said: "My sorrow is not occasioned by my enemies, but those souls who attribute themselves to Me but whose deeds and actions are conducive to the degradation of the Cause."[18]

We have been fortunate enough to find this Faith, but with this privilege we need to develop true humility and never display a "holier than thou" attitude which is not acceptable and abhorred in the sight of God. While working for this Faith we need to show the inner joy that grows from contributing to the building of a new civilization. The inner satisfaction we get should be matched by humbleness and joy without which we cannot hope to attract others.

When we are unhappy and miserable, we should ask

ourselves why? If we are honest, we would know that it is because we do not sufficiently get involved in the service of the Cause of God. What we don't understand is that as we get stronger spiritually we are better able to understand and cope with this material life.

> The Word of God is the storehouse of all good, all power and all wisdom. The illiterate fishermen and savage Arabs through it were enabled to solve such problems as were puzzles to eminent sages from the beginning of time. It awakens within us that brilliant intuition which makes us independent of all tuition, and endows us with an all- embracing power of spiritual understanding. Many a soul after fruitless struggles in the ark of philosophy was drowned in the sea of conflicting theories of cause and effect, while those on board the raft of simplicity reached the shore of Universal Cause, aided by favorable winds blowing from the point of divine knowledge. When man is associated with that transcendent power emanating from the Word of God, the tree of his being becomes so well rooted in the soil of assurance that it laughs at the hurricanes of scepticism violently attempting its destruction. For this association of the part with the Whole endows him with the Whole, and this union of the particular with the Universal makes him all in all.[19]

We need to learn and develop our understanding of faith, which will give us the capacity to accept with grace what we don't always understand or perhaps, even agree with. That doesn't mean we are forbidden to question, but we should do so only with a view to increasing our comprehension, not with a view to asserting our own perceptions. Faith is based on love, and a conviction that His word comes endowed with spiritual authority. It is not just abstract, and it works. This is not an existential concept. It is a spiritual reality which has successfully influenced the lives of thousands of believers. Why not have a little humility and try to submit to His will before insisting on yours. Try it!

But we need to learn the mysteries of these things and understand that the reality of how Bahá'u'lláh works is totally different from our experience of how the world works. We should appreciate how under the steward-ship of the beloved Guardian and the Universal House of Justice all the laws have been gradually applied in accordance with our capacity to obey them. Think of the rising sun which emerges gradually; slowly, slowly illuminating the sky rather than appearing fully risen immediately at the zenith. Even now, some of the laws won't be put into effect until we have a Bahá'í state. But personal laws have come into effect with the publication of the Kitáb-i-Aqdas. We have to endeavour to practise them, however difficult they may seem. The Universal House of Justice instituted the obligation of Ḥuqúqu'lláh (the Right of God) many years later in the West than in the East. Perhaps they waited until they were satisfied that we, in the West, fully appreciated the significance of this law. However, once the time is deemed appropriate for the Bahá'í world, our laws must be put into practice. We really have no excuse, and we have to understand that obedience contributes to our spiritual development.

No one knows whether our sacrifices will be accepted in the sight of God. However, we can be fairly confident that the act of sacrificing our own ego in order to maintain unity will be accepted by Bahá'u'lláh. It is natural for all of us to have our point of view but it is a real test of faith if, in the interest of avoiding discord and fostering unity, we are humble and submissive in the sight of God. We may be called upon to sacrifice in many different ways.

> . . . do Thou adorn them also with the ornament of Thine acceptance, through Thy grace and bountiful favour. For the doings of men are all dependent upon Thy good pleasure, and are conditioned by Thy behest. Shouldst Thou regard him who hath broken the fast as one who hath observed it, such a man would be reckoned among them who from eternity had been keeping the fast. And shouldst Thou decree that he who hath observed the fast hath broken it, that person would be numbered with such as have caused the Robe of Thy Revelation to be stained with dust, and been far removed from the crystal waters of this living Fountain . . . the virtue of every act is conditioned by Thy leave and the good-pleasure of Thy will, and may recognize that the reins of men's doings are within the grasp of Thine acceptance and Thy commandment.[20]

This quotation goes to show that it is only Bahá'u'lláh who knows the heart, soul and motive of each person. That is why we're told not to judge people, not even ourselves. He is the only judge.

Similarly with the forgiveness of God, and of Bahá'u'lláh, 'Abdu'l-Bahá and Bahá'u'lláh say we NEVER remain static spiritually. We're either moving forward or going backwards. Consider your spiritual journey as the ascent of a ladder but one on which you rise a few steps and invariably fall down a few steps. But the trick is to keep going up however many times we falter. And that's how we progress. The question is: if we fall off the ladder, is it possible that Bahá'u'lláh threw us off? As a matter of fact, there are very few of us who do not succumb to our egos and weaknesses from time to time, and will find ourselves having to retrace our steps, having fallen once again, up the ladder. I know I frequently have been pushed down the rungs of the spiritual ladder. There are of course some who keep ascending and ultimately become martyrs in death or in life. The majority of us, on the other hand, either fall off or are unceremoniously thrown off the ladder. However, Bahá'u'lláh in His mercy doesn't let that happen permanently or cushions the fall when we are sincere. If our heart faces God with a view 'To love Thee and to serve Thee', God will deal with us mercifully. But if we want to feed our own egos or selfish purposes because we want to be 'SOMEONE', then heaven help us.

It is very important to understand what 'Abdu'l-Bahá means when he says "We are ourselves the means of our degradation and exaltation". We have to accept that we cannot be degraded unless and until we are disobeying the laws and ordinances of Bahá'u'lláh, or not meeting the standards hoped for in a Bahá'í. None of us should think that when we follow the laws and ordinances we are doing something exceptional or difficult. Firstly, there are relatively few restrictions. Mostly, it is those positive endeavours asked of us which, perhaps, are the most difficult. Why? Because they highlight our weaknesses as individuals and focus on the need to improve ourselves and in relation to the world we find ourselves in.

Secondly, these laws and ordinances have been fashioned in such a way that every single human being on this planet is equipped to follow them, no matter what his status or condition. In my experience, it is often the simplest of people who most successfully live up to the standards required of us. How? Because of love. Their commitment to Bahá'u'lláh is pure and uncomplicated. But then I would also suggest that any one of us who is in love is prepared to do anything to demonstrate that love to our loved one. So why would we not be able to do the same for Bahá'u'lláh, if we claim to believe in Him and love Him? Why should we find it difficult to follow the laws of Bahá'u'lláh? Of course, we may fail. But all that is asked of us is that we get up and try again. And again we may falter. But if we keep going, every time we take a few more steps we are further along in the journey to achieving our objectives. If we are sincere in our endeavours, Bahá'u'lláh is always there to give us a hand and to pick us up so that we may try again. But if we don't try, that is pride or if we make excuses such as – "this instruction is given for the future and not for now" – there will be no assistance and we are the creators of our own "degradation". Remember this Faith is not just for the future! It is for NOW and the future. It is wise to remember that our personal spiritual future is in the next world, but preparation for that future starts here and now if we are to protect that promise of "exaltation".

If it is of any comfort, 'Abdu'l-Bahá said that nobody is without an ego, except the Manifestations of God.

Every single assured and firm believer will consider himself the servant of all the friends of God, nay rather, the servant of the world of humanity. The honour of man depends upon this. The everlasting glory of mankind lies in this. For this reason his Holiness Christ says: "The last shall be first; the least among you in the Kingdom is the greatest." Whosoever desires to walk in the path of the Kingdom, so that he may reach the court of the Almighty he must be a true servant, the path of God cannot be compared with the paths of men. The humbler man is in the path of God, the more exalted is he; the greater his meekness and submissiveness the more beloved is he; the more he is surrounded with tests and trials the vaster the tranquillity and composure of his spirit. Nay rather in the path of God humility is honour, trouble is rest, affliction is bestowal, poverty is wealth, indigence is sovereignty and lowliness is nobility. Truly, I say, whosoever is a real servant of the believers of God is their assistant and helper. We must all walk in this divine path. [21]

We have to control our ego and I know this first hand: once after conducting a class in Wales I needed to catch the train, and was running out of time, so I said: "Will someone say a short prayer," and people started looking in their prayer books. In a fit of frustration I said: "For goodness sake, you people can't even say a small prayer. I will say it!" And guess what, I couldn't remember a prayer that I say ten times a day. Clearly, Bahá'u'lláh wasn't pleased with my impatience and I was being shown a lesson. I wish I could say that was the only time my reaction was less than gracious but, unfortunately, I have frequently had to be humbled.

Unfortunately, far too frequently we Bahá'ís don't always understand why humiliation or disappointment comes to us. If we fully understood how it is that we are expected to behave, then we would appreciate that we have to learn to curb our less attractive traits. I could have put it down to – oh, I'm tired, my mind is not as well as it used to be and that's why I couldn't say the prayer . . . NO WAY! It's just because of my attitude and how I expressed myself to the Bahá'ís, that Bahá'u'lláh said: "I'll teach her a lesson she won't forget!"

He is the prayer-hearing, prayer-answering God, and His presence is always there but we are not conscious of it. We put it down to all sorts of things. I can assure you I have often been embarrassed, humiliated and generally shown up, and why? Because my ego got the better of me and Bahá'u'lláh was on my case in very short order. It is inevitable that we will all fall into the trap sometimes of thinking we are better than others or we do things better than others, but beware. There is nothing wrong in trying to do anything as well as you can or being as good as you can, provided it is not because you think you want to set yourself above others. Bahá'u'lláh encourages us to strive for perfection, but beware of your motives and your ego, otherwise you will pay heavily.

Bahá'u'lláh says, don't look towards yourself: "Where is Paradise, and where is Hell? Say: 'The one is reunion with Me; and the other thine own self.'"[22] Turning to Bahá'u'lláh and His Writings is the only way you can see what He wants you to do. He says go and teach. Then go and teach. He doesn't say how. I say, open your mouth. That's how! Some of us don't teach. Even Baha'is of long standing sometimes fail to teach, because they are consumed with themselves and their own lives. You are not with Bahá'u'lláh if your concerns are always focused on yourself, and believe me in that case your problems will only increase. Do you find yourself constantly making excuses? I can't teach because I don't have time; I don't teach because I don't understand and so on and so on. What we have to understand is that Bahá'u'lláh simply asks us to open our mouths and if there is sincerity in our hearts, He will do the rest. But we have to stop this constant self-absorption and excuse-making.

It is essential that we actively teach the Faith, otherwise our prayers don't get answered. It's like the telephone; unless you pick up the handset and dial the number, looking at it will not give you access to a conversation. However, if you are sincerely teaching the Faith, even if you feel inadequate Bahá'u'lláh will help you be successful. The confirmation is within the following quotation:

> Dost thou deem thyself a small and a puny form,
> when thou foldest within thyself the greater world.[23]

We should take comfort that we have within us an enormous capacity to tap into that universe. In following Bahá'u'lláh's exhortations, and being obedient to the Universal House of Justice's requirements, we will find indeed that we have the whole universe within us. We must not focus on our perceived limitations when we have the assurance that we are capable of great things in the name of God.

Individually and collectively, mankind encapsulates enormous potential. Who ever imagined we would be able to land on the moon, and that via a satellite those of us on earth would be able to witness the event of man walking on the moon's surface? My aunt told me that once when she was in the presence of 'Abdu'l-Bahá, He was telling some pilgrims how people will be able to see what is happening in other parts of the world, hear prayers said . . . and they were thinking, what is He talking about? He said, don't worry about it, and changed the subject. I can assure you that with the advancement of science and with successive generations within the Faith, your children and grandchildren will create a new race of men who are able to achieve things beyond our wildest imagination.

The Bahá'í Faith like all other Divine Religions is thus fundamentally mystic in character. Its chief goal is the development of the individual and society, through the acquisition of spiritual virtues and powers.[24]

Most of us Bahá'ís who are down to earth and practical (not a bad thing), think that to talk about mysteries and mystical things is reducing the Faith to a cult. Of course, if we get carried away and just dwell on "idle fancies and vain imaginings", it is; but Bahá'u'lláh is saying, Divine Religions being spiritual in nature, they embody elements and powers which are beyond our earthly knowledge. When we pray consistently and sincerely we are assisted to understand the mysteries in the Holy Writings, and offer to the world the gems contained there with wisdom and love.

SPIRITUAL GROWTH

After reading and praying, it is important to meditate – this entails reflecting upon the meaning of what we have read during the day whenever we can, and then acting. The primary action is to try and change or develop our own character, but that change is nurtured by accessing every opportunity to share with all of those around us the message of Bahá'u'lláh. Our growth is dependent upon giving, not upon taking. What we have to give is the love of Bahá'u'lláh. We need to recognize that we live in a time of the development and growth of the Faith, which requires us to focus our efforts on teaching the Faith. It doesn't matter if you mess it up or if it isn't correct. God will put it right. Our prime objective should be the offering of the Cause to a thirsty and suffering mankind. All we are required to do is try our best and leave the rest in His hands.

> Prayer and meditation are very important factors in deepening the spiritual life of the individual, but with them must go also action and example, as these are the tangible results of the former. Both are essential.[25]

> It is known and clear that today the unseen divine assistance encompasseth those who deliver the

> Message. And if the work of delivering the Message be
> neglected, the assistance shall be entirely cut off, for
> it is impossible that the friends of God could receive
> assistance unless they be engaged in delivering the
> Message.[26]

It is chilling to note that "if the work of delivering the
Message be neglected, the assistance shall be entirely
cut off". Only when we pray, meditate, read the Holy
Writings, act, and give to the Fund can we benefit our
souls and other people. We must always remember that
our whole purpose is to know and worship God, and then
to serve Him. However, we cannot serve Him unless we
serve His creatures.

'Abdu'l-Bahá and Bahá'u'lláh often speak about the
way a tree should grow; the branches should stretch east
and west; it should bear abundant flowers and fruits. The
analogy of trees is helpful. Imagine that the seed of a tree
which has been planted by a farmer is like the spiritual
seed planted by God in our soul when you declare your
belief in Him and commit to doing all you can in His service. Now consider the growth of that seed taking root
and sprouting. In the early stages nobody notices, only
the farmer knows the care he is taking. And if it grows the
farmer is even more happy, and takes more care of it, as it
begins to have more shoots. Still no one else notices. It is
growing; it is now a sapling and it even has a few leaves.
Still nobody has paid any attention. But the farmer knows
and he knows that it is well rooted. The tree continues to
grow until it has many leaves and then it gets flowers. The

leaves and flowers represent the character of the person. When the flowers come people take notice – especially of the fruit trees when they blossom. They gaze at the flowers, saying how beautiful, how fragrant, and soon they will have fruits! There is the anticipation that a tree should bear fruit. Flowers alone are not enough. While it is essential that we have a good character, it is not enough. The fruits are how many people we have helped to find and accept the Faith. When they do, they're our fruits and the blessing we'll take into the other world with us.

We have to bear fruit. All of the Manifestations of God have asked this of mankind. A fruit tree without fruits is ultimately only fit to be cut down and burned. Perhaps this is something we can all meditate on for a while and carefully consider the results of our own endeavours during the time we have been Bahá'ís. 'Abdu'l-Bahá when travelling in the West said that each person should aim to attract at least one person to the Faith every year. There is no farmer on the face of this earth that will keep a fruit tree that only brings in one fruit a year but by the mercy of God that is all that He is asking of us.

We all know of people who, no matter where they are, have succeeded in guiding many, many, many souls to the Faith. No one, however successful we are in teaching, should ever assume they are the ones who have brought someone into the Faith. Let's be clear, the tree doesn't even know that it has fruits. The seed doesn't even know that a tree could grow out of it. If you cut open the tree, you can't see the fruit. The tree is the medium within which the fruit is developed. All we have to be is as healthy a tree as possible. We don't know how many fruits have grown, or how they have grown, but we do know that it is only through the care of the gardener, or the farmer, that the tree will flourish. It is essential to understand that it is entirely through the nourishment of the love and care of Bahá'u'lláh and God that we have the potential to bear fruit. 'Abdu'l-Bahá says:

> To enter the Kingdom is easy, but to remain firm and constant is difficult. The planting of trees is easy but their cultivation and training to strengthen their roots to make them firm is difficult. Now as thou art a firm tree, thou shall certainly grow and send out branches, leaves, and blossoms and bear fruits.
>
> These branches leaves, blossoms, and fruits are the souls who may be guided through the providence of God, by thee. Therefore, thou are confirmed and strengthened.[27]

> The life of man will at last end in this world. We must all take out of this life some fruit. The trees of one's existence must bear some fruit. If a tree has no fruit, you must cut it down and burn it. It would be useless for other purposes.
>
> What is the fruit of the human tree? It is the love of God. It is the love of humankind. It is to wish good for all the people of the earth. . . It is virtues and good morals. . . It is devotion to God. It is the education of souls. Such are the fruits of the human tree. Otherwise it is only wood, nothing else.[28]

As to human souls, unless they acquire the Light, they are unable to shine upon other individuals. But when a man ariseth to expound the arguments of God and invite people to enter into the religion of God, and when he uttereth those arguments and advanceth consummate proofs concerning the appearance of the great Kingdom, then intense love shall become manifest in his heart. This love causeth the development of his spirit by the Grace of the beneficent Lord.[29]

PRAYER

Spiritual intoxication

People often assumed that praying and meditating came to me naturally. But that's absolutely not true. During my courses on prayer and meditation, I tried to explain that to really be able to pray and meditate meaningfully is a learning process which takes practice over a lifetime. It is conditioned upon a lot of things, all of which are interconnected. We can't be half-hearted and distracted or pick our own methodology, particularly in circumstances when we are given specific guidance, such as in the case of the obligatory prayers. Everything has to be properly done and is interconnected to make it one. When we say "I'm well", we are saying the whole body is functioning: that all of our senses and organs are working well together. In the same manner, when you pray or meditate, you need to fulfil all of the other conditions in order to ensure that your prayers and meditation are productive.

We have to become, as Shoghi Effendi says, an intoxicated lover of Bahá'u'lláh. You know when a man is intoxicated, he doesn't see or hear anything else. He only sees the contents of his bottle. In the same way, we always have to focus on Bahá'u'lláh. And then life, whatever the obstacles, seems manageable and purposeful. I've known people who have overcome difficulties that could drive a person into the ground or a mental institution, but they were able to overcome almost insurmountable difficulties, because they constantly relied on their spiritual helping hand – a connection with Bahá'u'lláh.

How do some people find the strength to become martyrs? They have the strength because they have an internal force and love in their lives, which is not motivated by personal gain, but reinforced by an undeviating devotion. Understanding love nowadays is not easy, because love is so often confused with lust. The love of which all of the Manifestations of God speak is so pure, so divine, so beautiful, so life-giving, that when you tap into it you're prepared and able to do anything. People often misconstrue this unconditional love as madness, or deeply admire the capacity for sacrifice and wish their lives too could be equally spiritually ignited.

We really have to understand that we can't do without the obligatory prayers. We have to learn to long to pray, thereby giving us that much-needed connection to God. As a consequence not only do we feel more energized and at peace, but we are also able to deal with life so much better, no matter what is thrown at us. 'Abdu'l-Bahá says:

> There is nothing sweeter in the world of existence than prayer. Man must live in a state of prayer. The most blessed condition is the condition of prayer and supplication. Prayer is conversation with God.

The greatest attainment or the sweetest state is none other than conversation with God. It creates spirituality, creates mindfulness and celestial feelings, begets new attractions of the Kingdom and engenders the susceptibilities of the higher intelligence. The highest attribute given Moses is the following verse: "God conducted a conversation with Moses."[30]

Prayer and supplication are two wings whereby man soars toward the heavenly mansion of the True One. However, verbal repetition of prayer does not suffice. One must live in a perennial attitude of prayer.[31]

We need to consider what 'Abdu'l-Bahá means when He says that "One must live in a continual state of prayer."

Once in a village in India, there was a young man who mentioned in the class, "How can one live in a continual attitude of prayer? I work in an office, I have to attend to phone calls, my boss wants me, he wants this file, that file, visitors come and go and it's non-stop disturbance. How can I live in a prayerful attitude?" Of course, all of us would think the same way, because our idea and understanding of a prayerful attitude is to sit quietly in a quiet room, close our eyes, and "think of God" and meditate. That's not always possible. Then a young lady, from the same village, got up and said: 'I don't work in an office, but I have to carry a big pot and go to the well to fetch water. I have this pot of water on my head, a baby on my side and I have a shopping basket in the other hand. I also go shopping and talk to people on the street. I do my shopping and come home, without dropping the pot from my head. How? Because I'm conscious all of the time that I have this pot of water up on my head and I must not drop it. No matter what I'm doing, I'm conscious of this and I keep my head straight while I move around normally. Not only that," she said, "but when I put the pot down, I look at it, and take care that I don't use it all up until I am able to go get some more the next day. In the same way," she said, "why can't we be in a prayerful attitude? We may be doing anything, but always remember that we are Bahá'ís and what would Bahá'u'lláh and 'Abdu'l-Bahá want of us in our everyday actions. That then is the way to behave."

How simple, how realistic, how fantastic! Coming from an ordinary village woman in India. In addition to the physical and focused act of praying and meditating, a prayerful attitude is one which pervades every second of our lives and determines our actions.

Why pray?

Why should I pray? Why should I use the revealed prayers and not use my own words to communicate with God?

> Know thou verily these Divine Teachings are heavenly and spiritual. They penetrate in the heart as the penetration of the heat of the sun, the outpouring of clouds and the blowing of vernal winds at morning-time upon the trees. When the lights (of these Teachings)

arose, they became spread, just as the shining dawn spreads upon the horizons. These wonderful traces shall surely appear throughout all regions and their lights will shine forth during centuries and ages forevermore.

As to thy question: "Why pray? What is the wisdom thereof? For God has established everything and executes the affairs after the best order, and He ordains everything according to a becoming measure and puts things in their (proper) places with the greatest propriety and perfection – therefore, what is the wisdom in beseeching and supplicating and stating one's wants and seeking help?"

Know thou, verily, it is becoming of a weak one to supplicate to the Strong One, and it behoveth a seeker of bounty to beseech the Glorious Bountiful One. When one supplicates to his Lord, turns unto Him and seeks Bounty from His Ocean, this supplication is by itself a light to his heart, an illumination to his sight, a life to his soul and an exaltation for his being.

Therefore, during thy supplication to God and thy reciting, "Thy Name is my healing"– consider how thine heart is cheered up, thy soul delighted by the spirit of the Love of God, and thy mind becomes attracted to the Kingdom of God! By these attractions, one's ability and capacity increase. When the vessel is widened the water increaseth, and when the thirst grows the bounty of the cloud becomes agreeable to the taste of man. This is the mystery of supplication and the wisdom of stating one's wants (i.e. praying).[32]

In every age God sends His Messengers with an evolving message which matches the needs and capacity of man for that particular time. These teachings have always gone hand in hand with the act of praying. The prayers which we have in the Faith have for the first time been revealed by the Manifestations of God themselves, in this case the Báb and Bahá'u'lláh. Through these revealed words we can reach Him because mankind has potentially reached the required stage of maturity. Believe it or not, we have spiritually grown up, and the words in the revealed prayers of Bahá'u'lláh are of far greater potency than anything we might invent ourselves, but more importantly, are better suited to nourish and inform our souls. Our souls need nourishment as do our bodies. While our body is sustained by oxygen, sunshine, food and water, prayers revealed by the Manifestation of God in this Day, Bahá'u'lláh, together with those revealed by the Báb and 'Abdu'l-Bahá, are the ones that refresh our souls, keeping us spiritually healthy, strong and happy in the same way as we wish our physical bodies to be well and happy. This increasing spiritual health enables us to grasp and understand more clearly the spiritual dimension of our existence.

Bahá'u'lláh has revealed many prayers for all our purposes in life, enabling us to communicate with God and Bahá'u'lláh. Muhammad likened prayer to a ladder to heaven. You can't just get there on your own.

You have asked whether our prayers go beyond Bahá'u'lláh: it all depends whether we pray to Him directly or through Him to God. We may do both, and also can pray directly to God, but our prayers would certainly be more effective and illuminating if they are addressed to Him through His Manifestation, Bahá'u'lláh.[33]

It is the Manifestation of God which is the go-between, providing a connection between you and your God. But the trouble is that almost all of us tell God what we want Him to do. Give me this, give me that, please do this, please do that. And of course, maybe He hears us, and maybe not. Some of us will say: hope for the best. We seem to think it is all a bit hit and miss. But Bahá'u'lláh says that God is a prayer-hearing, prayer-answering God.

Who is there that hath cried after Thee, and whose prayer hath remained unanswered? Where is he to be found who hath reached forth towards Thee, and whom Thou hast failed to approach? Who is he that can claim to have fixed his gaze upon Thee, and toward whom the eye of Thy loving-kindness hath not been directed?[34]

That means that He can hear whatever we say. If prayer is communication with God, then that means the conversation is two-way traffic. Otherwise, we would just say our piece and leave it at that. But God is prayer-hearing, prayer-answering. I suggest that when we've said our prayers and we've opened our hearts, that we trust and have faith. The answer may not always be what we want, but the outcome will be what is good for us, because He knows best. We are sick and He is after all the Divine Doctor.

'Abdu'l-Bahá gives a very nice example. He says there was a patient who was sick and in the hospital. The doctor attended the patient who said, "Doctor, they've stopped all my food and given me only water and I want a steak. I want solid food." "Alright, alright," says the doctor, "turn over", and he gives the patient an injection! "What kind of doctor are you? I asked for food and you gave me pain!" But we all know the doctor knows best.

We don't always know what is best for us. We may sit down and say, this is what I want, give it to me. Sometimes we may even demand it immediately. It doesn't work like that! It's a childish way of looking at things because we are incapable of understanding all the implications for the present and for the future.

We have to learn how to pray, because 'Abdu'l-Bahá says that the language of prayer is as different as the human language is from the animal language. Can you imagine how much we have to learn? This language of prayer, this language of the spirit, is the food for our soul. It is a comfort for our sorrow-laden heart.

There is a "language of the Spirit", which is independent of speech or writing, by which God can commune with and inspire those whose hearts are seeking after truth, wherever they are, and whatever their native race or tongue . . .

We should speak in the language of heaven – in the language of the spirit – for there is a language of the spirit and heart. It is as different from our language as our own language is different from that of the animals, who express themselves only by cries and sounds.[35]

The language of prayer is really the language of love, and we should allow our prayers to transform us. Otherwise, it is as 'Abdu'l-Bahá says, you play a beautiful instrument and it gives out beautiful music, but has no effect on itself. We must not be like an instrument that gives out the beautiful Words of God, without having any effect on our own selves. When the prayers begin to transform us and others begin to see a change in who we are and how we behave – that is the proof of our having improved and that our prayers have been offered appropriately.

Teaching is the source of Divine Confirmation. It is not sufficient to pray diligently for guidance, but this prayer must be followed by meditation as to the best methods of action and then action itself. Even if the action should not immediately produce results, or perhaps not be entirely correct, that does not make so much difference, because prayers can only be answered through action and if someone's action is wrong, God can use that method of showing the pathway which is right.[36]

Frequently, we think, I must pray now, but then say, no, I must finish what I am doing and then I must go somewhere. Or we say, I'm too tired, I don't feel too good. I won't pray now, maybe later.

> I bear witness that Thou hadst turned toward Thy
> servants ere they had turned toward Thee, and hadst
> remembered them ere they had remembered Thee. All
> grace is Thine, O Thou in Whose hand is the kingdom
> of Divine gifts and the source of every irrevocable
> decree.[37]

What does this mean? This means that He is calling to
communicate with me, to give me strength, to give me
energy, because He knows my soul. I need this now, but
what do we do? we postpone the moment because we
think we are too busy. Time passes, and we go deeper
into weakness and possibly miss the opportunity.

> Just as there are laws governing our physical lives,
> requiring that we must supply our bodies with cer-
> tain foods, maintain them within a certain range of
> temperatures, and so forth, if we wish to avoid physi-
> cal disabilities, so also there are laws governing our
> spiritual lives. These laws are revealed to mankind in
> each age by the Manifestation of God, and obedience
> to them is of vital importance if each human being,
> and mankind in general, is to develop properly and
> harmoniously. Moreover, these various aspects are
> interdependent. If an individual violates the spiritual
> laws for his own development he will cause injury not
> only to himself but to the society in which he lives.
> Similarly, the condition of society has a direct effect
> on the individuals who must live within it.
>
> As you point out, it is particularly difficult to follow

the laws of Bahá'u'lláh in present-day society whose accepted practice is so at variance with the standards of the Faith. However, there are certain laws that are so fundamental to the healthy functioning of human society that they must be upheld whatever the circumstances. . .[38]

It is interesting to note that if an individual violates the spiritual laws, he will cause injury not only to himself but to the society in which he lives. That shows that in this age we cannot isolate ourselves. We live in society and we are responsible to society. Similarly, the condition of society has a direct effect on the individual who must live within it. That means that we cannot be protected just by ourselves. We need spiritual assistance and need to endeavour through prayer and service to contribute to a change in society.

When you come into the Bahá'í Faith, you come in of your own free will. No one forces you to come in, or for that matter, to stay within the Faith. Your entry into the Faith is predicated on the acceptance of Bahá'u'lláh as the Manifestation of God for this day and age, Whose Revelation provides the means to your spiritual well-being and the security of mankind. If we come across something in the Writings that we don't understand, the answer is not to reject it. We can certainly seek clarification. However, if we still don't understand, we have to recognize our own limitations with a degree of humility which some of us might find difficult, particularly if we are highly educated or successful. It is important to remember that it would be a contradiction in terms to say a Manifestation of God doesn't get everything right and might be wrong occasionally; in which case He would be a clever man, not a Manifestation of God. I make no apologies for re-emphasizing this, as it is the foundation of releasing ourselves from our egos and protecting and developing our spiritual well-being. 'Abdu'l-Bahá says:

> We are ourselves the means of our degradation and exaltation. . . A person through his own actions and deeds makes himself loved or disliked by the people; or through his own unselfish conduct and behavior, refined morality and selfless intention, trustworthiness and rectitude he suffers himself to become favored and beloved at the threshold of God.[39]

It is very important that we develop into what Bahá'u'lláh desires for His followers so that we are able to attract others, and not just for our own personal satisfaction. Together we are in the process of building a new civilization. Given that this really is the whole purpose of our lives, how can we, with this monumental endeavour on our plate, find the time to be unhappy or miserable? Perhaps it is because we do not get totally involved in the service of the Cause of God? We cannot treat being a Bahá'í as a part-time job!

I implore you to have faith. A faith which you have to recognize is endowed with spiritual authority and is not just abstract. Believe me, it works. Try it and keep working on forgetting yourself and trusting in the Word of God. I know it is not easy but there is no other way that you can understand these things. I've said it in many places and I shall repeat myself over and over again; one has to try these things for oneself.

Whenever you want to speak, teach anybody or give any form of service for Bahá'u'lláh, first I suggest you mentally transport yourself to 'Akká, in the Holy Land, say a prayer and then act. You may well ask, how practical is that? I am fairly confident that everyone has been somewhere they have been happy or dream of going and let their imagination wander as if they are there. We live in a world where we can send messages around the world, even before the traffic light changes. If mechanical or electronic things can function so quickly, why can't the spirit, which is free of time and space, not be faster than any material device? We all have imagination: just tap into it. Every time you try, it becomes easier. If you've been on pilgrimage, it is even easier: all you have to do is remember. If you haven't been on pilgrimage, look at a photograph of Bahjí, Bahá'u'lláh's Holy Shrine. I urge you to keep trying and I know, if you are sincere, you will succeed and it will become like second nature to you.

With your voice, you can now remotely close the curtains, turn the music on, open the door, shut the door, so why can't it be possible when you say "Yá Bahá'u'l-Abhá", and think of Him, that it's done. He's heard and the reply comes to strengthen and guide you appropriately. Believe me, with time you will come to appreciate that there are far greater things in the spiritual worlds than any technological advancement you now consider amazing. You just need faith.

What is real faith? Faith outwardly means to believe in the message a Manifestation brings to the world and accept the fulfilment in him of that which the prophets have announced. But in reality faith embodies three degrees: to confess with the tongue; to believe in the heart; to show forth in our actions. These three things are essential to true faith.[40]

All that I am sharing with you, by the grace of God, I have experienced. Bahá'u'lláh and the invocation "Yá Bahá'u'l-Abhá" will always help you, if your call is sincere and with conviction. That's how I went pioneering in 1953 to Madagascar where I knew no one and I didn't even know how to get there. But I did believe that since this was God's work, it would succeed. It was amazing, although I admit not easy and not without difficulties.

The beloved Guardian, Shoghi Effendi, said to me: "You will be successful. Follow in the footsteps of the apostles of Jesus Christ." They had nothing, and I had nothing. I reckoned if they can be successful, why can't I, if I believe in Bahá'u'lláh? I'm not an apostle of Bahá'u'lláh, but I am His humble maidservant, and results came by the grace of Bahá'u'lláh, 'Abdu'l-Bahá, and Shoghi Effendi who prayed for me as he did for all the pioneers. Despite the enormous barriers, we all succeeded.

After returning to the United Kingdom from Madagascar, I almost immediately went to the French Cameroons in Africa. Again, I didn't know anything or anyone and there were lots of restrictions, but somehow I survived and the Faith was established. Success depends not upon how clever we are or how much money we have but solely upon the purity of our motive and faith and on our willingness implicitly to rely on the bounty and guidance of Bahá'u'lláh. Anything short of this and we are doomed to failure. These successes are not miracles nor are they reserved for a selected few; they are promises made to each and every one of us, provided we trust in Him and serve.

I share with you my personal experiences or you might think I am talking about some existential concept that is not a reality. Yes, dear friends, I do know what I'm talking about. That is why my wish is that you might also experience this joy at which you can marvel in this world but which you can take with you to the other world as well.

Bahá'u'lláh has said that God will assist all those who arise in His service. The more we labour for His Faith, the more He will assist us.

It is in Our power, should We wish it, to enable a speck of floating dust to generate, in less than the twinkling of an eye, suns of infinite, of unimaginable splendor, to cause a dewdrop to develop into vast and number-less oceans, to infuse into every letter such a force as to empower it to unfold all the knowledge of past and future ages.

We are possessed of such power which, if brought to light, will transmute the most deadly of poisons into a panacea of unfailing efficacy.[41]

By the righteousness of God, should a man, all alone, arise in the name of Bahá and put on the armor of His love, him will the Almighty cause to be victorious, though the forces of earth and heaven be arrayed against him.[42]

The source of courage and power is the promotion of the Word of God, and steadfastness in His Love.[43]

He, verily, will aid every one that aideth Him, and will remember every one that remembereth Him. To this beareth witness this Tablet that hath shed the splendor of the loving-kindness of your Lord, the All-Glorious, the All-Compelling.[44]

Every single letter proceeding from Our mouth is endowed with such regenerative power as to enable it to bring into existence a new creation – a creation the magnitude of which is inscrutable to all save God. He verily hath knowledge of all things.[45]

We all have failings which we may try to rationalize and in respect of which we make self-serving excuses. A person may think: "If I drink a little, what does it matter? Nobody is looking. I'm just drinking for my pleasure," or they may say to themselves: "I'm just having a little affair in secret. What does it matter? I'm not hurting anyone." Little by little, you start to drink more or find yourself deeper in and getting away with situations which fundamentally you are ashamed of. It's like playing with a

tiger cub. That cub is so sweet, little, playful, not ferocious, great fun and you are convinced you are in control.
Slowly, that tiger grows and then he devours you. This is
what happens when you break the laws of Bahá'u'lláh.
Eventually, it will damage you. Not only your mind, but
your soul as well. You risk damaging your soul's progress
in the Abhá Kingdom. Just think about it – is it worth it?

Do we want a short life of so-called "fun" or enduring serenity? The choice is ours. That's why we have been
given willpower.

On the other hand, why do we think that we don't hurt
others? Eventually, people do find out, particularly those
who are near and dear to us. They find out because our
actions change, our attitudes change. People say that the
person closest to us is the last to know, but that is because
they are the last to really believe we could have done such
a thing. They are the last to accept the proof of our indis-
cretions. So why do we choose to lose our moral compass
in any area of our lives?

> The root cause of wrong doing is ignorance, and we
> must hold fast to the tools of perception and knowl-
> edge. Good character must be taught. Light must be
> spread afar, so that, in the school of humanity, all
> may acquire the heavenly characteristics of spirit,
> and see for themselves beyond any doubt that there is
> no fiercer hell, no more fiery abyss, than to possess a
> character that is evil and unsound; no more darksome
> pit nor loathsome torment than to show forth quali-
> ties which deserve to be condemned.

The individual must be educated to such a high degree that he would rather have his throat cut than tell a lie, and would think it easier to be slashed with a sword or pierced with a spear than to utter calumny or be carried away by wrath.

Thus will be kindled the sense of human dignity and pride, to burn away the reapings of lustful appetites. Then will each one of God's beloved shine out as a bright moon with qualities of the spirit, and the relationship of each to the Sacred Threshold of his Lord will not be illusory but sound and real, will be as the very foundation of the building, not some embellishment on its façade . . .[46]

Erroneously, we think that our characters are unalterable and if, for example, you have a temper, it's part of your nature and there is nothing that you can do about it. But this is not so, it is our animalistic nature which we have allowed to get out of hand and which we have to overcome with the assistance of daily prayers. This is a conscious process which is accompanied by pure prayers and sincere thoughts to correct our aggression and impatience. You cannot just empty your mind and say, ok, I'm good now!

Examine for a minute the relentless and daily chore of housework. You do it because you love your family and your children for whom you would do anything. They come first, then you take care of yourself afterwards. Most parents are like that. In everything, love comes first. In other relationships, if I don't like you or love you,

I don't want to talk to you. If you don't love me or like me, then you won't want to talk to me. We would make a hundred and one excuses to avoid each other. This is quite natural. The basis of anything we do for others as Bahá'ís in the world is out of love, whether it comes easily or we have to make a great effort. On the other hand, it doesn't change the nature of a chore or your dislike of doing it but your desire to do what is for the benefit of others motivated by a spiritual love is greater and takes priority over your own comfort.

> O SON OF BEING! Love me that I may love thee. If thou lovest me not, My love can in no wise reach thee. Know this O servant.[47]

We all understand that God will look after and shower love upon humanity in general. But equally we each have a need to feel a love which is specific to us. The purest love is that which comes from giving love. It's two-way traffic. Love is not enduring if it is one-way. Perhaps for a while, but after some time it is clear that it is not sustainable and not constructive. This is true of our relationship with God. If we want to be the beneficiaries of His Grace and Love we have to prove consistently that we love Him, otherwise we risk being left to our own devices. So, we must ask ourselves, do I really, really love God and Bahá'u'lláh? Do I really want to communicate that love?

What is the purpose of communicating and praying? It's certainly not going to benefit God. However much we love Him or we don't love Him, let's be clear; God doesn't need us. But God's love is going to benefit our souls, enabling our whole being to change. It's just like eating healthy food, taking care of our clean clothes, living in a clean house, and breathing in fresh air. All of these things add to our health and beauty. If we have the choice and access to a healthy productive environment, why would we want to exist under conditions that are to our detriment?

Five steps of prayer

Here is a quotation from Shoghi Effendi that was shared with a Bahá'í in Haifa. It is a pilgrim note but it is printed in *Principles of Bahá'í Administration*, obviously it has been checked and it is very helpful, as it clarifies in detail the approach and the impact of the act of praying:

> After emphasising the need for more prayers and meditation among the friends, the Beloved Guardian said to use these five steps if we had a problem of any kind for which we desired a solution or wished help.
>
> First step. Pray and meditate about it. Use the prayers of the Manifestations, as they have the greatest power. Then remain in the silence of contemplation for a few minutes.
>
> Second step. Arrive at a decision and hold this. This decision is usually born during the contemplation. It may seem almost impossible of accomplishment but if it seems to be as an answer to a prayer or a way of solving the problem, then immediately take the next step.

Third step. Have determination to carry the decision through. Many fail here. The decision, budding into determination, is blighted and instead becomes a wish or a vague longing. When determination is born, immediately take the next step.

Fourth step. Have faith and confidence that the power will flow through you, the right way will appear, the door will open, the right thought, the right message, the right principle or the right book will be given you. Have confidence, and the right thing will come to your need. Then, as you rise from prayer, take at once the fifth step.

Fifth step. Then, he said, lastly, ACT; act as though it had all been answered. Then act with tireless, ceaseless energy. And as you act, you, yourself, will become a magnet, which will attract more power to your being, until you become an unobstructed channel for the Divine Power to flow through you. Many pray, but do not remain for the last half of the first step. Some who meditate arrive at a decision, but fail to hold it. Few have the determination to carry the decision through; still fewer have the confidence that the right thing will come to their need. But how many remember to act as though it had all been answered. How true are those words – 'Greater than the prayer is the spirit in which it is uttered' and greater than the way it is uttered is the spirit in which it is carried out.[48]

And elsewhere Shoghi Effendi wrote:

Thus, when a person is active, they are blessed by the Holy Spirit. When they are inactive, the Holy Spirit cannot find a repository in their being, and thus they are deprived of its healing and quickening rays.[49]

Even after reading this some of us get confused. We think that when we ask for help for teaching or for doing something, or when we are stuck and have nobody and don't know what to do, if we say a prayer, sit in silence, and meditate, some fantastic plan will be given right up to the smallest detail. Then we can go and work on it. That's not so. In my humble experience – I don't know about others – but in the fifty years of my travelling and in trying to pray and meditate and get things done, I find that sometimes we are given a little nudge, and it may be a very small thing that we are directed to do.

For example, in the 1950s while we were in the United States I travelled with my small child to many states including Arizona where we were visiting Amos and Mary Gibson and stayed in a boarding school on an Indian Reservation. Although Amos and Mary were pioneering there they were restricted in their teaching endeavours because as school teachers they were government servants and subject to certain constraints. Amos and Mary were both away at a conference when I arrived totally exhausted after a journey of several hundred miles. So I had a bath and bathed my baby and we both said our prayers. I often say, "Now, Bahá'u'lláh, what would you like me to do?" And, you know, the thought came to me, why don't you go and do your washing. Then

I thought, no! I'm too tired for washing, I'm going to bed. I tried to get into bed, and put my head on my pillow, and an inner voice said to me, "Meherangiz – go and do your washing."

So, although my body just wanted to lie down I conceded that I'd better do what my instincts were telling me. I got out of bed, collected my washing, came out and there was a Native American Indian lady standing there. I said, "Could you please tell me where can I do my laundry?"

"Oh", she says, "sure, I'll show you."

Then I said: "I wonder who did my room, because I would like to thank that person."

So she said: "I did."

"Oh," I said, "thank you very much."

She said: "Nobody ever thanks me."

"Well, I'm not responsible for anybody but for my own self and I thank you."

Then she took me into the room where there was an old-fashioned washing machine. You had to put in the water, put in your clothes, put in the powder, then she switched it on and said, "I'll be back in 15 to 20 minutes. Please sit here."

I waited and the machine was making such a racket, and I said to myself, you see, after all there isn't anything inspirational about this, I should have gone to bed and rested. What am I doing here with all this dreadful noise going on in this washing machine. I sat back and said, maybe, maybe not; let's see what happens. In any event I had no choice, because my laundry was in the washing machine.

Twenty minutes later, this woman – her name was Lola – came with eight Native American men and women. They sat down and to my total astonishment said: "Please tell us what is your religion." Who would have imagined that a chance meeting around a washing machine would have prompted anyone to ask about religion!

Now if I had gone to sleep at that moment, I would have missed this opportunity. I might never have met this woman again. I would not have this opportunity to speak to eight Native Americans who were anxious to know about the Faith. On my own, I was unlikely to have come across them collectively.

You have to trust in your inner self, particularly if you are sincere when you implore Bahá'u'lláh to assist you. You have to go ahead and act on the slightest thought and see what happens – however small it may be or for that matter how ridiculous it may be. It may not always work but with faith the most remarkable and unexpected things happen.

Another time in the middle of a lot of work, I prayed and said, "Bahá'u'lláh, what can I do? I want to do so much for the Cause, and I cannot do much. What may I do for you, please?" And the thought came – go and telephone a lady Bahá'í friend. I rang her up and I realized that, in error, I rang her home instead of her office. As soon as she answered, she started to cry at the other end. I asked, "Why are you crying?"

She said: "How did you know that I was home?"

"Oh, I didn't know. I rang by mistake. Why are you crying? What's the matter?"

She said: "I don't know. My faith is shaken, and I need help and I've been crying. I need Bahá'u'lláh to help me."

"All right," I said, "Talk to me."

She said: "No! I've been asking Bahá'u'lláh to help me."

I jokingly said: "Bahá'u'lláh told me that He was busy and He sent me. Now you tell me, what you want me to do and what happened."

And she laughed and then we talked for an hour on the phone and she settled down and she became a very good pioneer in other countries and to this day remains very, very firm in the Faith.

You see, it was just a little phone call. Now I could have said "Oh, come on, I've got so much work to do, I'll call her tomorrow." Well, even five minutes would have been too late. We never know. Bahá'u'lláh and the Concourse on high do not always give us the whole plan. He just gives us a nudge, a tiny flash of inspiration, to see whether we will obey and act upon the hint. I have experienced hundreds of such incidents.

At one stage, again, I was extremely busy. I was to prepare dinner for prominent people coming to my house. After prayer a thought came to me about a lady I had recently met for the first time. She was not a Bahá'í and she had come to my house and had tea with her family and gone away and left me her address so that we might correspond someday. I had put her address somewhere in my address book and the thought came: "Go and write to this lady." I did not know what to write and I had so much work to do. Can you imagine this, in the middle of the day, in the middle of cooking with no help and my guests were coming at seven o'clock, and I have thought that I should go and look for the address? I did, I wrote a letter and, to my horror, I found that I had no postage stamp. I ran all the way to the Post Office, put a stamp on it, put it in the box. Then I ran all the way back, and on the way I thought, "Thank God at least my friends and family can't see me in this condition. I am running like a lunatic just to go and post a letter."

By return of mail a reply came. She said: "I was about to commit suicide, when I said 'God, help me or here I come,'" and she wrote and said: "Your letter came through the letter box and I am alright." And I heard later that she became a Bahá'í and so did her family.

There was an English lady, Mabel Joseph, who came from a Christian background and was excommunicated by her family on becoming a Bahá'í. She was unmarried and lived alone in an apartment in Bournemouth. One day after saying my prayers I felt I had to go to visit Jo (her nickname) because I felt she was in trouble. Jo didn't have a phone and there was no such thing as a mobile phone. I did not drive and my family said, "You mean to say that you are going to go on an arduous journey to Bournemouth, which is 172 kilometres by train, not even knowing if Jo will be at home, just because you 'feel' something is wrong?" I insisted and agreed it was a little crazy but off I went. When I arrived I found Jo very unwell to the extent that she had to be hospitalized. Since there was no one else in Jo's life I stayed in Bournemouth until Jo was discharged and then brought her back to our home until I was satisfied that she had fully recovered.

Perhaps it is difficult to believe in the power of prayers but I learned that it was better to be guided by them than to ignore them. But I will say it a hundred times: there is nothing special about me and that the potency and influence of prayers is open to everyone who is committed to connecting with Bahá'u'lláh through His words.

So please, dear friends, do not ignore your inner voice when it says "Try it." If it works, it's inspiration, if not it's your imagination or it may be even indigestion. It doesn't matter, we will learn to carry on. Study carefully all of the five steps given by the Guardian properly and understand them and have faith.

Action means act; act upon your feelings. Almost all of us have said: "I have this gut feeling," or "I feel it". But you put it off and you decide to analyse it intellectually. These things cannot be analysed intellectually. It has to be put into action. Put it into action and see what happens.

This next story is well known by many Bahá'ís but I repeat it for the benefit of those who don't. During the Ten Year Crusade, between 1953 to 1963 the Bahá'ís were charged with spreading the Faith all over the whole of this planet. In one town in Africa the friends were longing to proclaim the Faith but they did not have the money. At one of the Nineteen Day Feasts someone explained the spiritual nature of giving and how universal participation by the friends in donating to the Funds can produce wonderful results. So that evening every single member of the community, even the children, put something in the Fund box. There were very few Bahá'ís there, I don't know precisely how many, but only a handful and sadly they were only able to collect three dollars and ten cents. Now even in the early fifties $3.10 didn't go very far and it certainly wasn't enough to launch a publicity campaign. So they decided they would buy a Bahá'í book. The book was bought and the secretary thought: "Well, I haven't read this one so I'll read it as I am going home in the bus." She took it with her, sat in the bus, and started to read. It was a rainy evening and a gentleman came and sat next to her. Many of you know how there is often the inclination to want to read over someone's shoulder to see what they are reading. For some reason one becomes very uncomfortable when this happens, so when the gentleman who was sitting next to her started to do this she tried to sort of not let him read. But by then he had already read the caption and a sufficient amount to prompt him to say, "Excuse me, Madam, this book seems very interesting. What is it all about?"

Then she realized, "Oh how stupid I am. I mean, after all, this is why we got the book; for others to read." So, she told him about the Bahá'í Faith and lent him the book.

"You know," he said, "for six or seven years my wife has always picked me up but, as one of my children was ill, she could not come today so I was forced to catch this bus." As it transpired he was the editor of a newspaper in which he wrote two articles about the Faith with thirteen articles to follow. He also gave the Bahá'ís a large hall in the newspaper building to hold a proclamation meeting as well as arranging two radio programmes and two television shows. In the event the three dollars and ten cents they had all contributed provided about fifteen thousand dollars' worth of publicity. You see when we pray sincerely we are guided and extraordinary things happen, but we must know when to act.

When you consistently rely on prayers you will notice that you are prompted with rational and sometimes irrational thoughts but the important thing is to ACT, and don't worry about how absurd or insignificant the inspiration might be. There is a greater power in this Cause than we will ever understand, but we have to rely on it with faith and sincerity.

I would like to refer you to a Tablet of 'Abdu'l-Bahá, entitled 'Reason is Spiritual':

> Reason, which comprehends (or detects) the realities of things, is a spiritual reality, not physical (or material). Therefore the animal is deprived of reason, and it (reason) is specialised to mankind. The animal feeleth realities which are perceptible to the senses, but man perceiveth intellectual realities (or things perceptible to reason). Consequently, it has become evident that reason is a spiritual faculty, not physical (or material).[50]

You see, if you are intelligent and endowed with reason then it's a double blessing. Not everyone, however, may have had the blessing of an education such as in the villages or even in cities where they may have been neglected or been deprived of an education. It is a cardinal mistake to believe that a lack of education means someone is not intelligent or is incapable of making decisions for themselves. As humans we have this reasoning power which is a spiritual gift of which no one is deprived, and by that we can be guided and are able to lead fruitful and inspirational lives.

Why pray aloud?

Why should it be necessary for him to repeat prayers aloud and with the tongue?

One reason for this is that if the heart alone is speaking the mind can be more easily disturbed. But repeating the words so that the tongue and heart act together enables the mind to be concentrated. Then the whole man is surrounded by the spirit of prayer and the act is more perfect.[51]

'Abdu'l-Bahá says that it is necessary that we pray aloud so that we can concentrate. In another place he says that when we pray aloud, sometimes we pay attention to the words and other times to the melodies. So when we're chanting or singing, or saying it beautifully, then it has a very great effect because our thoughts are not disturbed and we can concentrate better.

'Abdu'l-Bahá also says that when reading for a group the reader must make the effort to ensure that the prayers are read beautifully, so that every word has an effect on the souls present. How often we find ourselves straining to hear the words of a prayer or reading when someone is mumbling or racing through the devotional as if they need to catch a bus. We need to remember that we are praying with and for everyone in the room and it is essential that they can clearly hear what is being said so that they are able to meditate on the words.

Why pray in groups?

Some of us question, why should I go and pray in a group organized by a Local Spiritual Assembly, Bahá'í group, community or individuals? Sometimes we don't feel like praying in a group at a time, place and date prescribed by others. Some may even resent praying with those that they don't like very much. We may be quite happy sitting on top of a hill, or near the beach, just saying our own prayers by ourselves. 'Abdu'l-Bahá is quite clear about this:

> To think this way is useless imagination for where many are gathered together their force is greater. Separate soldiers fighting alone and individually have not the force of a united army. If all the soldiers in this spiritual war gather together, then their united spiritual feelings help each other, and their prayers become acceptable.[52]

> Thou hast asked about places of worship and the underlying reason therefore. The wisdom in raising up such buildings is that at a given hour, the people should know it is time to meet, and all should gather together, and, harmoniously attuned one to another,

engage in prayer; with the result that out of this coming together, unity and affection shall grow and flourish in the human heart.[53]

And the Universal House of Justice has written:

Responding to the inmost longing of every heart to commune with its Maker, they carry out acts of collective worship in diverse settings, uniting with others in prayer, awakening spiritual susceptibilities, and shaping a pattern of life distinguished for its devotional character.[54]

Obligatory prayers

Obligatory prayers are obligatory for Bahá'ís from the age of 15. Think of these prayers as similar to your requirement to take in oxygen, sunshine, food, water; if you don't, you get sick and you die, in this case spiritually. That's why Bahá'u'lláh has given us obligatory prayers. 'Abdu'l-Bahá says:

O thou spiritual friend! . . . Know thou that prayer is indispensable and obligatory, and man under no pretext whatsoever is excused from performing the prayer unless he be mentally unsound or an insurmountable obstacle prevent him.[55]

In another place it says:

Exemption from offering the Obligatory Prayers is granted to those who are ill, those who are over 70, and women in their courses provided they perform their ablutions and repeat a specifically revealed verse 95 times a day.[56]

The laxness in saying our obligatory prayers comes because we have not got into the habit of praying, leaving the soul weak and vulnerable. I think it would be helpful if each home were to have a picture of a starving man or woman as a reminder of the condition of our souls. Look at it and say, "That's my soul, that's my soul." However, in the case of these starving bodies someone will either help them or they will die. But with our souls only we can provide nourishment – we cannot rely on others. Looking at these starving images we should be mindful that our souls are also at risk of being weak and emaciated and only we can feed them and provide the energy required on a consistent basis. I often picture my own soul like that picture of the starving man or woman and I get on the double to nourish it, as I don't want my soul to be like that or even worse go into a coma. Condemning our souls through eternity is not clever, particularly when it is so easily avoidable. Many people these days practise mindfulness regularly. While this is beneficial physically and often mentally, it does not enhance our spiritual condition. Through praying and meditating and reciting the obligatory prayers, we are able to benefit all three dimensions of our being.

So, even if in the beginning the fire of your love is

not burning that strongly, at the very least, nurture your soul by reciting any one of the three obligatory prayers revealed for us. It may be self-serving but it is also self-protecting. Why does Bahá'u'lláh say we are obliged to pray? The soul needs spiritual sustenance, even though we may not be fully aware of its impact, in the same way as we are not conscious of the air we breathe. The obligatory prayer is the essential lifeforce for our soul. It takes time and depends on how emaciated our soul has become. The longer the soul has been like that, the longer it will take to revitalise, but even that process will be influenced by our sincerity and of course God's mercy.

When the soul has been starved, it may not be able to take initially too much prayer, just as a starving body can't take too much food at one time. It may not be immediately capable of assimilating it. We are fortunate that Bahá'u'lláh has given us three different obligatory prayers to choose from. Also, Bahá'u'lláh has cautioned that we should not tire and exhaust our soul. So take as little as you can, and step by step you will find that you are growing and feeling better and gaining spiritual strength. Your stamina strengthens in every aspect, and in time you will find the longest prayer will seem short. God is my witness, often after saying the long obligatory prayer, I can't believe I have come to the end and I start all over again, making sure I am conscious and certain of what I am doing. A little like exercising, the more you practise, the more repeats you are able to do with less and less effort.

I can remember when my husband first became a

Bahá'í and he started saying the Tablet of Aḥmad. He said: "O my God, when will I ever finish this?". And after a few months, he said, "It now seems so short! I keep going back to make sure I haven't missed a page." It happens to everybody. We begin to enjoy it. It's like someone you love or a favourite food that you enjoyed. You say – oh, I didn't really have very much, did I? But, yes you did.

> In truth, I say that obligatory prayer and fasting occupy an exalted station in the sight of God. . . Blessed be such men and women as pay heed, and observe His precepts.[57]

> He saith: "Obligatory prayer is a ladder of ascent for the believer." Within it are concealed a myriad effects and benefits. Indeed they are beyond computation.[58]

> Should the garb of anyone be visibly sullied, his prayers shall not ascend to God, and the celestial Concourse will turn away from him.[59]

> . . . the obligatory prayers are by their very nature of greater effectiveness and are endowed with a greater power than the non-obligatory ones.[60]

> You should rest assured that your strict adherence to the laws and observances enjoined by Bahá'u'lláh is the one power that can effectively guide and enable you to overcome the tests and trials of your life, and help you to continually grow and develop spiritually.

The Guardian particularly appreciates the fact that you have been faithfully observing Bahá'u'lláh's injunction regarding the recital of the daily obligatory prayers, and have thereby set such a high example before your Bahá'í fellow-youth. These daily prayers have been endowed with a special potency which only those who regularly recite them can adequately appreciate. The friends should therefore endeavour to make daily use of these prayers, whatever the peculiar circumstances and conditions of their life.[61]

Given the nature of these specific prayers which are classified as obligatory, we really shouldn't be making any excuses. There are exemptions though, particularly for women who experience pain or fatigue when menstruating. As a substitution there is a special prayer in the Codification of the Kitáb-i-Aqdas that can be said ninety-five times, after ablutions: "Glorified be God, the Lord of Splendour and Beauty."

As most of you know, there are three obligatory prayers, one long one which you say once every twenty-four hours; a medium one which you say three times a day – which means during the intervals from sunrise to noon, from noon to sunset, and then from sunset till two hours after sunset; and the short one which is to be said anytime from noon, twelve o'clock, until before sunset.

The short obligatory prayer doesn't even take a minute to recite. You have to wash your hands and face; you may wish to take your shoes off if you are at home (although there are no specific instructions for shoes). Turn towards 'Akká, and no matter where you are, no one need know you're even praying. It has no genuflections so that you won't look funny or conspicuous. Just say it, in your heart; you can just say it softly within yourself. Frankly, these days anyone observing you would probably assume you are talking on your mobile phone. You can't say that you cannot find one minute to spare between midday and sunset. We are fortunate to have been given a choice of how long we choose to spend remembering God, depending on the circumstances we find ourselves in, but remembering Him is imperative.

In answer to a specific question, the Guardian said:

He would advise you to only use the short midday Obligatory Prayer. This has no genuflections and only requires that when saying it the believer turns his face towards 'Akká where Bahá'u'lláh is buried. This is a physical symbol of an inner reality, just as the plant stretches out to the sunlight – from which it receives life and growth – so we turn our hearts to the Manifestation of God, Bahá'u'lláh, when we pray: and we turn our faces during this short prayer, to where His dust lies on this earth as a symbol of the inner act.

Bahá'u'lláh has reduced all ritual and form to an absolute minimum in His Faith. The few forms that there are – like those associated with the two longer obligatory daily prayers, are only symbols of the inner attitude. There is a wisdom in them, and a great bless-ing, but we cannot force ourselves to understand or feel these things, that is why He gave us also the very short and simple prayer, for those who did not feel the desire to perform the acts associated with the other two.[62]

Bahjí, where Bahá'u'lláh is buried, is located at:
35 Degrees East Longitude
33 Degrees North Latitude

My observation is that once you start saying the long obligatory prayer, it even affects the children in the home. When they see you praying regularly they learn it is natural and then when the time comes for them, they also are able to pray naturally. Again it is not dissimilar to a household where everyone exercises daily, so the children join in naturally. You won't have to tell them.

People often get confused because it says in the "privacy of one's chamber".[63] Privacy of your chamber does not mean a private room, just for prayers. Who can afford that? In developing nations there are often 10 people living in one room. What do they do? Don't they pray? While these prayers might be obligatory it does not mean that we have to make an exhibition of ourselves. If you are at home, take a little corner, anywhere, and start praying, and your family, friends or guests will respect your special time. They will naturally move away or stay silent.

It is not compulsory to say your prayers out loud. 'Abdu'l-Bahá says that you can pray aloud or softly. But when you pray aloud, you hear yourself and because you hear what you say, you can concentrate better. By contrast, when you are just reading, often your mind may wander elsewhere. So, I suggest you begin by praying aloud. Firstly, it helps you to focus and secondly it helps you to start memorizing the prayer. You may have to use the prayer book in the beginning when saying the medium or long obligatory prayers even though it is a little awkward while you do all the genuflexions. The important thing is the sincerity of your heart when praying. My memory, after a profound illness, is almost non-existent so I always have to use the prayer book. But in the part where I place my forehead to the ground, I begged Bahá'u'lláh to allow me to remember that part and fortunately I can. Really, how stupid was I, instead I should have asked to be able to memorize the whole thing! But I foolishly didn't.

Bahá'u'lláh says that you must wash your hands and face before saying your prayers; wash means wash – not that people should sprinkle water on themselves. There is a purpose in the physical act of cleansing. Do you think that Bahá'u'lláh cares if or how you pray? I have frequently stayed in people's homes and if I say anything about following the guidance given for the manner of praying, I have been told to mind my own business. Usually their retort is "What I do as a Bahá'í is my business." So naturally I kept quiet even though all I was trying to do, was to share Bahá'u'lláh's instructions.

My perception of the tremendous power of prayer is that it is comparable to nuclear power. Have you ever heard of anybody messing around with nuclear power? No, you have to wear your gloves, protect yourself from head to toe, use specially designed tools, and be very careful. You'd be crazy not to follow the instructions. You can't discover the atom and then just play around with it. It is the same thing with the power of prayer. It is very powerful. If guidance has been given, it is for a reason and it makes no sense to mess around with it. My feeling is that you should very humbly just follow the instructions clearly laid out for us, none of which is very difficult.

With time you will find that the genuflexions, which are the physical manifestations of turning with your whole being to God, have a power which might initially elude you:

> Shouldst thou come with the whole of thy being to God and be attracted to the light of the Kingdom of God and be enkindled by the fire of the love of God, then wilt thou see that which thou canst not see today, will comprehend the inner significance of the Word of God and thoroughly understand the mysteries contained in the holy Books.[64]

Shoghi Effendi says there's a mystery in the genuflexions that no one can understand and, in my opinion, with time you will lose any self-consciousness and awkwardness and find it increasingly natural.

The whole body is built in such a way that when you raise your hands with your palms upwards, it is as if you were asking for bounties and His love and you are offering Him your love. Think about it, where do you put your hands when you want to receive and give something? It's so natural to do it this way.

What do you do when you see someone you respect? To offer a comparison, a worldly comparison: what do you do when you're presented to the Queen or someone important? You bow or you curtsy. When we pray, we're in the presence of Bahá'u'lláh and He is the King of Kings, King of the Universe, and through Him we make our connections with God so we put our hands on our knees and bow before Him.

Then there are the times when you want to sit down and talk to Him. I prefer to put my feet under me, just like the camels sit, and your feet become a cushion for your seat and your back, but this is only a personal preference and is not required. But if you can't do all of the specific genuflexions and movements, and there are many people who can't, then you should do the short or medium obligatory prayer.

> Concerning other positions prescribed in the Obligatory Prayers the House of Justice has instructed us to inform you that one of the believers asked the Guardian a question about the correct position for sitting. From the context it seems clear that this question is related to the medium Prayer, but this is not explicitly stated. The Guardian's reply states that sitting on a chair is permissible, but to sit on the floor is preferable and more fitting.[65]

So although you of course can sit on a chair, it is preferable, if possible, to sit on the floor or ground. You could put your feet tucked under on one side, or for those of you who are more flexible you could sit cross-legged. The important thing is that you are in a relaxed, submissive position which allows you to be totally focused on conversing with your Maker.

Then, there is the action of raising your hands while you say Alláh-u-Abhá, Alláh-u-Abhá, Alláh-u-Abhá. This is God's Most Great Name. How should we say it? When you love someone very much, it is natural to call their name repeatedly. There is nothing to feel embarrassed about repeatedly calling God's Name. Every religion that God has sent has asked man to humble himself, for example by kneeling or prostrating, thereby manifesting his love and respect. This is simply an outward expression of humility. It additionally facilitates our ability to focus on the Manifestation of God.

When you look to the right and turn to the left in order to supplicate mercy from God, in the beginning of the prayer, it is of course symbolic. In the narrative to the long obligatory prayer: "Whoso wisheth to recite this prayer, let him stand up and turn unto God, and, as he standeth in his place, let him gaze to the right and to the left, as if awaiting the mercy of his Lord, the Most Merciful, the Compassionate." Clearly, this is a time for us to reach the depths of our humility while waiting for the power of God to reach us and for us to be in His Presence, while communicating with Him through this most powerful of prayers.

The bounties and benefits for the soul that we derive from using the genuflexions are more numerous than we can imagine.

Know thou that in every word and movement of the obligatory prayer, there are allusions, mysteries and a wisdom that man is unable to comprehend, and letters and scrolls cannot contain.[66]

'Abdu'l-Bahá says:

Know thou, verily, it is becoming in a weak one to supplicate to the Strong One, and it behoveth a seeker of bounty to beseech the Glorious Bountiful One. When one supplicates to his Lord, turns to Him and seeks bounty from His Ocean, this supplication brings light to his heart, illumination to his sight, life to his soul and exaltation to his being.

During thy supplications to God and thy reciting, "Thy Name is my healing", consider how thine heart is cheered, thy soul delighted by the spirit of the love of God, and thy mind attracted to the Kingdom of God! By these attractions one's ability and capacity increase. When the vessel is enlarged the water increases, and when the thirst grows the bounty of the cloud becomes agreeable to the taste of man. This is the mystery of supplication and the wisdom of stating one's wants.[67]

It is all too easy to come up with a variety of excuses for not praying. But we shouldn't forget that the privilege of praying could be taken away from us in an instant. Don't be the person who only implores God when things go wrong, and dares to ask, "Oh my God, why do you do this to me?"

Often during my travels, people have asked me: "Why does God create earthquakes, floods, natural disasters etc.?" We seem to blame God for all the distressing things which happen but never seem to attribute all the good things which happen in our lives. What about our health, our family and all of the other beautiful things in our life. Do you think we are the exclusive creator of these things? Does it ever occur to us that instead of blaming God, we should constantly be remembering to be grateful to God for all the beautiful things in this life.

"Prayer", says 'Abdu'l-Bahá, "is conversation with God." In order that God may make known His Mind and Will to men, He must speak to them in a language which they can understand, and this He does by the mouths of His Holy Prophets. While these Prophets are alive in the body they speak with men face to face and convey to them the Message of God, and after their death their message continues to reach men's minds through their recorded sayings and writings. But this is not the only way in which God can commune with and inspire those whose hearts are seeking after truth, wherever they are, and whatever their native race or tongue. By this language the Manifestation continues to hold converse with the faithful after His departure from the material world. Christ continued to converse with and inspire His disciples after His crucifixion. In fact He influenced them more powerfully than before; and with other Prophets it has been the same. 'Abdu'l-Bahá speaks much of this spiritual language. He says, for instance:

We should speak in the language of heaven – in the language of the spirit – for there is a language of the spirit and heart. It is as different from our language as our own language is different from that of the animals, who express themselves only by cries and sounds.

It is the language of the spirit which speaks to God. When, in prayer, we are freed from all outward things and turn to God, then it is as if in our hearts we hear the voice of God. Without words, we speak, we communicate, we converse with God and hear the answer . . . All of us, when we attain to a truly spiritual condition, can hear the Voice Of God.[68]

Prayer is very important if we want to grow spiritually. It's not a question of fear. It's not a question of reward. It's a question of love.

'Abdu'l-Bahá explains that when we turn to God, we must turn with our heart, soul, mind and body. The way I understand this is like meeting someone who is an old friend. We don't just say "hi", we express our love by embracing, with joy and radiance. But if someone comes and holds your hand like a wet fish, and says: "How are you?", you don't want to converse with that person. Approaching our prayers without enthusiasm and love is not the way to talk to God or to Bahá'u'lláh. If our conversation is to be meaningful, let's pray with all our heart, all of our mind and all of our soul.

It doesn't matter if your mind is distracted while you are praying. Bring it back. It'll happen and it's quite natural until you get into practice, when your soul will realize that it's important to concentrate to the exclusion of your environment and extraneous thoughts. No matter how much noise is going on around us, we should be able to still pray and not get disturbed by any distractions, in the same way as we manage to have conversations even in a noisy party, restaurant or airport. But we need to recognize the importance of what we are trying to achieve. If we want to communicate we find a way and nothing stops us. So should it be with praying; we just need to get our priorities straight.

Our intellectual, emotional and material commitment may be there but spiritual inertia is a universal condition. This inertia deprives us of accessing the very source of development and vitalization of our souls, leaving us in an unnecessarily sorry and weak state. There is nothing unique about this condition but the sadness is that we can only recognize and remedy the situation on our own.

Unfortunately, because we are told that prayer is private, a conversation between you and your God, people have made the subject so personal that nobody is willing to talk about it and if you try to raise the subject you are considered weird. We talk for hours about everything: sex, weather, gossip; and the world's problems and all and any of the trivial and passing things of this life. But we need to remember that prayer helps our souls, our minds, our bodies and all those who fall with the radar of our spirits. This is what makes us a magnet that people are attracted to. Nothing else. That's the only thing. Then people want to know, "How come you always look so radiant?" They cannot help but be drawn to you. So perhaps we can do

ourselves a favour and seek to discover ways and means
of improving our approach to praying.

The Tablet of Visitation of 'Abdu'l-Bahá

*Whoso reciteth this prayer with lowliness and fervor
will bring gladness and joy to the heart of this Servant;
it will be even as meeting Him face to face.*

He is the All-Glorious!

O God, my God! Lowly and tearful, I raise my sup-
pliant hands to Thee and cover my face in the dust of
that Threshold of Thine, exalted above the knowledge
of the learned, and the praise of all that glorify Thee.
Graciously look upon Thy servant, humble and lowly
at Thy door, with the glances of the eye of Thy mercy,
and immerse him in the Ocean of Thine eternal grace.

Lord! He is a poor and lowly servant of Thine,
enthralled and imploring Thee, captive in Thy hand,
praying fervently to Thee, trusting in Thee, in tears
before Thy face, calling to Thee and beseeching Thee,
saying:

O Lord, my God! Give me Thy grace to serve Thy
loved ones, strengthen me in my servitude to Thee,
illumine my brow with the light of adoration in Thy
court of holiness, and of prayer to Thy kingdom
of grandeur. Help me to be selfless at the heavenly
entrance of Thy gate, and aid me to be detached from
all things within Thy holy precincts. Lord! Give me
to drink from the chalice of selflessness; with its robe

clothe me, and in its ocean immerse me. Make me as dust in the pathway of Thy loved ones, and grant that I may offer up my soul for the earth ennobled by the footsteps of Thy chosen ones in Thy path, O Lord of Glory in the Highest.

With this prayer doth Thy servant call Thee, at dawntide and in the night-season. Fulfill his heart's desire, O Lord! Illumine his heart, gladden his bosom, kindle his light, that he may serve Thy Cause and Thy-servants.

Thou art the Bestower, the Pitiful, the Most Bounti-ful, the Gracious, the Merciful, the Compassionate.[69]

The Tablet of Aḥmad

We must pray for understanding and little by little we comprehend not only why we are praying but what the words signify. Nowhere does it say that we should say this Tablet daily, but within the Tablet itself, it says "Learn well this Tablet, O Aḥmad; chant it during thy days and withhold not thyself therefrom."[70]

This Tablet and the obligatory prayers "have been invested by Bahá'u'lláh with a special potency and sig-nificance".[71] In my opinion I recommend that this prayer be recited daily and we should remember the sufferings of Bahá'u'lláh, because again in this Tablet it says:

O Aḥmad! Forget not My bounties while I am absent. Remember My Days during thy days, and My distress and banishment in this remote prison.[72]

The whole Tablet shows the power which was given to Aḥmad to go and teach in Iran, which he did. And this is a prayer which can now be accessed and said by all of us around the world when teaching is of paramount importance. Understandably, we encounter difficulties when we try to teach, but rather than giving up we should access this potent Tablet that has within it the power to overcome obstacles, provided we are sincere. I keep emphasizing the importance of sincerity: it is not enough just to speak the words; you have to feel and ache for them to give you the strength and opportunity to offer those around you this healing Faith. We should also be immensely grateful that we have such a powerful prayer within our grasp.

> These favours have We bestowed upon thee as a bounty on Our part and a mercy from Our presence, that thou mayest be of those who are grateful.[73]

The Tablet says that it will remove our difficulties, but we must have Faith.

> By God! Should one who is in affliction or grief read this Tablet with absolute sincerity, God will dispel his sadness, solve his difficulties and remove his afflictions.[74]

Remember that time is relative. Spiritual time and physical time here are different. We can't expect everything instantly. If it is meant to be, things will happen quickly;

otherwise, we have to be patient. Patience is one of the virtues that some people are blessed with and some people aren't. Some of us regrettably have to cultivate it, as I do. In 1952, when I was in the presence of Shoghi Effendi, he told me "Mrs Munsiff, in the service of the Cause, one has to be very patient, so please be patient." Over the decades this has been a constant struggle for me but when I am able to tap into this virtue, the results clearly show the wisdom of exercising patience.

The Fire Tablet

This is one of Bahá'u'lláh's most potent Tablets, possessing great power, and believers often recite it at times of difficulties and suffering, when they feel they are in acute need.

In the final verses of the Tablet Bahá'u'lláh says:

O 'Alí-Akbar, thank thy Lord for this Tablet whence thou canst breathe the fragrances of My meekness, and know what hath beset Us in the path of God, the Adored of all the worlds.

Should all the servants read and ponder this, there shall be kindled in their veins a fire that shall set aflame the worlds.[75]

The Remover of Difficulties

Concerning the prayer for difficulty revealed by the Báb; he [Shoghi Effendi] wishes me to inform you that it is not accompanied by any instructions for its recital.[76]

On page 1 of your October Newsletter you have quoted the Báb's prayer for the removal of difficulties and have added: "Bahá'u'lláh has said to repeat this prayer 500 times by day and by night that it may aid us to recognize Him and our souls will be illumined."

The above statement gives the impression that the repetition of the said prayer 500 times is one of the prescribed devotionals of the Faith and has a specified effect on the believer who observes this form of prayer.

We do not feel it is justified to infer such conclusions from the reference in "God Passes By", page 119, which you mention. The passage in question obviously refers to a specific circumstance in the life of Bahá'u'lláh in Baghdád before the declaration of His Mission, and should not be presented to the believers as one of the prescribed observances of our Faith.[77]

This is an example of how careful we must be in the Faith not to make custom and dogma out of things which one person might find successful but which at the end of the day is particular to that person and should not be assumed to have universal application, even more so now that we might be victims of the viral impact of social media.

Dawn prayer

Engage ye in the remembrance of God at dawn; rise ye up to praise and glorify Him.[78]

At every instant, I beg for your assistance, bounty, and a fresh favour and blessing, so that the confirmations of Bahá'u'lláh may, like unto the sea, be constantly surging, the lights of the Sun of Truth may shine upon you all and that ye may be confirmed in service, may become the manifestations of bounty and that each one of you may, at dawn, turn unto the Holy Land and may experience spiritual emotions with all intensity.[79]

Encourage, where feasible, the practice of dawn prayer.[80]

Clearly the quietness and stillness of the early hours, free of activity and daily routine, is a desirable time to pray. It probably gives us the best chance of concentrating and focusing on communing with our God. Mindfulness and meditation are very popular at the moment with recognized emotional and physical benefits, all the more so when our prayers and meditation are focused on connecting and communicating with God.

Midnight prayer

O seeker of Truth! If thou desirest that God my open thine eye, thou must supplicate unto God, pray to and commune with Him at midnight . . .[81]

The prayerful condition is the best of all conditions, for man in such a state communeth with God, especially when prayer is offered in private and at times when one's mind is free, such as at midnight. Indeed, prayer imparteth life.[82]

If you are able to switch off the TV, computer and all your hand-held devices this clearly is another opportune time to pray and have the additional advantage of allowing your soul to permeate your dreams with insight.

Healing prayers

O handmaid of God! The prayers which were revealed to ask for healing apply both to physical and spiritual healing. Recite them, then to heal both the soul and the body. If healing is right for the patient, it will certainly be granted, but for some ailing persons, healing would only be the cause of other ills, and therefore wisdom doth not permit an affirmative answer to ailments.

O handmaid of God! The power of the Holy Spirit healeth both physical and spiritual ailments.[83]

Perhaps one of the clearest signs of spiritual maturity is acceptance of events in our lives which are not what we wished for or for those we love, and indeed are the very opposite of what we earnestly prayed for. This of course is often the hardest when it comes to illnesses and death. I learned early on in my pioneering days that the outcome

of my prayers was neither predictable nor always welcome but with the hindsight of minutes or sometimes
even years, my wishes turned out not to be the wisest nor
would they have taught me the lessons I needed to learn.
It is one of the signs of our progressive spiritual growth
when we are able to accept that what we desperately want
and sincerely believe will be good for us or others may
not always be the case. This is one of the hardest but most
crucial lessons to learn in our earthly existence.

Prayers for parents

It is seemly that the servant should, after each prayer,
supplicate God to bestow mercy and forgiveness
upon his parents. Thereupon God's call will be raised.
"Thousand upon thousand of what thou hast asked
for thy parents shall be thy recompense!" Blessed is he
who remembereth his parents when communing with
God. There is, verily, no God but Him, the Mighty, the
Well-Beloved.[84]

O God, my God! I implore Thee by the blood of Thy
true lovers who were so enraptured by Thy sweet
utterance that they hastened unto the Pinnacle of
Glory, the site of the most glorious martyrdom, and
I beseech Thee by the mysteries which lie enshrined
in Thy knowledge and by the pearls that are treasured
in the ocean of Thy bounty to grant forgiveness unto
me and unto my father and my mother. Of those who
show forth mercy, Thou art in truth the Most Merciful.

No God is there but Thee, the Ever-Forgiving, the All-Bountiful.[85]

The station of parents is very important in the Faith. The effort and sacrifices on our behalf that our parents have endured, particularly during the early years of our lives, and the silent anxieties and pain they suffered while we stumbled and made mistakes, deserves to be remembered and appreciated. How gracious is God that we are able through remembering our parents in our prayers to enhance their existence during their continuing spiritual journey. It would seem that we are also able to derive a benefit.

RECITE THE VERSES OF GOD MORNING AND EVENING

Reciting the obligatory prayer is not the end of our obligations. We are also required to read the Holy Writings morning and evening. No one is suggesting you exhaust yourself or read more than you are able to absorb. You don't have to tire yourself or your soul. Just a few verses from the *Hidden Words*, for example, or even a single paragraph from the Writings may be sufficient. Often I find that although I think I am very tired, once I start reading my fatigue goes away and I continue reading far longer than I would have thought at the beginning. It is also important to contemplate what you have read and perhaps you might do that later while you're washing dishes, or driving to work, or performing some other mundane task. You need time to think about those words so that they have an opportunity to have an effect on your soul. In the morning before you get up, if you read a little you will find yourself inspired or guided, and then right before going to bed at night, you have those sweet words in your soul all night.

You will see in the quotation which follows that there is a fairly stark reminder regarding the obligation to commune with God on a daily basis.

Recite ye the verses of God every morn and eventide. Whoso faileth to recite them hath not been faithful to the Covenant of God and His Testament, and whoso turneth away from these holy verses in this Day is of those who throughout eternity have turned away from God.[86]

One should not think, "Well, I've read a couple of books now and I can go without reading for a few weeks." That is not how it works.

Pride not yourselves on much reading of the verses or on a multitude of pious acts by night and day; for were a man to read a single verse with joy and radiance it would be better for him than to read with lassitude all the Holy Books of God, the Help in Peril, the Self-Subsisting. Read ye the sacred verses in such measure that ye be not overcome by languor and despondency. Lay not upon your souls that which will weary them and weigh them down, but rather what will lighten and uplift them, so that they may soar on the wings of the Divine verses towards the Dawning-place of His manifest signs; this will draw you nearer to God, did ye but comprehend.[87]

It is very important that we do not overtire ourselves by

reading too much at one time and say: "I've prayed for two hours and I have read from the Writings every day so I have done what I am supposed to do." Of itself, going through the motions is of no value. It is the quality of our approach which is more important than how much we have read and for how long. The prayers should be to inspire and uplift us. The readings should make us feel so happy – and then we should meditate upon them so that they may influence us as we work or go about our daily life. This is very important. It's like food which is the sustenance that we have every day, rather than when we sit and gorge ourselves so much that afterwards we feel ill and cannot eat any more. There is no point in that. Bahá'u'lláh says:

Intone, O My Servant, the verses of God that have been received by thee, as intoned by them who have drawn nigh unto Him, that the sweetness of thy melody may kindle thine own soul, and attract the hearts of all men. Whoso reciteth in the privacy of his chamber, the verses revealed by God, the scattering angels of the Almighty shall scatter abroad the fragrance of the words uttered by his mouth, and shall cause the heart of every righteous man to throb. Though he may, at first, remain unaware of its effects, yet by the virtue of the grace vouchsafed unto him must needs sooner or later exercise its influence upon his soul. Thus have the mysteries of the Revelation of God been decreed by virtue of the Will of Him who is the Source of power and wisdom.[88]

We might well wonder how that is possible and who are these angels. First of all, let's agree they are not people with wings and halos flying around. However, they are holy souls in the other world. Another dimension of our Faith is accepting that in the next phase of our existence there are far, far greater things than in this world. While we are limited in our ability to know of the next realm, our Faith should give us the assurance that the unblemished creative power of these worlds is infinitely greater and more sublime than for example nuclear power which is the most powerful force we have here on earth. When there was the meltdown of the nuclear plant in Chernobyl, the fallout travelled from Russia to Scotland, to the meadows, to the seas, to the livestock all over Europe: everyone and everything was affected. So it is with the power of the Words of God scattered by the holy souls and put into the hearts of other pure souls on earth. Since Bahá'u'lláh says it is possible, we can only believe that it is so.

The art of successful praying and meditating can for many of us be a slow process, during which we gradually discover the effect it has on our lives and actions. First of all, we should not approach our devotional time as a chore. If you can't do it with sincerity and joy, I suggest you leave it till you can. When engaging with the verses of God you can read, chant, sing, or just say them quietly, but be happy so that your soul has a chance to grow spiritually and influence the souls of others with the Words of God.

Shoghi Effendi says:

When a person becomes a Bahá'í, actually what takes place is that the seed of the spirit starts to grow in the human soul. This seed must be watered by the out-pourings of the Holy Spirit. These gifts of the spirits are received through prayer, meditation, study of the Holy Utterances and service to the Cause of God. The fact of the matter is that service in the Cause is like the plough which ploughs the physical soil when seeds are sown. It is necessary that the soil be ploughed up, so that it can be enriched, and thus cause a stronger growth of the seed. In exactly the same way the evolution of the spirit takes place through ploughing up the soil of the heart so that it is a constant reflection of the Holy Spirit. In this way the human spirit grows and develops by leaps and bounds.

Naturally there will be periods of distress and difficulty, and even severe tests; but if that person turns firmly toward the Divine Manifestation, studies carefully His Spiritual teachings and receives the blessings of the Holy Spirit, he will find that in reality these tests and difficulties have been the gifts of God to enable him to grow and develop.[89]

MEDITATION

We have to understand that love is not only of paramount importance but it is also the tool which enables us to pray and access a meditative state. It is only through prayer and meditation we are able to change our lives and help other people change their lives. Underestimating the power of love in our lives is a big mistake. 'Abdu'l-Bahá says:

> Love revealeth with unfailing and limitless power the mysteries latent in the universe.[90]

Perhaps the meaning of love is very difficult for people to understand. True love is selfless. Even when we pray, Bahá'u'lláh says, we must not pray because we fear hell or we want heaven or we want this or that. We should pray because we love Bahá'u'lláh, we want to communicate with Him and through Him with God. The essence of this love is eternal and it brings a happiness which is eternal. It is only through comprehending this truth that we can move forward. Let's see what 'Abdu'l-Bahá says about love:

> Love is the most great law that ruleth this mighty and heavenly cycle, the unique power that bindeth together the divers elements of this material world,

the supreme magnetic force that directeth the movements of the spheres in the celestial realms.[91]

Another by-product of praying and meditating is that it brings order, peace and purpose to our lives, enabling us to understand the essence of all the religions of the world which in turn prepares us for spiritual existence in the next world. "What is he in need of in the Kingdom which transcends the life and limitation of this mortal sphere?", asks 'Abdu'l-Bahá, and then immediately answers:

That world beyond is a world of sanctity and radiance; therefore it is necessary that in this world he should acquire these divine attributes. In that world there is need of spirituality, faith, assurance, the knowledge and love of God. These he must attain in this world so that after his ascension from the earthly to the heavenly Kingdom he shall find all that is needful in that life eternal ready for him.

That divine world is manifestly a world of lights; therefore man has need of illumination here. That is a world of love; the love of God is essential. It is a world of perfections: virtues or perfections must be acquired. That world is vivified by the breaths of the Holy Spirit; in this world we must seek them. That is the kingdom of life everlasting; it must be attained during this vanishing existence.[92]

Can you imagine that? Many think that meditation is

only for special people, but that is not true. Every time a Manifestation of God has come to this world, He has prescribed that mankind pray and meditate. Why? Because we have the faculty. You meditate, not in your physical form, but you meditate with your mind and your spirit and your heart. It has nothing to do with the body. 'Abdu'l-Bahá said you cannot talk as well as meditate, so, naturally, silence is necessary. Not silence around us, but silence within us. One has to be silent and listen to the inner voice. Shoghi Effendi, the Guardian of the Faith, wrote to an individual and he said:

He thinks it would be wiser for the Bahá'ís to use the meditations given by Bahá'u'lláh and not any set form of meditation recommended by someone else . . .[93]

So you see there is no formula for meditation because that is left entirely to the individual as to where, when and how they wish to meditate upon what they have read, and subsequently put into action. 'Abdu'l-Bahá explains it this way:

Chant the Words of God and pondering over their meaning, transform them into actions. I ask God to cause thee to attain a high station in the Kingdom of Life for ever and ever.[94]

Therefore, know thou that the True One possesseth invisible worlds which human meditation is unable to comprehend and the intellect of man hath no power to imagine. When thou wilt purify and clarify thy spiritual nostrils from every worldly moisture, then thou wilt inhale the holy fragrances diffusing from the merciful gardens of these worlds.[95]

In another place He says:

When man allows the spirit, through his soul, to enlighten his understanding, then does he contain all Creation . . .

But, on the other hand, when man does not open his mind and heart to the blessing of the spirit, but turns his soul towards the material side, towards the bodily part of his nature, then is he fallen from his high place and he becomes inferior to the inhabitants of the lower animal kingdom.[96]

Bahá'u'lláh says there is a sign (from God) in every phenomenon: The sign of intellect is contemplation, and the sign of contemplation is silence, because it is impossible for a man to do two things at one time – he cannot both speak and meditate.

It is an axiomatic fact that while you meditate you are speaking with your own spirit. In that state of mind, you put certain questions to your spirit and the spirit answers: the light breaks forth and reality is revealed.

You cannot apply the name 'man' to any being void of this faculty of meditation; without it he would be a mere animal, lower than the beasts.

Through the faculty of meditation man attains to eternal life; through it he receives the breath of the Holy Spirit – the bestowal of the Spirit is given in reflection and meditation.

The spirit of man is itself informed and strengthened during meditation; through it affairs of which man knew nothing are unfolded before his view. Through it he receives Divine inspiration, through it he receives heavenly food.

Meditation is the key for opening the doors of mysteries. In that state man abstracts himself: in that state man withdraws himself from all outside objects; in that subjective mood he is immersed in the ocean of a spiritual life and can unfold the secrets of things-in-themselves. To illustrate this, think of a man as endowed with two kinds of sight; when the power of insight is being used, the outward power of vision does not see.

This faculty of meditation frees man from the animal nature, discerns the reality of things, puts man in touch with God.

This faculty brings forth from the invisible plane the sciences and arts. Through the meditative faculty inventions are made possible, colossal undertakings are carried out; through it governments can run smoothly. Through this faculty man enters into the very kingdom of God.

Nevertheless, some thoughts are useless to man; they are like waves moving in the sea without result. But if the faculty of meditation is bathed in the inner light and characterised with divine attributes, the results will be confirmed.

The meditative faculty is akin to the mirror; if you put it before earthly objects it will reflect them. Therefore if the spirit of man is contemplating earthly subjects he will be informed of these.

But if you turn the mirror of your spirit heaven-wards, the heavenly constellations and the rays of the Sun of Reality will be reflected in your hearts, and the virtues of the Kingdom will be obtained.

Therefore, let us keep this faculty rightly directed – turning it to the heavenly Sun and not to earthly objects – so that we may discover the secrets of the Kingdom and comprehend the allegories of the Bible and the mysteries of the spirit.

May we indeed become mirrors reflecting the heavenly realities, and may we become so pure as to reflect the stars of heaven.[97]

Let us consider the elements of what we are trying to achieve: first of all, you put the question to your spirit or your conscience and your conscience answers. Some of us may wonder: "What is this conscience? Where is it? How do I talk to my conscience? Are there any pre-scribed conditions for this sub-conscious dialogue? Do I have to be in a particular environment or in a particular posture?" 'Abdu'l-Bahá says that you are putting these questions to your spirit all the time, and you don't even know it and your spirit keeps answering. For example, someone has given you too much change and they don't realize it. Your conscience kicks in and tells you that you know it is too much so you must give it back. And when we want to do greater things, with peace in our heart and we call upon our inner being to be inspired to serve humanity or do something meaningful, that is when we should meditate upon the words of Bahá'u'lláh and 'Abdu'l-Bahá after praying or reading the Holy Writings. Peoples of all religions can contemplate and meditate upon the words of their holy scriptures, but this is completely different from what any mortal gives you. Besides, Bahá'u'lláh says you must pray in the language you understand, so that when you pray you can clearly comprehend and absorb what you are reading and then can act accordingly.

But let us not be deluded. Let us not think that if we sit down and really meditate that we will be given such a power that we can do fantastic things and change everything. This is not realistic, because those world-changing events are set in motion by the Manifestation of God. They have already stamped their influence on the world, now we have to act upon them. It is really to take modest steps which will help the great process of development of the whole world. It is very important that we should seek the answer in our meditative state. The Guardian said that the true worshipper, while praying, should endeavour not so much to ask God to fulfil his own wishes and desires, but rather to adjust these and make them conform to the Divine Will. Only through such an attitude can one derive that feeling of inner peace and contentment which the power of prayer alone can confer.

While meditating, you should remain silent but this

doesn't mean that you empty your head. 'Abdu'l-Bahá said in one place that your mind will be like the waves of the ocean beating, and it will calm down, but you must not try to completely stop it, because that is not possible and you will only be wasting your time. 'Abdu'l-Bahá explains that, when once He was looking from the window in Haifa, He said:

We hear the murmur of the sea always continuing, it never ceases. Were it to cease, the world would be dead, stagnant, lifeless. But the waves of the mind of man are far greater than those of the sea; they also are ceaseless. They never stop for one instant. This movement is good. If these waves of the mind are few, the man is dull and quiet. What pearls and jewels are contained in the depths of the sea! But the pearls and jewels hidden in the mind of man are the knowledge, virtues, capabilities, etc., These pearls can grow and increase in lustre for ever, but the pearls of the sea remain always the same. These waves from our minds go forth and create movement and thought in other minds. From one strong thought of love what great results may be produced.[98]

At the same time, 'Abdu'l-Bahá also says that when we get these ideas, thoughts or feelings during meditation, it is important to distinguish between inspiration and imagination. He says:

Inspiration is in conformity with the Divine Texts

but imaginations do not conform therewith. A real spiritual connection between the True One and the servant is a luminous bounty which causeth an ascetic (or divine) flame, passion and attraction. When this connection is secured (or realized), such an ecstasy and happiness become manifest in the heart that man doth fly away (with joy) and uttereth a melody and song. Just as the soul bringeth the body in motion, so that spiritual bounty and real connection likewise moveth (or cheereth) the human soul.[99]

He explains in another place:

Many ideas rise up in the human mind; some of them concern truth and some untruth. Among such ideas those which owe their source to the Light of Truth will be realized in the outward world; while others of a different origin vanish, come and go like waves on the sea of imagination and find no realization in the world of existence.[100]

You can only know whether your ideas are inspiration or imagination by acting on them. If the results are positive, you will know that you were inspired, and if they yield no results, it was probably your imagination. As with many things in life, practice makes perfect and with the passage of time you will be able to distinguish between inspiration and imagination. The key thing is not to give up.

As previously mentioned, Shoghi Effendi wrote:

He thinks it would be wiser for the Bahá'ís to use the meditations given by Bahá'u'lláh, and not any set form of meditation recommended by someone else: but the believers must be left free in these details and allowed to have personal latitude in finding their own level of communion with God.[101]

Many people spend fifteen minutes or an hour daily, working very hard to blank out their minds; to think about nothing. This is rather like someone using an oven every day, heating it up, but never putting anything into it. Little by little the enamel burns, and it becomes less and less effective. Wouldn't it be more sensible to use the oven every day, to cook something specific for a specific amount of time. Then when it's done, you take it out and you eat it, or you give it to someone else to eat. It serves a purpose. The mind needs to be active and serve a purpose.

If the mind is always active, what is meant then that it must be emptied? Maybe it must be emptied of trivial things, in order to be refilled with meaningful thoughts?

I now assure thee, O servant of God, that if thy mind become empty and pure from every mention and thought, and thy heart attracted wholly to the Kingdom of God, forgetting all else beside God and coming in communion with the Spirit of God, then the Holy Spirit will assist thee with a power which will enable thee to penetrate all things, and a dazzling spark which enlightens all sides, a brilliant flame in the zenith of the heavens, will teach thee that which thou dost not know of the facts of the universe and all the divine doctrine . . .[102]

There are no set forms of meditation prescribed in the teachings, no plan, as such, for inner development. The friends are urged – nay enjoined – to pray, and they also should meditate, but the manner of doing the latter is left entirely to the individual . . .

The inspiration received through meditation is of a nature that one cannot measure or determine. God can inspire into our minds things that we had no previous knowledge of, if He desires to do so.[103]

The Guardian feels that, if the friends would meditate a little more objectively upon both their relationship to the Cause and the vast non-Bahá'í public they hope to influence, they would see things more clearly . . .

He fully realizes that the demands made upon the Bahá'ís are great, and that they often feel inadequate, tired and perhaps frightened in the face of the tasks that confront them. This is only natural. On the other hand, they must realize that the power of God can and will assist them; and that because they are privileged to have accepted the Manifestation of God for this Day, this very act has placed upon them a great moral responsibility toward their fellow-men. It is this moral responsibility to which the Guardian is constantly calling their attention . . .[104]

To be engaged in diffusing the fragrance of God

(teaching the Truth) in one hour of time, is better than the dominion of the World and all therein; for the latter is mortal and temporary, while the former is permanent and endless.

Thou hast written what shouldst thou do and what prayer shouldst thou offer in order to become informed of the mysteries of God: Pray thou with an attracted heart and supplicate with a spirit stirred by the glad tidings of God. Then the doors of the Kingdom of mysteries shall be opened before thy face, and thou shalt comprehend the realities of all things.[105]

I remember when I was in Ghana, West Africa, I was teaching young African men and women about prayer and meditation and how we should realize that He is always with us, and guiding us, but then we must act. Often, we make the critical mistake of assuming because people have no education and cannot read or write that somehow this precludes them from understanding the Faith or being able to call upon God to assist them. Our understanding of the Faith is not dependent on how intellectual we are. It is the hunger of the soul that you feed. And everyone has a soul, whether they are educated or not, and all souls are hungry and in need of nourishment. When I was sharing with these Africans of all ages the meaning of prayer and meditation, their grasp was often quicker and greater than with an educated audience. Receptivity is a function of a pure heart, not an educated mind.

On my second day with this West African group, the

Secretary of the National Spiritual Assembly said: "It is all very well, Mrs Munsiff, you teaching them how to pray and meditate and all that, but here we have problems, and what are we going to do about them?"

So I said, "Alright, what is the problem?"

The Secretary answered, "We have to have four Bahá'í centres before the end of the Plan." This was only a few months before the end of the Nine Year Plan. "How are we going to do it, because we can't buy the cement we need here? The government controls all of the cement. We even went next door to Togo and couldn't find any. What are we going to do? How can we build the centres without cement?"

I asked, "How much cement do you want?"

The Secretary answered, "Fifty sacks of cement. We could mix it together with sand and build them."

"No," I said, "We can't build this half-heartedly. If we build a centre, we build it properly. Anyway, bring me the letter of the Universal House of Justice where it says that you have to build four centres."

I was given the letter of the Universal House of Justice. I took it with respect, devotion, and love and looked at it. Word by word by word, I studied it carefully. Letters from the House of Justice need to be read thoughtfully and with attention to every word as every single sentence has a meaning and a significance. Looking at it, I found that what the Universal House of Justice wanted was two centres in the villages and two in the towns. By way of encouraging the Secretary and the others attending the class that day to use their imagination and think laterally

I asked those present "How do you build your houses in the villages?"

They said, "Mama, we just put four bamboos up, tying the roof on top with palm leaves, and then plastering all of it with mud and that's it."

"Right," I answered, "So, go and build a bigger one, just like that, for the Bahá'í centres in the village."

You see that this is what meditation is all about. I didn't go through this letter quickly, as if it were a newspaper, but studied it and I found out that within five minutes at least two of the problems were solved. You can build at least two of the Bahá'í centres with no cement, and with their expertise and experience these can be completed quickly. Now, the problem of the two centres in the cities remained, and for those centres clearly they needed cement.

Having spent the previous day in intense study of the Writings, I put the following proposition to them: "Alright, dear friends, we've had one day of studying the Writings of Bahá'u'lláh and we have developed our love for Him and we believe in Him completely. Now let's try to practise what we have learned. We will pray, and be silent, because we want inspiration as to how to go about building these centres and where to get the cement from. I don't want consultation and discussion afterwards. Is this acceptable?"

They all said "Yes."

We prayed and remained silent and after a little while, a young man got up and said: "Why don't we write to the government saying that we need cement." And everybody started to laugh.

I said, "Please, this is not a matter for laughing. We decided that we will follow the inspiration." So, I said, "All right, let's pray again and see what we should write – to write is fine, but what shall we write?"

So they prayed again, everybody remained silent and the same young man got up and said, "We should write to the government saying that we need cement to build our Bahá'í centres because as Bahá'ís we cannot take our Holy Books and read them in the Mosque or in the Temples or in the Churches and worship there. They won't let us. But if we have our own centres, anybody can come in and read their prayers, their Holy Books and study, and we can all study together. We believe in the oneness of God, the oneness of the Prophets, and in the oneness of religions. It is open to all."

Then the Secretary said, "They won't read it. They'll just throw it in the rubbish."

I said, "Please, we decided that we would do this. We don't need any debating afterwards. Don't say a word."

Then some of the pioneers and the others said, "We have to grease their palms and . . ."

I said "Please, don't ever say or consider such a notion as Bahá'ís. We have made a decision. Please go and type the letter and take it to the appropriate Government department."

The Secretary duly wrote it, typed it and got on a motor bike and delivered it, returning, all hot and tired and quite miserable, probably because he was convinced that all this effort would be for nothing.

I said, "Please, I don't want to see you looking

miserable. I want to see a happy face that the job is done. Now, it's in the hands of Bahá'u'lláh."

This programme finished and I left for Nigeria, then from Nigeria I went to the Cameroons. When I arrived in Cameroon, there was a letter waiting for me from the National Spiritual Assembly of Ghana saying that the youth were very happy. They divided themselves up so that half went to the villages, clearing the land and building the centres, and the other half went teaching and formed all the remaining Local Spiritual Assemblies. In addition, they had received cement from the government – 500 sacks of it and they were going to start building. Can you imagine, initially, they thought no one would even read the letter and, even if they were to have a response, they did not believe they would even get 50 bags of cement, let alone 500. Yet, when we had faith and unitedly did exactly as Bahá'u'lláh taught us to do, unimaginable results were achieved.

During another course in Cameroon, there was a man attending who had to return to his home after two days. On the third day, he brought his daughter, who was fourteen and said, "I'm sorry. I know that you don't allow people to come in and out of the class, and not to come in half-way through the class, but after saying my obligatory prayer and meditating deeply, I felt compelled to return home. My wife, who is a Catholic, has always been very much against the Faith, and is constantly shouting and telling me I'm a heathen. But today she said to me: "I don't know where you've been going, but when you go back take your daughter with you." Previously she would never have allowed him to take her but clearly something changed, both in him and in her, and she now wanted her child to be subject to the same influence as her husband.

Another man told me that the next morning after his prayers, all of the children started crying, saying, "We want food. There is no food in the house."

The wife said: "There is no food. What can we do?"

He said, "I don't know." He was so upset, and at a loss he said: "Well, raise your hands and ask Bahá'u'lláh to give you food. I don't have it. I must go to the office and I don't get paid till the end of the month."

So he went to the office and somebody came and put five hundred francs on his desk. He said, "What is this for?"

The man said, "This is for you," and walked away.

He bought food for two hundred and fifty francs and put the other two hundred and fifty francs in a box, saying: "Bahá'u'lláh, I don't need all this now, I will keep the rest for next time."

As a result of this inexplicable generosity he was able to feed his children. Despite his desperation, he had continued to pray and remain close to Bahá'u'lláh, and the constancy of his faith was rewarded.

THE POWER OF THIS CAUSE

Since the beginning of our history, the enemies of the Faith in Iran, its birthplace, thought that they could destroy this Faith and anything connected with it. But they could not even destroy an orange tree. On one occasion the authorities went to the House of the Báb in Shíráz and cut down a tree that the Manifestation of God had planted. What they didn't know was that some time before this, the tree looked as if it was failing, so the Bahá'ís had called in a tree-doctor. The arborist after examining the tree informed the Bahá'ís that the root system was weak; the tree was old and dying. But the friends were not upset, because so many of the Bahá'ís had already taken the seeds from this sacred tree and planted new orange trees. Now, the original orange tree in Shíráz is destroyed, but in many countries all over the world there are other orange trees, seeded by the one the Manifestation planted.

The enemies of the Faith cannot even kill a tree planted by the Manifestation. How can they imagine that they can kill the Faith of God?

Then, know that the power of the Word of God is effective, both in the spirit and the body, and the influence

of the Spirit of God is predominant over the material
as well as the essential and spiritual. And that, verily,
God is powerful in all things and that the signs (or
verses) have exoteric and esoteric meaning . . .[106]

In the time of 'Abdu'l-Bahá, there lived a man in Iran
who was a leader of highway robbers. As he was getting
old, he thought that he'd better consider the next life. He
went to see a Mullá and asked what he should do so that
when he died, he could go to heaven. The Mullá said, "If
you want to go to heaven, you must kill a Bahá'í."

He said: "Is that all?"

"Yes, that's all."

"Ok, that's easy."

He was a big, strong man. He said to himself: "I've
killed hundreds already, one more or so won't make any
difference." He remembered that around the corner there
was a bakery shop owned by a Bahá'í and he went there
and found a very humble, weak, small Bahá'í and he
thought: "Well, I won't kill him right away, but first I will
get him agitated then with one blow it will be easy to end
his life. He went in and started agitating but this Bahá'í
was kind, and said to him, "You're tired" and brought him
tea and some cookies and calmed him down. So he left,
thinking, "Well, that Bahá'í is not going anywhere, I'll get
him tomorrow." He came back the next day and started
doing the same thing and the Bahá'í again calmed him
down and brought him tea and cookies. Then the man
asked, "What is this Bahá'í Faith?" The Bahá'í explained
and the chief of the highway robbers was so impressed

with the teachings that he became a Bahá'í. However, not having completely transformed, he said: "Now the first thing that I must do is go and kill the Mullá!"

The Bahá'í said: "No, you can't kill anyone, even your bitterest enemy."

Slowly, through prayers and the power of Bahá'u'lláh, this man changed dramatically. Formerly, if he were walking on the street people would run in and lock their doors, but after he became a Bahá'í, people would come out of their homes to witness his transformation: he now walked humbly with his head down. Everybody was so surprised how this man had so totally changed from aggressiveness to submissiveness. Many people were so affected that they also became Bahá'ís.

RITUALS AND DOGMA

Frequently, Bahá'ís fail to understand the significance of prayer or how we should pray. We always say that we don't have priests in the Bahá'í Faith, we don't have rituals, we don't have ceremonies, we don't have dogmas and yet at the same time we fail to focus on the truly spiritual dimension of our Faith, which develops within us through the obligatory nature of prayer in our lives.

On becoming Bahá'ís we are excited; we think the Faith will give us comfort, we can help others find solutions, and come forward and build a new world and establish heaven on earth. Set against these aspirations, we maintain that we don't have rituals or dogmas which we consider the trappings of religion. But this is not totally correct. We do have dogmas but dogmas which are divine, not man-made; we have laws given by Bahá'u'lláh which are divine; and we have rituals. One ritual is the ritual of daily prayers including a selection of obligatory prayers, two of which require genuflexions; that is a ritual. We have specific requirements for the dead and for marriage. They may be very simple and uncomplicated but nevertheless they are embodied in ceremonies with essential prescribed elements.

So we do have these things, which have not been created by man but are divinely ordained, that is, they have been revealed by the Manifestation of God himself, not made up by priests or others later on. How can we build something, change our own heart, our own soul and attract other people, without an infrastructure and a solid foundation upon which our spiritual growth both individually and collectively is based?

In some places the Bahá'í friends have taken to holding hands and singing Alláh-u-Abhá. That's fine, but we must not make it a ritual any more than we should invent anything which can be perceived as a man-made ritual and which has not been prescribed specifically by Bahá'u'lláh. Within the Faith there are extremely few prescribed rituals and on the whole they are connected with praying.

Often people enter a room and always say Alláh'u'Abhá to the friends as if it were a prescribed greeting in the Faith. It isn't!

> We wish to draw special attention to the requirements set out above, namely, the verses and music should be appropriate and such singing should not be ritualized. We have received reports that some friends feel that the singing of "Alláh'u'Abhá" and forming a circle and holding hands at the same time may be developing into a ritual in some communities.[107]

The Universal House of Justice affirms that the friends can sing or pray in unison the Holy Words, but:

> . . . they should take the utmost care that any manner

they practice should not acquire too rigid a character, and thus develop into an institution . . .[108]

THE GREATEST NAME OF GOD

In May, 1959, in their Message to the Chicago Intercontinental Conference, the Hands of the Cause in the Holy Land asked us to recall these words and stressed again the importance of the using of the GREATEST NAME as an invocation.

The Guardian stated in 1949 that the Greatest Name is the name of Bahá'u'lláh and that both Yá-Bahá'u'l-'Abhá and Alláh'u'Abhá refer to Him. By the Greatest Name is meant that Bahá'u'lláh has appeared in God's Greatest Name, in other words, that He is the Supreme Manifestation of God.

With regard to the Greatest Name, 'Abdu'l-Bahá states that:

'By its use, the doors of the Kingdom of God open, illumination is vouchsafed and divine union results. . . The use of the Greatest Name, and dependence on it, causes the soul to strip itself of the husks of mortality and to step forth freed, reborn, a new creature.'[109]

Here, one wonders how this can be, when we Bahá'ís usually think that Alláh-u-Abhá is just a Bahá'í greeting. Frequently, we say it when meeting the Bahá'ís:

"Alláh-u-Abhá", and even then we often don't say it with meaning and love. We say it rather routinely, just as a common greeting, or even rush over it so no one else will understand what we've said. Sometimes we're too embarrassed, so we just say Hi! The beloved Guardian says that we don't have to say "Alláh-u-Abhá" and particularly when there are non-Bahá'ís present or in public meetings or spaces. They might think we are some kind of cult or that it is a magic word of some kind.

In all the religions of the world there have been certain words given that are to be said a prescribed number of times. Some have to be recited a hundred times, some five hundred times, some a thousand times, but Bahá'u'lláh has asked us to sit down and say "Alláh-u-Abhá" ninety-five times only, once in twenty-four hours. By doing that, it also teaches us concentration, and it helps us to get closer to the other world in a condition of tranquillity. We also must learn to depend upon it. Before we get up early in the morning and we open our eyes, why not say "Yá Bahá'u'l-Abhá"? By this means we call upon Him for assistance and protection. By invoking these words, which mean "O Thou Glory of the Most Glorious", it is almost like a spiritual S.O.S. which generates the most incredible power. The great thing is that you can say it anytime of the day or under any circumstances when you want to secure that spiritual connection with Bahá'u'lláh.

Human beings are funny creatures. We believe in everything we have in this world that does wonders. With our voice, we are now able to turn on the television; draw the curtains; open the door; because our voice registers on the electronic circuits. No matter how marvellous the things we have in this world, stop to think what we have in the other world – we have the Source. If He, the Supreme Manifestation, gives us something we can use, why should we be dubious or disbelieving? Our scientists have not truly created anything. Their "creations" already existed. They just found them and put them together for us. We get quite excited about these inventions, and hurry to tell everybody – "See, that works!"

If those material things work, why should we not believe that "spiritual" things, such as praying, work? Why, because we don't use them, that's why! When we sincerely rely upon them, then they achieve results. Again, it is important to realize that the results from praying and meditating will only be achieved when relied upon with implicit trust and conviction.

What does 'Abdu'l-Bahá mean when he says that the soul is able to emerge as "a new creature"? I believe it means we are accessing spiritual illumination; that we are united with the divinity in the other world. That does not mean directly with God, but with His love and protection we are united. With this protection we are like new creatures dependent on a powerful spiritual force.

There are hundreds of such stories from true experiences from the Bahá'í friends. When in Japan, in February 1991, in Fukuoka on the island of Kyushu, the Bahá'í Counsellor came to my course. She was so excited that she returned to her home and within two or three days rounded up roughly 50 or 60 people to attend, including seven members of the National Spiritual Assembly. This was highly unusual as the Japanese usually consider themselves too busy to go anywhere. The Board members and Counsellor Mrs Kimiko Shwerin came. At the end of the course, one of the Japanese ladies had to take a friend home whom she had brought to the meeting but who lived quite a long distance away. While driving back, in her mind she was asking herself, how can you say "Yá Bahá'u'l-Abhá" when you are in danger and be protected? Suddenly a car appeared in front of her. At the moment of impact she found herself saying "Yá Bahá'u'l-Abhá". Both cars were total write-offs. Both drivers and passengers were unharmed. The policeman on arrival said he found it impossible to believe, given the nature of the crash and the condition of the vehicles, that anyone was still alive. Immediately, the sceptical driver called the Counsellor and cried on the phone, "Tell Mrs Munsiff that I believe, I believe, I believe, I believe."

Once on one of the Pacific Islands, I was a passenger in a car driven by a friend and on that particular island the people really drive as if they are in carnival dodgem cars – you know the kind of cars they have in the fun fairs, where people intentionally try to hit each other. Every time another car came towards us, I would sit there and say "Yá Bahá'u'l-Abhá, Yá Bahá'u'l-Abhá, Yá Bahá'u'l-Abhá"! Finally, the woman who was driving turned towards me and said, "Madame Munsiff, please shut up, you are making me nervous." I apologized and kept quiet. Then a truck came directly towards us as if it would hit us in a second. I instinctively said "Yá Bahá'u'l-Abhá', and the truck stopped just a millimetre away from hitting us – so close, that the only thing that could pass between the two vehicles was a hair. The woman turned towards me again and said, "I'm sorry, Mrs Munsiff. Please keep right on."

The same thing happened when my daughter was about ten. We were returning home and my husband was having to drive in very bad snow and ice. I kept saying "Yá Bahá'u'l-Abhá, Yá Bahá'u'l-Abhá". She said, "Mummy, please do you mind. Could you stop saying Yá Bahá'u'l-Abhá." Instantly the car swerved and once again I instinctively said "Yá Bahá'u'l-Abhá", and the car stopped within a hair's breadth of the edge of a cliff. From then on both my husband and my daughter would also say "Yá Bahá'u'l-Abhá" when there was a perceived danger! These may all be coincidences, but it's strange how they all occurred immediately after the concept of invoking protection was being mocked. Perhaps the Concourse on high also likes to prove a point.

I remember the time when I was giving this course in a Summer School in Iceland. I was explaining about the power of the word "Yá Bahá'u'l-Abhá" as an invocation, especially in moments of danger. There was a youth who walked through my class just at that moment. He must have been 15–16 years old. I asked who he was as I don't permit people to walk in and out of my classes. They said, "No, don't worry, he's not a Bahá'í, he is just look-ing around." He left with his parents to continue their journey and on the way their car was hit by a truck. Just before impact, this young man cried out "Yá Bahá'u'l-Abhá!" Although the vehicles were seriously damaged, none of the people were hurt. His parents asked him: "What was that you said?"

He said: "I said 'Yá Bahá'u'l-Abhá.'"

They said: "What is that?"

"Oh, there was this old lady from India telling these Bahá'ís about it, and it flashed into my mind when the accident happened. I have no idea why."

The family came back to ask for Bahá'í books and investigate further.

There are thousands of such stories. The only thing left, is that it's up to you to try it. All I can say is to have faith in what you are saying. If you believe in it – it works. It has great power. You may use or know of those gadgets often used by the elderly which are connected to a receiving centre when if you fall or shout they come to you right away, to assist you. If these gadgets work, why shouldn't this spiritual gadget work? This is something in which one needs to have faith and then to try it. There's nothing to feel embarrassed about. You can experience dangers or trials or you can have faith – the choice is yours. 'Abdu'l-Bahá said:

The Greatest Name should be found upon the lips in the first awakening moment of early dawn. It should be fed upon by constant use in daily invocation, in trouble, under opposition and should be the last word breathed when the head rests upon the pillow at night. It is the name of comfort, protection, happiness, illumination, love and unity.[110]

Many of us start talking to people about the Faith, but we seldom first say "Yá Bahá'u'l-Abhá" in our heart. If we say it, then that person's heart is open, their mind is open and their soul is attracted, with the result that what we offer them enters their mind, heart and soul. They get interested. Even if they don't ask you a lot of questions, they're not going to forget the encounter. Often we have given up even before we have opened our mouths, not having the confidence to know what we are going to talk about. We focus on our limitations, convinced we have no power to come up with the right words.

Learning to be totally dependent upon Bahá'u'lláh and His Name is a difficult lesson to learn but it is an essential step in the process of sharing with those you come across the message of Bahá'u'lláh, which should be given to those who are interested with great love and great dignity. Also, when you refer to Bahá'u'lláh, translate immediately, explaining that the name means the "Glory of the Lord". This is important so that they are aware of the station and the meaning of the Name and you don't put them in a position of having to ask or grappling with a foreign-sounding name. Unfortunately, Bahá'ís often omit mentioning Bahá'u'lláh, referring only to the principles and leaving it to the listener to enquire "Who is the founder of your Faith or who said all this?" Our response too often is inaudible or unintelligible, rather than with clarity, dignity and love.

You will come to see that the name of the Manifestation of God for this day and age "Bahá'u'lláh" has great effect on those pure and searching souls. Shoghi Effendi says that all the teachings are like the body, but when you say "Bahá'u'lláh", the spirit goes into the teachings. Otherwise, if there is no spirit, of what good is the body?

Many organizations are now based upon the Bahá'í principles. Most of them don't even know they are from Bahá'u'lláh. But because His message was let loose in the world, like music from radio transmissions, they receive it. They don't know where it's coming from; they don't know the station because they didn't hear the announcement saying which station was transmitting, but they've heard it and they like the music, and say "O well, we like this, we'll go on playing it. It's my music." But there's no spirit. It is the spirit that we are duty bound to impart and constantly keep the relevance of His title in our hearts, minds and souls. It is very important that we understand that the Name has power and we must try to release that power by mentioning it when appropriate and with dignity.

Over and over again, there are hundreds of such stories demonstrating how this strategy has helped people. It helps you to become a new creature, if you beg of Him and say it to Him with utter humility and love and sincerity. It is of the utmost importance that we realize that the power of His Name opens the hearts of pure souls.

During the Ten Year Crusade we Bahá'ís conquered, not conquered physically, but spiritually by uttering the word Bahá'í so that it was heard in many, many countries, islands and territories. At that time, in 1953, we had twelve National Spiritual Assemblies in the world. With them and a handful of workers, the Faith was established throughout the whole of this planet. With what? With this cry: "Yá Bahá'u'l-Abhá".

We were asked during the Ten Year Crusade that when we were travelling and teaching and establishing the Faith, that we should use "Yá Bahá'u'l-Abhá, Yá 'Alíyyu'l-A'lá!" "Yá Alíyyu'l-A'lá" is an invocation meaning "O Thou the Exalted of the Most Exalted," and refers to the Báb. So we used both. We called upon both Bahá'u'lláh and the Báb during the Crusade. So, the Bahá'ís at that time were crusaders – spiritual crusaders, covering spiritually the whole planet, which was achieved in ten years. Admittedly at a cost, but how wonderful it was, and how effective Yá Bahá'u'l-Abhá, Yá Alíyyu'l-A'lá was! We should remember that these invocations can still be used in our teaching work and in our lives.

It is important that you access and use these names and expressions if you want to put faith into the hearts of men. Shoghi Effendi says that we have to feed the hunger of the soul first, and the soul will help the mind to understand, and if the soul is happy, the heart is happy and then the mind relaxes and grasps what it has to do. When the soul is tired, the heart is not open and the mind is closed, even with all of its learning, making receptivity impossible.

There's an easy way and a hard way. The easy way is to trust in Bahá'u'lláh and follow the instructions that He has given, and the hard way is to knock your head against a wall, and keep knocking to no effect.

Some people ask if you can use the Greatest Name too much or inappropriately. Obviously, it should not be used in the bathroom. This is a lack of reverence, unless you perceive an immediate danger. If you use the Greatest Name with respect and devotion and use it acknowledging your dependence on God, there is no limit to its use, rather it is right and correct in order to bring you closer to Him.

> O My Name! Hearken Thou unto by My Voice coming from the direction of My Throne. He wisheth to make mention of thy name at all times inasmuch as thou hast proved thyself steadfast in extolling His virtues amongst men. Indeed thy Lord loveth fidelity as found in the realm of creation, and He hath given it precedence over most of the praiseworthy qualities. Verily, He is Potent and Powerful.
>
> Know thou moreover that We have heard the praise thou hast uttered in thy communion with God, thy Lord, the Exalted, the Gracious. Great indeed is the blessedness awaiting thee, inasmuch as thou hast curtailed thine own affairs in favour of this inviolable, this mighty and enlightened Cause. We entreat God to make thy call a magnet which will attract the embodiments of names in the world of existence that all beings may spontaneously hasten to heed it. No God is there besides Him, the Exalted, the Pre-Eminent, the Ever-Blessed, the Sublime, the Most August, the Most Glorious, the Most Bountiful, the All-Knowing, the All-Informed.[111]

> O maid-servant of God! The Lord of the Kingdom hath raised His voice with the utmost power and

strength and is conquering the realms of hearts and souls with the hosts of the Supreme Concourse. All holy souls in the kingdom of existence respond unto this voice and cause the call, "Yá-Bahá'u'l-Abhá!" to reach the Lofty Apex.[112]

THE CONCOURSE ON HIGH

As you are aware, as Bahá'ís we are forbidden to go into trances, or become a medium and talk to the spirits in the other world. However, we can still access the holy spirits, the holy Bahá'ís that are in the other world and are referred to as the Concourse on high. Those who are in the other world are always waiting to help us, whenever we need help. It would be foolish not to call on them to help us in our teaching endeavours simply by saying "Yá Bahá'u'l-Abhá, help me!"

> The invisible hosts of the Kingdom are ready to extend to you all the assistance you need, and through them you will no doubt succeed in removing every obstacle in your way, and in fulfilling this most cherished desire of your heart. Bahá'u'lláh has given us [a] promise that should we persevere in our efforts and repose all our confidence in Him the doors of success will be widely open before us.[113]

You can call on an individual, a specific person. Again, here is a true story. But you have to try it out for yourself. You don't have to believe me.

When I was in Ghana, I wrote a report to the Universal House of Justice. Brian O'Toole, who was in Ghana, was going back to England so I asked him to post my envelope with a local stamp which was addressed to my husband, who would then send the report on to Haifa. On his arrival in London, Brian sent me a cable saying that the bag in which he was carrying my report was stolen. I was not well at the time and I was absolutely devastated. I had no copy of the handwritten report. I didn't know what to do and was totally desperate.

Before I continue the story of the missing report, I need to take you back to an earlier incident which has a bearing on the outcome. When I was in Benin earlier in the year, someone told me about a young American, Patricia Moore. I think she was 28 years old or so, and she had come to Benin to pioneer. As she was travelling in the train, it got stuck in the desert for many hours and she had a bottle of water which she gave to some African children, and sadly, she died of dehydration. She was duly buried in Benin, and so I thought I must visit her grave and salute her as a true example of a pioneer. By chance I asked, "what was her profession?" and was told she had been a post woman in California.

When I was in Ghana and had heard that this man had lost my report, I thought, I'll call on Patricia in the Concourse on high. I did nothing extreme: I simply said the Greatest Name and called on Patricia Moore, telling her what had happened to my report and that I needed it sent to the House of Justice. I walked around and said this a few times. Then after a few days I received a letter from my husband. He told me, "How strange, I received your letter with the report for the Universal House of Justice, without any postage stamp!" You may call it yet another coincidence, I call it affirmation.

I was in Sweden, during the time the Bahá'ís were experiencing persecution in Iran. A friend of mine living there said that letters sent to Iran never got to their loved ones. Although she kept writing to her brother, it seemed that he was not receiving anything. She was quite distressed at not being able to communicate with her brother and would I please pray about it. I told her that there was nothing special about me or my prayers but that I would call on the Concourse on high and Patricia Moore, the post woman. She would make sure it was delivered. So in her presence I called on Patricia, and a letter was posted and that was the end of the story as far as I was concerned. A month and a half later she phoned me and she said that her brother received the letter. You can call it another coincidence if you like, but you don't have coincidences repeatedly, with so many people in so many places experiencing the same result.

Some time later, together with an Indian friend of mine, we went on a three-day pilgrimage. While visiting the Shrine of Bahá'u'lláh, we bumped into the custodian of the Shrine who happened to be the lady who was now successfully communicating with her brother. Because my companion was a little sceptical, I asked for confirmation of the events. She not only confirmed the past incident but said she had continued to call on Patricia Moore with success. Not only that, she also said that she had given Patricia's name to so many Bahá'ís who had suffered the same disappointment in the past and who were now so pleased that their correspondence was getting through. I exclaimed "You shouldn't have done that! She'll curse my name!" But then I thought, "But no, they don't get tired there. Spirits don't get tired. Maybe she's enjoying it. It's also timeless there, and she's been helping so many, so we can call on her."

I call on many different people in the Concourse on high to help in difficulties. Whether we know it or not, we are connected with the other world, and when you say "Yá Bahá'u'l-Abhá", the doors of the Abhá Kingdom are opened, illumination is vouchsafed unto you. Having that communication and unity with the other world highlights how close it is. It's like the child in the mother's womb. The child in the womb cannot see us, but we can see the child, now even more so with all the scanning and the advancement of science. We can even tell the sex of the child or diseases that might be carried. Our closeness is not matched by the baby's, it has no concept of the world outside its mother's womb. In a similar fashion we do not fully understand nor are we conscious of what is going on in the next world. The only thing is that if we are spiritually attuned, we Bahá'ís should rely on our faith because Bahá'u'lláh has confirmed its power. We are so blessed that Bahá'u'lláh has given us a glimpse of the next existence and assured us that help is to be had just for the asking. I would like to recommend that children should be taught to say "Abhá", even at the age of a few months. When they start to say mama, papa, why not teach them to say "Abhá".

In Korea, there was a two-and-a-half year old, and the nanny said "Come, I have to do some shopping." The child answered: "No, you go and I can wait here and say Abhá. Nothing will happen to me." She had so much faith. That is what Christ meant when He said, "Come unto me like a child," not childish, but pure like a child.

There is this prayer, "O God, guide me, protect me, make of me a shining lamp," and so on. This two-and-a-half year old little girl was rather naughty during a fireside, so the father said: "Come on, come on – you're going to bed," and as she was going up the steps, he tapped her bottom. So as she continued up the stairs in a toddling hop, she started saying: "O God, guide me" – and put both of her hands on her bottom – "protect me". Of course, everyone laughed, including her father. She had faith. She got protection instantly.

If only we had faith like that child – but tragically so many of us don't. I am not suggesting that we have blind faith nor stop using the qualities of wisdom or discernment, but once you believe in Bahá'u'lláh, then you have only to follow and do what He says. It couldn't be simpler.

The supreme cause for creating the world and all that is therein is for man to know God. In this Day whosoever is guided by the fragrance of the raiment of His mercy to gain admittance into the pristine Abode, which is the station of recognizing the Source of divine commandments and the Dayspring of His Revelation, hath everlastingly attained unto all good. Having reached this lofty station a twofold obligation resteth upon every soul. One is to be steadfast in the Cause with such steadfastness that were all the peoples of the world to attempt to prevent him from turning to the Source of Revelation, they would be powerless to do so. The other is observance of the divine Ordinances which have streamed forth from the wellspring of His heavenly-propelled Pen. For man's knowledge of God cannot develop fully and adequately save by observing whatsoever hath been ordained by Him and is set forth in His heavenly Book.[114]

I have travelled to many countries, particularly to first-world countries in the West, and Bahá'ís frequently complain that they are too tired to pray and to teach. It is not for me to judge, and I understand that for many life, work and commuting can be consuming and exhausting, but it strikes me that if they really followed the laws and ordinances of Bahá'u'lláh they would be surprised at the opportunities which arise and how they would regain their energy. But it does need a constant desire to teach His Faith and rely on His support. Without that commitment, no matter how much effort is expended, the results will keep eluding us. In some ways this total reliance on prayer is a concept which we really do not discuss amongst ourselves and therefore it is hardly surprising that prayer is not our first port of call. But my experiences have fashioned my actions. I am not an educated woman and almost always have been by myself in my endeavours to serve the Faith, so I have had no choice but to implicitly rely on prayers and the subsequent guidance

I receive. I must emphasize there is absolutely nothing special about me, other than that together with many others, I have an unshakeable conviction in the power of prayer. This is why I try to share my experiences to give those who are less convinced a taste of how prayers have been instrumental in guiding me through difficult, and what often seemed like impossible, obstacles.

But, as I keep saying, there is nothing special about me. My friend Janet Alexander, who had listened to me endlessly going on about the power of prayer and calling upon the Concourse on high related the following experience to me.

I've had lots of wonderful experiences calling on Them, but one that possibly surprised me the most was during an extremely rainy night in Asuncion, Paraguay. It was literally pouring cats and dogs, and the streets were flooding. A friend had been visiting me from Resistencia, Argentina and she could not get a taxi, in order to get her bus back home, and we were getting pretty desperate. The taxis just don't run when there are floods. After half an hour of continually calling every cab stop in town, we decided that as a last resort we'd call on the Concourse on high. We wondered who we'd get up there. I thought about Jessie Revell, because she must have been highly organized and efficient and reliable to be on the International Council and to have been blessed with helping the Guardian. This was about 12:30, late at night. We said Yá Bahá'u'l-Abhá, and called on Jessie Revell on high, and then dialled to get a cab. Nothing happened. We hung up, wondering what went wrong; nothing happened – no answer again! Just in that short pause, one of our Bahá'í friends, Mrs Mahin Balazadeh, called and her first words were: "Do you need a cab?" We gasped, "Yes – how did you know?" Her husband had awakened and had dreamt that we needed a cab. So he got out of bed, drove over and chauffeured my friend so that she could catch her bus. I owe many thanks to Jessie Revell for helping and to Mrs Munsiff for telling me in the first place how to tap into the Divine Resources.

Often people don't believe that calling on the Concourse on high and using the Most Great Name produces any results. I remember that some years back I was in Zaire in Dr Guy's house. He was a Canadian Bahá'í pioneering in Zaire with his family. We were sitting at the breakfast table. He's a scientific man, and I was talking about how the Concourse on high can help us in everything and how we can get through to them. I could see on his face that he wasn't buying my explanation and he was just humouring me. I stopped and didn't say any more. You can tell from people's faces if they are interested or think you are a "little strange". But Dr Guy's luggage had not yet arrived from Canada after many months, and all they had in their house was their hand luggage. As he was driving to the Custom House to investigate his lost luggage, he thought, "Why not, I might as well test this thing Mrs Munsiff is explaining."

First, he went to the warehouse, but they wouldn't let him in, so he continued saying "Yá Bahá'u'l-Abhá", and finally the man let him in. It was a huge place, completely filled with luggage and no one could care less about helping him. He thought, how on earth can I ever find my baggage if it is in here; it's impossible! As he walked, he looked up and thought – "Who do I know in the Concourse on high that could help me?" He thought of Mr Blackwell, a pioneer to Zaire who had recently passed on, and was buried in Zaire. As he was walking, he hit his leg rather badly against the edge of a trunk. He said: "Ouch!" And he looked down to see whose trunk it was, and it was Mr Blackwell's trunk, addressed to Mrs Blackwell in the United States, and it had been sitting there for three years. And right next to that trunk was his own luggage. So he brought his baggage out successfully and made sure that Mrs Blackwell received her trunk. I later saw Mrs Blackwell in Haifa, and she confirmed that she finally did get the trunk after three years of waiting.

Dr Guy was quite excited. He said: "Wow, this is easy!" So he decided again to try to see the Minister of Health, who had not been able to see him for the last six months. He needed his permission to practise in Zaire. He went to his office and the secretary said: "*Très occupé*" – very busy. He thought, "All right – I don't know anyone in the Concourse on high who's a doctor, but never mind, I'll just call on anybody. Dear doctor, whatever doctor – in the Concourse on high, please make sure that I meet this Minister today." But the secretary confirmed that no – he can't see anyone today. Just as Dr Guy was walking out, thinking, the Concourse on high isn't working today, the Minister at that moment came out of his office and said: "Oh, Dr Guy, please come in and see me!" "He welcomed me and gave me the authorization to carry on my project." When he came home that day, Dr Guy was on cloud nine – to this day he doesn't forget. Now, he finds all of his work is done quite easily.

But remember this – don't think that if you don't have faith, if you don't say your obligatory prayers, if you don't teach, and if you don't recite the Holy Writings daily that the Concourse on high is still going to help you when you have consistently failed to maintain your spiritual connection. There are billions of people in this world, and there are millions of Bahá'ís. How are those in the Concourse on high going to be aware of you? Why should they even care to find you, since you didn't care to know them? Very simply, we must always do what Bahá'u'lláh asks of us, because Bahá'u'lláh says of the person who obeys His ordinances and laws, "I am his!" Bahá'u'lláh and all His wealth and the Concourse on high are there to help us. This is the key.

In another place, Bahá'u'lláh says that "those who teach My Cause, their name is better known in the Abhá Kingdom than to their own selves". So for people who are constantly teaching, sacrificing, working in the Cause, they and their endeavours are known in the next world. Imagine trying to make a call to the President or the Queen of England. When you phone and ask to speak to the Queen, first of all they'll never put you through, and secondly, even the secretary won't know who you are. The process will of course be unsuccessful. Unless you have achieved something which has attracted media attention or you have done something truly special which is known to the person you are talking to, you will be met with a polite but disappointing rejection. This analogy, of course, is my simple attempt to make the process more vivid. I have based it on Bahá'u'lláh's warning that if you don't teach, the power is taken away from you, and the more you teach, the more power is given to you. Where do you think you get this power from? From Bahá'u'lláh and the Concourse on high – they are your power, they are your armaments, they are your soldiers. So, the more you teach, the more support you have. If you don't teach, if you don't pray, you remain unknown to the other world and your power to attract others is non-existent, and you are left not being able to do anything. I would suggest you get yourself known.

If you pray sincerely, begging Bahá'u'lláh, He's always merciful. Bahá'ís are counselled not to dwell on guilt, or to beat ourselves up, focusing on our omissions and convincing ourselves that our prayers won't be answered. Nothing could be further from the truth. As soon as you sincerely feel contrition and start praying, then there is the connection. If you consistently do not serve the Faith and yet have a constant expectation, just because you say these prayers, that they should work for you, I believe you will experience only disappointment. Prayer and action have to go hand in hand in order to have success.

I was in Nigeria where a pioneer told me to get ready as we were going to take a picnic lunch and meet a Nigerian who was interested in the Faith and promised to meet us with his children at an agreed location. Everybody got into the car, with their lunch, and when we arrived, we went and sat in the garden. We waited, had lunch but the man didn't show up. Everyone was so disappointed that we had come for a two-hour drive for nothing. I saw a pub, a sort of bar across the street and said I bet he's in there, but let's not worry about it. I said "Yá Bahá'u'l-Abhá, what are we supposed to do?" I told them to get into the car and we'd drive on. I got us lost very quickly, but continued saying – go straight on, go straight on. The Bahá'í driver laughed, saying, you don't know the roads. I answered that it made no difference. After a while 1 told him to turn right and keep driving. Shortly a young man in a school uniform approached the car. I asked him where his school was, and he informed us that it wasn't far. Where's your principal's office? The first gate on the right. We went in, and I asked permission to speak after telling the principal what the Bahá'í Faith was all about. He agreed and called the teacher to round up all the boys. But it was recess time and the principal warned "If they're called now, they may be very aggressive, so watch it, Madame." I said, don't worry about it. Being Indian, my usual form of dress was a sari which the children had probably never seen, they all came forward out of curiosity. As I walked in, I internally said "Yá Bahá'u'l-Abhá", and all of the students stood up in respect and that of course was the power and glory of Bahá'u'lláh. Then I gave a talk which seemed to capture their interest. The teacher spontaneously took us to his house and gave us tea and asked the Baháʼís to come again and talk more about the Faith. All were very happy. So, we missed out on one person who didn't meet us, but we never gave up hope and said, "Oh well, it's not working, we might as well go back." My plea to you is to call on Baháʼuʼlláh and He will guide you.

Baháʼís all around the world who have put these thoughts into practice have succeeded. So, why don't you try it? If it doesn't work, go back to your own way of life. But at least give yourself a chance and prove it to yourself, one way or the other.

> The meaning of "angels" is the confirmations of God and His celestial powers. Likewise angels are blessed beings who have severed all ties with this nether world, have been released from the chains of self and desires of the flesh, and anchored their hearts to the heavenly realms of the Lord. These are of the Kingdom, heavenly; these are of God, spiritual; these are revealers of God's abounding grace; these are dawning-points of His spiritual bestowals.[115]

THE PRACTICAL APPLICATION OF THE SPIRITUAL LIFE

Transformation

The power of God can entirely transmute our characters and make of us beings entirely unlike our previous selves. Through prayer and supplication, obedience to the divine laws Bahá'u'lláh has revealed, and ever-increasing service to His Faith, we can change ourselves.[116]

Let each morn be better than its eve . . .[117]

When I was in Western Samoa, the Bahá'ís gave a big dinner. There was a small open-air pavilion and about 300 of us sat down on the floor to eat. A man walked in and others followed with different dishes and everyone started to applaud. I asked if it was the Samoan custom to applaud when the food arrives, and the person sitting next to me said, that no, it is not our custom, but you see – the first man who brought in the food has a fishery business and before he was a Bahá'í, if a fish would fall

off of his truck and a child would pick it up – he would
smack the child and put the fish back into the truck.
Today he is feeding 300 Bahá'ís totally free!

Know thyself

Bahá'u'lláh says if you know yourself, you know God.
However, Shoghi Effendi explains that the self of which
Bahá'u'lláh speaks is your own soul, which we of course
can never know. But then there is the other self that we can
know – namely, our own character and our shortcomings.

> The believers, as we all know, should endeavour to set
> such an example in their personal lives and conduct
> that others will feel impelled to embrace a Faith which
> reforms human character. However, unfortunately, not
> everyone achieves easily and rapidly the victory over
> self. What every believer, new or old, should realize
> is that the Cause has the spiritual power to re-create
> us if we make the effort to let that power influence us,
> and the greatest help in this respect is prayer. We must
> supplicate Bahá'u'lláh to assist us to overcome the fail-
> ings in our own characters, and also exert our own
> will power in mastering ourselves.[118]

> Humanity, through suffering and turmoil, is swiftly
> moving on towards its destiny; if we be loiterers, if we
> fail to play our part, surely others will be called upon
> to take up our task as ministers to the crying needs of
> this afflicted world.

Not by the force of numbers, not by the mere exposition of sets of new and noble principles, not by an organized campaign of teaching – no matter how world-wide and elaborate in its character – not even by the staunchness of our faith or the exaltation of our enthusiasm, can we ultimately hope to vindicate in the eyes of a critical and sceptical age the supreme claims of the Abhá Revelation. One thing, and only one thing, will unfailingly and alone secure the undoubted triumph of this Sacred Cause, namely the extent to which our own inner life and private character mirror forth in their manifold aspects the splendour of those eternal principles proclaimed by Bahá'u'lláh.[119]

We often talk about the heart in an emotional context, or having a feeling in the heart. We might say: "Oh, I feel uneasy in my heart." Prayers mostly affect the heart. And I often wondered why we are always talking about the heart. For example, all the Manifestations of God say: "Keep Me in your heart. Keep My love in your heart." Therefore, the heart is so important. But I personally could not understand how a heart can meditate. The Writings say: "Meditate in your heart."

Ismá'íl enquired, "Where is the seat of thought?" The Master replied, "It is generally understood that the seat of thought, consciousness and volition is in the brain. The brain is the organ of the intellect and understanding. The heart also plays a part through the central nervous system."[120]

Now the psychiatrists and doctors and surgeons have found out how important the central nervous system is. Even the heart, through the central nervous system, can coordinate the thoughts with your brain. Thus the activities of the brain and the heart by means of afference, and afferent fibres, are linked together. When both head and heart coincide then that is truly wonderful.

Intellect is a good thing, using your head is helpful, but the inner feeling in the heart is very important. All the Manifestations of God speak about your heart and they want to stay in your heart. Even when you fall in love with someone you have fallen in love with your heart, not your head. You never hear anybody say "You are my sweethead", it is always "my sweetheart". So the heart is of great importance and one can fall in love and understand with your heart and confirm your emotions in your mind. Whether it's physical love, spiritual love, material love; the seat of love is the heart, so keep your heart pure.

And how can you cleanse your heart?

O SON OF GLORY! Be swift in the path of holiness, and enter the heaven of communion with Me. Cleanse thy heart with the burnish of the spirit, and hasten to the court of the Most High.[121]

Faith

Regard not the all-sufficing power of God as an idle fancy. It is that genuine faith which thou cherishest for the Manifestation of God in every Dispensation. It is such faith which sufficeth above all the things that exist on the earth, whereas no created thing on earth besides faith would suffice thee. If thou art not a believer, the Tree of divine Truth would condemn thee to extinction. If thou art a believer, thy faith shall be sufficient for thee above all things that exist on earth, even though thou possess nothing.[122]

This is a story well-known to the Persians. There was a man working for an iron smithy and he had to stand all day and pump the bellows. When the boss came, he said "Boss, I'm tired of pumping these bellows, standing up all day long."

"All right," said the boss, "Sit down and pump."

After a few days, the boss came back again, and he said to the boss: "Boss, I'm tired of pumping these bellows, even sitting down all day long."

"All right," said the boss, "Lie down and pump."

Then after a few weeks when the boss came again, he said to the boss: "Boss, I'm tired of pumping these bellows, even lying down all day long."

"All right," said the boss, "Drop dead, but pump."

Often we behave like this worker, making all sorts of excuses every time we are given something to do. "Oh, I have to do this, but I'm tired, but . . ." Really? We have a job to do and we'd better do it.

What is real Faith? Faith outwardly means to believe the Message a Manifestation brings to the world and

accept the fulfilment in Him of that which the Prophets
have announced. But in reality faith embodies three
degrees: To confess with tongue; to believe in heart;
to give evidence in our actions. These three things are
essential in true Faith. The important requirement
is the love of God in the heart. For instance we say
a lamp gives light. In reality the oil which burns produces the illumination, but the lamp and the chimney
are necessary before the light can express itself. The
love of God is the light. The tongue is the chimney
or the medium by which that love finds expression.
It also protects the Light. Likewise the members of
the body reflect the inner Light by their actions. So
the tongue confesses in speech and the parts of the
body confess in their actions the Love of God within
the soul of a true believer. Thus it was that Peter con-
fessed Christ by his tongue and by his actions. When
the tongue and action reflect the Love of God, the real
qualities of man are revealed. Christ said "You will
know them by their fruits" that is, by their deeds. If
a believer shows forth divine qualities, we know the
true Faith is in his heart. If we do not find evidence
of these qualities; if he is selfish or wicked, he has not
the true kind of Faith . . . Many claim to possess the
true Faith, but it is rare, and where it exists it cannot
be destroyed.[123]

Faith in God is not intellectual yielding to argument
through being convinced that certain statements are
correct, but it is rather from a hunger of the soul, a

knowledge of personal helplessness and the perception of a possible Mighty Helpfulness. Faith cannot
rely on any man, but in God only; the required help
must come from a higher power than man. The soul
is craving that which does not pertain to humanity in
itself. The latent spark of divine longing is awaking to
seek its promise, and it turns heavenward for the dawn
of hope. It is looking for its Father, God.[124]

Devotion

It is very important that we have devotion. If we are not
going to commit with our heart and soul our endeavours
are going to be very difficult.

> Intellectual assent to a creed does not make a man
> a Bahá'í nor does outward rectitude of conduct.
> Bahá'u'lláh requires of His followers wholehearted
> and complete devotion. God alone has the right to
> make such a demand, but Bahá'u'lláh speaks as the
> Manifestation of God, and the Revealer of His Will.
> Previous Manifestations have been equally clear on
> this point. Christ said: "If any man will come after me,
> let him deny himself, and take up his cross and follow
> me. For whosoever will save his life shall lose it, and
> whosoever will lose his life for my sake shall find it . . ."
> The gateway of spiritual birth, like the gateway of nat-
> ural birth, admits men only one by one, and without
> encumbrances. If, in the future, more people succeed
> in entering that way than in the past, it will not be

because of any widening of the gate, but because of
a greater disposition on the part of men to make the
"great surrender" which God demands; because long
and bitter experience has at last brought them to see
the folly of choosing their own way instead of God's
way.[125]

Religious history shows us that every Manifestation of
God had an expectation of mankind to prove their faith;
to have love, devotion and sacrifice.

> Sacrifice of life is of two kinds. To be killed for the
> Cause is not so difficult as to live for it in absolute
> obedience to the commands of God. To attain to the
> condition of Mírzá Abu'l-Faḍl who cares for nothing
> of this world save to write something for the Cause
> that will be of benefit or Mírzá Haydar-'Alí who cares
> not for money, clothes, or even food, but only to teach
> someone something about the Kingdom, is real attain-
> ment to the plane of sacrifice! And without attaining
> to this condition, all effort is without any final result.
> One who cares for love, of husband, wife or children
> more than the Cause of God has not attained.[126]

It is crucial that we learn to appreciate what is intrinsi-
cally good for ourselves and our family. If it is not good
for the Cause, no matter how much we may think that
this is good for me, it will amount to nothing – nor, if
that is our aspiration, will it turn out ultimately to be of
benefit to the family. Consequently, we have to curtail

our carnal inclinations, bad habits, and those behaviours which run counter to the Baháʼí teachings. When obeying the laws of Baháʼuʼlláh, with time it becomes easier but YOU NEED TO START PRACTISING and don't be over-analytical.

How often do we think, "Oh well, maybe I can't do it. Let someone else do it." In all probability someone else will do it, but what happens when the end comes, why miss out on that precious opportunity to strengthen our spiritual development? How comfortable will you feel about meeting your Maker and saying: "I let someone else do it"? We have to understand not only the privilege of serving our Faith but also the importance of constant endeavour in the promotion of the teachings. Everything Baháʼuʼlláh has said is practical and is not difficult once you learn to have faith and serve with joy. Don't make it a chore. Make it a pleasure and then it's not difficult at all. But remember, this can be a slow process and you must avoid being disheartened.

The trouble is sometimes all of us want to do everything very fast because we live in this push-button age. Push-button is alright for technical, medical, material things, but spiritual things have to be done by individuals slowly, step by step, with sincerity and conviction. ʼAbduʼl-Bahá says, never rush. There's no point in rushing. Gradually as you take each step, the realization will become apparent. If we have to confront an obstacle, a problem, or a difficulty in our life, pray about it, and remember, "This too shall pass." Believe me, I have endured many tribulations which seemed unbearable and everlasting but with prayer they do indeed pass. Everything passes. Nothing is static. All we have to do is to have patience and focus on that which is positive in our lives, always relying on the support of prayer which strengthens our conviction that we will ultimately prevail.

How does having complete love and devotion for Bahá'u'lláh work in practice? In the time of 'Abdu'l-Bahá, an American Bahá'í travel teacher came to India. He was in Lucknow where cholera broke out. A friend who was not a Bahá'í sent a telegram to the Local Spiritual Assembly of Bombay, saying "Please send someone to look after this man. He has cholera and is very sick." Mr R..., an Indian believer who was a member of the Local Assembly immediately got up and said: "I'm going", to which the other members said: "Sit down and let's consult."

"There's nothing to consult about," he responded.

"But why are you in such a hurry to go?" asked his fellow Assembly members.

He said: "Because I love Bahá'u'lláh, and this man can teach better than I can and he's teaching and he's sick. It's my duty to go and nurse him."

Now, this is what is called devotion and love for Bahá'u'lláh. Not just sitting there and closing your eyes and saying "Bahá'u'lláh, I love you." That doesn't mean anything. Mr R. immediately acted. Everybody said: "But you have a shop, you have four children, what about your wife? Who will take care of them?"

He said: "God will or all of you will. I don't care, I'm going." He threw his keys on the table, telling them to take them to his wife. He went right away and nursed that man. The American Bahá'í teacher, Sydney Sprague, recovered, but the other man got cholera and died, leaving a poor wife and children. In those days women were not highly educated and trained in business so the situation was desperate. How was she going to care for her four children? Immediately, out of the blue a telegram came from 'Abdu'l-Bahá declaring the Bahá'í a martyr and with instructions to send his wife and children to Haifa where He took care of them.

When we act with the right motivation and in a spirit of devotion and sacrifice in the service of Bahá'u'lláh, we and our loved ones are immediately under God's protection. 'Abdu'l-Bahá assured us that Bahá'u'lláh takes care of His own, like a hen takes care of her chicks. What more do we want? But we have to have faith. If we have the slightest doubt or hesitation then it's finished; faith means faith. You cannot deviate, but must remain firm and do what your heart and head tell you to do, right away. That's one part of devotion.

Another part of devotion is to make sure that you never, ever do a blameable deed that will reflect upon you, no matter how great the loss may be. I remember again in the early years of the Faith in India, there were two Indians, one of whom owed a lot of money to the other. The one who owed the money was not paying so the other one decided quite naturally to take this man to court. But the National Spiritual Assembly decided that they shouldn't do this as it would reflect badly on the reputation of the Faith and that this was not how Bahá'ís should resolve difficulties. In obedience to the Assembly the man withdrew his claim. With time everything was sorted out and both of them matured into wonderful Bahá'ís and served well. We have to understand that the institutions are there to guide us and after consultation will provide spiritual solutions, rather than necessarily conventional or obvious solutions.

It is important not to look at the individuals serving on our institutions. They are like nuts and bolts in a radio or television put together by the engineer and connected with whatever is at the broadcasting station – you then have transmission from the radio or television. What we must always remember is that it is not the individual parts that are of any significance but when the institutions function in accordance with the principles of the Faith, there is a spiritual power which when it gives rise to a decision we are duty bound to obey.

Obedience doesn't come easily if you don't have love. But if you have love and trust, obedience is easier. Your measure of obedience shows the measure of the love that you have for Bahá'u'lláh. That is the bottom line.

Sometimes, one becomes caught up in such a situation that it becomes impossible to obey the laws of Bahá'u'lláh. It may seem that way at the time. I have experienced this myself. [This story is also briefly related in Part One, but we will repeat it here – Ed] In 1953 when I was pioneering in Madagascar, then a French territory, I was the only Bahá'í there, the first to settle. I met most of the people, the government officials, ambassadors and everybody, and I worked there. At first, of course, the government and the church didn't like me. They were suspicious of me, until they noticed that I was serving humanity all the time, loving, caring, uniting them, and not a political person. After some months the Governor of Madagascar invited me to a banquet. He made me sit on his right-hand side. The British Consul knew me, because I came from England and my husband worked there in the Indian High Commission. Actually, at that time, my husband was the Vice-Consul from India to the United Kingdom. The British Consul said to me, since he knew that, as a Bahá'í, I didn't drink alcohol, "Now, I would like to see, how are you going to avoid the toast." The French will not drink a toast with anything else but champagne at such banquets, and if you don't drink too it will be considered an insult. I think he was intrigued to see how I would get out of this situation. And, indeed, how would I? I was the guest of honour and after dinner, the Governor raised his champagne glass and wished me well with a toast. When he sat down, I had to respond. So, I just kept on silently saying, "Yá Bahá'u'l-Abhá" repeatedly, and I stood up, taking my glass of water. Looking at the other guests, I could see from their faces that many were quite shocked. However, I found myself raising the glass of water and saying: "Your Excellency, champagne is only for the rich people, and after a while it goes flat, and after drinking it, some go home, not remembering much, and get up with a headache. But water is eternal, sweet and life-giving. Everybody in the world drinks water, and I wish and I pray that your name will remain forever in this world. Rich and poor all over the world will know of you." And

I saluted him and toasted him and drank the water, and everybody else drank the champagne.

Now, most people thought that it would be a disaster, but the Governor was so pleased with me that afterwards he said that if I wanted anything, I had but to ask his aide-de-camp. If I wanted a car or help, it was there for me to have. You see, I didn't hesitate, I didn't pretend, I didn't make any excuses. I didn't protest. Bahá'u'lláh always helps if you remain firm. But if we start doubting or being apologetic or trying to find a way out for a moment then we are stuck and risk our downfall.

How often do we think that Bahá'u'lláh is far away, and that He doesn't hear our prayers; He's not with us; He's abandoned us. None of this is true. In the *Hidden Words* Bahá'u'lláh says:

> O MOVING FORM OF DUST! I desire communion with thee, but thou wouldst put no trust in Me. The sword of thy rebellion hath felled the tree of thy hope.[127]

Our lack of faith is a lack of trust which results in an internal resistance which deprives us of His support when we assert, "He's not doing this – He's not near me – He's not listening." But Bahá'u'lláh says that "the sword of thy rebellion hath felled the tree of thy hope".

> At all times I am near unto thee, but thou art ever far from Me.[127]

We are far from Him. He is never far from us. He continues:

Imperishable glory I have chosen for thee, yet boundless shame thou hast chosen for thyself. While there is
yet time, return, and lose not thy chance.[127]

What is boundless shame? Not obeying the laws of
Bahá'u'lláh, by not working for the unity of mankind
and bringing peace and happiness to the world. That is
our shame. And what is our glory? He says that I have
chosen imperishable glory – imperishable glory – for
thee. What is this imperishable glory? Just look at the
apostles of Jesus Christ or of any of the early followers
of Manifestations of the past; they are remembered even
after thousands of years. Their glory never ends. So when
we work for a Cause such as ours with all of our heart
and soul, this is our imperishable glory. You have to be
confident that Bahá'u'lláh is always with us.

Verily, I pray God to make thy home a center for the
radiation of light and the glowing of His love in the
hearts of His people. Know that in every home where
God is praised and prayed to and His Kingdom proclaimed, that home is a garden of God and a paradise
of His happiness.[128]

Love

O SON OF MAN! Veiled in My immemorial being
and in the ancient eternity of My essence, I knew My
love for thee; therefore I created thee, have engraved
on thee Mine image and revealed to thee My beauty.[129]

O SON OF BEING! Thy Paradise is My love; thy heavenly home, reunion with Me. Enter therein and tarry not. This is that which hath been destined for thee in Our kingdom above and Our exalted dominion.[130]

O SON OF MAN! If thou lovest Me, turn away from thyself; and if thou seekest My pleasure, regard not thine own; that thou mayest die in Me and I may eternally live in thee.[131]

This love is not of the body but completely of the soul. And those souls whose inner being is lit by the love of God are even as spreading rays of light, and they shine out like stars of holiness in a pure and crystalline sky. For true love, real love, is the love for God, and this is sanctified beyond the notions and imaginings of men.[132]

Love is of course something which cannot be forced. But the essence of your belief in Bahá'u'lláh has to be your love for Him. Without this love your ability to develop and sustain all the varied qualities required of a Bahá'í will be severely hampered. More importantly, the sustenance required for the spiritual enhancement and progress of your soul will be diminished. Love for God and Bahá'u'lláh is like your love for anyone else: you either have it or you don't. I neither have the ability nor the desire to advise you how to develop this love other than if, you are sincere, pray to increase it and I am confident your prayers will be answered.

Truth

It is the Word of God which has the power to change us profoundly as individuals in a way that our own words can rarely achieve to affect others.

For the first time in religious history, it is enjoined upon us as Bahá'ís not to falsify our identity as Bahá'ís even in the face of danger. Adherence to this simple truth is more impactful than we can ever imagine.

> Truth is the Word of God, which gives life to humanity; it restores sight to the blind and hearing to the deaf; it makes eloquent those who are dumb, and living beings out of dead beings; it illumines the world of the heart and soul; it reduces into nothingness the iniquities of the neglectful and erring ones. Beauty, perfection, brilliancy and spirituality in this existence comes from or through the Word of God. For all it is the supreme goal, the greatest desire, the cause of life, light, instruction. The road to attain to this Truth is the Love of God. When the light of the Love of God is burning in the mirror of the heart, that flame shows the way, and guides to the Kingdom of the Word of God. As to that which causes the growth of the love of God – know that it is to turn one's self towards God. [133]

When I was in a very small Pacific island, a Hindu from Fiji came to a fireside at which I was speaking. He became a Bahá'í and then he asked me what he should do. I told him he should teach and tell others what he knew about the Faith. The next morning at 6 a.m. he brought a teacher from the school, telling me that he had explained all he knew to the teacher and that I should tell him the rest. Then I asked him if he had a family.

"Yes, I have a wife and seven children."

I asked him if he had told his wife that he had become a Bahá'í.

He said: "Not yet."

I asked, "Why are you afraid of her?"

He answered: "She is a Christian and she and the priest are always nagging me to become a Christian and I told them that I would not become a Christian. I'm waiting for Krishna to return. You Christians are always fighting among yourselves – what good is that?" He said, "She beats me and throws me out of the house."

I said "Oh, that is not true – you must be getting drunk and for that reason she throws you out of the house and not because you're not a Christian."

He told me, "Well, I get so frustrated that I go out and get drunk."

I told him that he should not be drinking any more and he said: "Yes, I know and I will give up drinking."

In the meantime, his wife walked in. This man was no more than five feet in stature and his wife was a big woman. As soon as he saw her, he straightened himself upright in the chair, looking very authoritative. She walked right up to him and started saying in a loud voice: "Come on, come on, come on home!"

He in a very soft, but firm voice, said: "Go home woman, go home. I am not afraid of anybody, I have

304

Bahá'u'lláh with me and the whole world is mine."

She turned around, and went away. After he left, an hour later she came back and she said to me, "I apologize."

I really told her off, saying that she did not know how to behave herself. "You were most discourteous to both me and your husband."

She profusely apologized and said: "I want to know what you did to my husband."

"I didn't do anything."

"Yes, you did, he never had the courage to stand up to me before."

I kept on saying that I had done nothing – it was Bahá'u'lláh's power, not mine. She asked me when I was leaving the island. I said tonight. She came to the airport with her seven children, all lined up, and she said: "Give them the power that you gave to my husband."

I said that I had no power. She was very tall and strong; she grabbed my hand and forcibly put my hand on each of her seven children herself. Later, I heard that she was sending her children to Bahá'í children's classes.

The revealed words of the Báb and Bahá'u'lláh are the foundation of truth upon which all of humanity's well-being depends. For the first time in religious history, mankind is blessed with the original writings of the Manifestations of God. As a Bahá'í community we are also blessed with the enormous legacy of the translation of the Writings into English by Shoghi Effendi, and his voluminous writings and correspondence. Furthermore, the authority to elucidate on the writings has been exclusively vested in the Universal House of Justice. It is not for us as individuals to interpret, modify or compromise these spiritual truths.

Humility

Set against the station of and the support we derive from the institutions of the Faith, there is no room for individuals to endeavour to acquire power or assert superiority in the community. Furthermore, the all-embracing nature of the Message of Bahá'u'lláh imposes on us an obligation to offer these teachings to those we come across, with the grace, patience, understanding and love exemplified by 'Abdu'l-Bahá.

> They who are the beloved of God, in whatever place they gather and whomsoever they may meet, must evince, in their attitude towards God, and in the manner of their celebration of His praise and glory, such humility and submissiveness that every atom of the dust beneath their feet may attest the depth of their devotion.[134]

> They should approach their task with extreme humility, and endeavour, by their open-mindedness, their high sense of justice and duty, their candour, their modesty, their entire devotion to the welfare and interests of the Friends, the Cause, and humanity, to win, not only the confidence and the genuine support and respect of those whom they serve, but also their esteem and real affection.[135]

The teacher, when teaching, must be himself fully enkindled, so that his utterance, like unto a flame of fire, may exert influence and consume the veil of self and passion. He must also be utterly humble and lowly so that others may be edified, and be totally self-effaced and evanescent so that he may teach with the melody of the Concourse on high – otherwise his teaching will have no effect.[136]

Thankfulness

Thankfulness is of various kinds. There is a verbal thanksgiving which is confined to a mere utterance of gratitude. This is of no importance because perchance the tongue may give thanks while the heart is unaware of it. Many who offer thanks to God are of this type, their spirits and hearts unconscious of thanksgiving. This is mere usage, just as when we meet, receive a gift and say thank you, speaking the words without significance. One may say thank you a thousand times while the heart remains thankless, ungrateful. Therefore, mere verbal thanksgiving is without effect. But real thankfulness is a cordial giving of thanks from the heart. When man in response to the favours of God manifests susceptibilities of conscience, the heart is happy, the spirit is exhilarated. These spiritual susceptibilities are ideal thanksgiving.

There is a cordial thanksgiving, too, which expresses itself in the deeds and actions of man when his heart is filled with gratitude. For example, God has conferred upon man the gift of guidance, and in thankfulness for this great gift certain deeds must emanate from him. To express his gratitude for the favours of God man must show forth praiseworthy actions. In response to these bestowals he must render good deeds, be self-sacrificing, loving the servants of God, forfeiting even life for them, showing kindness to all the creatures. He must be severed from the world, attracted to the Kingdom of Abhá, the face radiant, the tongue eloquent, the ear attentive, striving day and night to attain the good pleasure of God. Whatsoever he wishes to do must be in harmony with the good pleasure of God. He must observe and see what is the will of God and act accordingly. There can be no doubt that such commendable deeds are thankfulness for favours of God.

Consider how grateful any one becomes when healed from sickness, when treated kindly by another or when a service is rendered by another, even though it may be of the least consequence. If we forget such favours, it is an evidence of ingratitude. Then it will be said a loving-kindness has been done, but we are thankless, not appreciating this love and favour. Physically and spiritually we are submerged in the sea of God's favour. He has provided our food, drink and other requirements; His favours encompass us from all directions. The sustenances provided for man are blessings. Sight, hearing and all his faculties are wonderful gifts. These blessings are innumerable; no matter how many are mentioned, they are still endless. Spiritual blessings are likewise endless – spirit, consciousness, thought, memory, perception, ideation and other endowments. By these He has guided us, and we enter His Kingdom. He has opened the doors of all good before our faces. He has vouchsafed eternal glory. He has summoned us to the Kingdom of heaven. He has enriched us by the bestowals of God. Every day He has proclaimed new glad tidings. Every hour fresh bounties descend.[137]

Severance

Devotion to God also implies severance from everything that is not of God, severance that is from all selfish, and worldly, and even other-worldly desires. The path of God may lie through riches or poverty, health or sickness, through palace or dungeon, rose-garden or torture-chamber. Whichever it be, the Bahá'í will learn to accept his lot with "radiant acquiescence". Severance does not mean stolid indifference to one's surroundings or passive resignation to evil conditions; nor does it mean despising the good things which God has created. The true Bahá'í will not be callous, nor apathetic nor ascetic. He will find abundant interest, abundant work and abundant joy in the Path of God, but he will not deviate one hair's breadth from that path in pursuit of pleasure nor hanker after anything that God has denied him. When a man becomes a Bahá'í, God's Will becomes his will, for to be at variance with God is the one thing he cannot endure. In the Path of God no errors can appal, no troubles dismay him. The light of love irradiates his darkest days, transmutes suffering into joy, and martyrdom itself into an ecstasy of bliss. Life is lifted to the heroic plane and death becomes a glad adventure.[138]

For whoso cherisheth in his heart the love of anyone beside Me, be it to the extent of a grain of mustard seed, shall be unable to gain admittance into My Kingdom.[139]

O SON OF MAN! If thou lovest Me, turn away from thyself; and If thou seekest My pleasure, regard not thine own; that thou mayest die in Me and I may eternally live in thee.[140]

I would like to share a story about a family that went pioneering. Having arrived at their destination they went to visit their neighbours. The neighbours answered: "Yes, we know that you are Bahá'ís, and if you don't get out we'll come and kill you tonight."

The pioneers answered: "All right, as you wish, we're not going anywhere." They prayed together and then went to bed.

The next morning in the marketplace, the father of the Bahá'í family saw his neighbour. He asked: "What happened? You didn't come?"

The neighbour answered: "How could we? There were a few of us and we came. But you had a priest standing outside your door."

The Bahá'í answered: "But we have no priest. We don't believe in priests."

"You did. We knew that you Bahá'ís were liars."

"Look, I'm here in the market with you. Let's go together to my house. I can't very well warn the priest to leave, now can I? Come along and see if he's there."

They went to the man's house, and looked in every room. When they went into the bedroom, they saw a picture of 'Abdu'l-Bahá. The man said: "Here you are, you liar. This is the man that was standing outside the door."

The Bahá'í answered that this man passed away in 1921.

You see, they were afraid to come in because they had seen 'Abdu'l-Bahá who was protecting the family. I can't pretend to be able to explain this.

In the 1940s, there was constant fighting between the Arabs and Jews in Israel. At that time it was known as Palestine. There was a little girl of seven years old, whose grandmother was a Bahá'í, but her parents were not. She used to go to her grandmother's house often. Her grandmother put the love of 'Abdu'l-Bahá in the child's heart and gave her a picture of 'Abdu'l-Bahá. She brought this picture home and put it on the mantlepiece.

In this house in the basement, they had a special place to hide for safety. One day, they heard a lot of commotion outside. This occurred every time when the Arabs would come into the Israeli sector with the intention of killing anyone Jewish. This day, when the Arabs came into the Jewish sector, the parents ran down into the cellar and called out to the daughter. But the daughter didn't go and hide, she stayed in the living room. Two Arabs entered, with blood running down their swords, and yelled at her: "Who are you?"

The child pointed to the picture of 'Abdu'l-Bahá, and said: "I love 'Abdu'l-Bahá." So they left her. They did not harm the child.

When everything calmed down, the parents came up from the cellar and said: "Thank God, you're alive. We must quickly go to the synagogue and light candles in thanksgiving."

The child stopped them, however, and said: "Mummy, daddy – it's because of your synagogue that we're being killed. Go to Granny and ask about 'Abdu'l-Bahá. It was 'Abdu'l-Bahá who saved me!"

Impressed by what had happened they went to the grandmother to learn more about the Faith and subsequently became Bahá'ís. Shoghi Effendi said that this girl would grow up to be a modern Ṭáhirih. I asked Rúḥíyyih Khánum about this story when I was in Haifa in 1952. She said: "Yes, that was true. They came here too. The mother was 40 years of age. She felt that her daughter being an only child would get spoiled, because she was so brave and courageous. They prayed to Bahá'u'lláh to have another child, and they gave birth to a son when the mother was 40."

Sadly, I don't know where this girl is, but I'd love to meet her.

When I was a young girl and I used to hear these amazing stories, I'd talk to Bahá'u'lláh, and say: "When can I experience these wonderful things?" Needless to say, I did experience these wonderful miracles when I was pioneering in Madagascar and the French Cameroons. If I were to sit down and relate all those stories, that would require a few more books. The stories here I hope will whet your appetite and I pray that during the course of your life and service you too may have similar experiences.

'Abdu'l-Bahá gave the following advice to some friends who visited him:

> If the friends of God listen to my first word, they will find the success of this and the next world therein. But there are some who prefer their own thoughts above mine, and when they fall they beg me to save them. Progress and prosperity are in the first word. For example, should I say to so and so, "Go thou to America", and should he reply "I beg to remain a few days more", I give him permission to do as he wishes. But this is not my thought; it is his thought. All of the opinions in the world are useless for the believers. I am the one whose heart burns for them and who sympathizes with them. I wish for them absolute good. I desire of them ideal advancement.[141]

At no time are we ever left alone. We have 'Abdu'l-Bahá with us, who guides us. But many of us never listen.

When the Guardian asked the Bahá'ís to go and teach in different parts of the world; for the Bahá'ís to leave the cities; or the Bahá'ís to leave Iran because there would be persecution, many failed to listen, and then sadly they suffered. When they suffer, they complain to Bahá'u'lláh: "Why am I suffering?" What we don't always understand is that all too often even when we are warned or guided to take certain actions we fail to listen and live to regret our actions. The Universal House of Justice continues to tell us so many things which can help us and others, indeed the whole world, and still we don't listen. In the future when we get caught up in the inevitable chaos the world will experience, there is no point lamenting what is happening if we have failed to actively respond to the repeated calls for action.

You see, some of us really don't read the Writings sufficiently and it's always too easy to make excuses. We really have to try hard to increase our understanding. Once we begin to understand the essence of the Writings and the implications of the prayers, then we find we are not only able to enjoy the deepening process but we love it, and we're enabled to act, as I have said many times before.

How much trouble the beloved Guardian took to translate into English the epic book, *Nabíl's Narrative*. It's true, there are so many names there that confuse us. Forget the names. Just read the stories and remember the events and the sacrifices which occurred during this historic time in the Faith. The stories are important, the names aren't crucial. As a young girl I used to get so confused by the names but through my life I continued to be inspired by the actions of those whose names I couldn't remember.

Indeed the chief motive actuating me to undertake the task of editing and translating Nabíl's immortal Narrative has been to enable every follower of the Faith in the West to better understand and more readily grasp the tremendous implications of His exalted station and to more ardently admire and love Him.[142]

Turn thy face sincerely towards God; be severed from all save God; be ablaze with the fire of the love of God; be purified and sanctified, and beseech and supplicate unto God. Verily, He responds unto those who invoke Him, is near unto those who pray unto Him. And He is thy companion in every loneliness, and befriends every exile.[143]

Bahá'u'lláh says that He really is our companion in every loneliness and He befriends us in every exile. He never, never, never deserts us. Unless, God forbid, we desert Him.

Detachment

During my life, detachment has been perhaps the most difficult of states to achieve. The tests never ended and the failures were painful and heart-breaking. My sorrow from being separated from my family I was never totally able to overcome. We all have attachments which may prevent us from being as victorious in our service as we might be otherwise. My only advice is to be aware of them and pray that you are given the strength to carry on serving.

Whosoever loves money does not love God, and whosoever loves God does not love money . . .

The souls must be detached from the world. Those souls who are attached to this world and its wealth are deprived of spiritual advancement.[144]

I desire every Bahá'í to be severed and detached. If he passes between two mountains of gold, he must not look to either side. These souls who have entered under the shade of the Blessed Perfection must show such independence as to astonish the people of the world. If men come to them with money and supplicate them to accept it, they must reject it.[145]

Muhammad the Prophet has said: "Man in this world must be so attentive to his worldly affairs and temporal necessary pursuits, that it may seem as though he thinks he is going to live forever in this world, and he must, at the same time, be so submerged in the love of God and occupied with the thoughts of the hereafter, that it may seem as though he is going to die and leave this earth at the very moment."[146]

It behoveth the people of Bahá to die to the world and all that is therein, to be so detached from all earthly things that the inmates of Paradise may inhale from their garment the sweet smelling savour of sanctity, that all the peoples of the earth may recognize in their faces the brightness of the All-Merciful, and that through them may be spread abroad the signs and tokens of God, the Almighty, the All-Wise. They that have tarnished the fair name of the Cause of God, by following the things of the flesh – these are in palpable error![147]

Sacrifice

We only need to look to our history as Bahá'ís to know the degree to which thousands have willingly paid and are continuing to pay the ultimate sacrifice of their lives and their freedom. I suggest it behoves all of us constantly to consider our own service for this Cause set against the background of this sacrifice.

> Until a being setteth his foot in the plane of sacrifice, he is bereft of every favour and grace; and this plane of sacrifice is the realm of dying to the self, that the radiance of the living God may then shine forth.[148]

> Thus I exhort each of you . . . to sacrifice all your thoughts, words and actions to bring the knowledge of the Love of God into every heart.[149]

Trust

Often we say – what can I do? The job is so big. I cannot do it alone. No one is helping me. No one is coming to do anything. Frequently we are looking to blame others for our inaction and fail to take responsibility. This reminds me of a sweet story.

Once there was a very big fire in the forest and there was a little bird who would go and wet her wings and would come and flutter over this huge fire. Every time, she would fly quickly to wet her wings, and then fly back and flick a few more drops of water on this huge fire.

God, looking down on this tiny bird, asked her, "Do you think that you can put out the fire in the whole forest by just doing this?"

"No, my God," answered the little bird, "I try my best and I am hoping that you would help me to put this fire out!"

You see she did attract God's attention, and then she got help. In the same way we as individuals must do what we can. God knows and He will send help. When He sees that here is one Bahá'í, one person who is doing whatever that person can do, He gives assistance and then things get achieved. But if that bird had said: "I can't do anything – I am too small," little by little as the trees and bushes got burnt and the other animals got burnt, she would have been burnt and that would have been the end. In essence, she truly saved the forest.

Like the bird, however small or insignificant our actions, when we trust that our service will be recognized as sincere, our faith will be rewarded. We do what we can, then trust in God and Bahá'u'lláh to take notice and send assistance.

If the heart turns away from the blessings God offers how can it hope for happiness? If it does not put its hope and trust in God's Mercy, where can it find rest? Oh, trust in God! for His Bounty is everlasting, and in His Blessings, for they are superb. Oh! put your faith in the Almighty, for He faileth not and His goodness endureth for ever! His Sun giveth Light continually, and the Clouds of His Mercy are full of the Waters of Compassion with which He waters the hearts of all who trust in Him. His refreshing Breeze ever carries healing in its wings to the parched souls of men![150]

It is incumbent in this Day, upon every man to place his whole trust in the manifold bounties of God, and arise to disseminate, with the utmost wisdom, the verities of His Cause. Then, and only then, will the whole earth be enveloped with the morning light of His Revelation.[151]

Sincerity

I declare by the bounty of the Blessed Perfection, that nothing will produce results save intense sincerity! Nothing will be productive of fruit save complete advancement toward God! Everything is condemned save severance, and every idea is fruitless and unacceptable save supplication, communion, prayer and obedience. We must entirely collect our scattered thoughts, purify and sanctify the house of our existence from every attachment, and make the palace of our hearts the nest and shelter of the dove of holiness. Then and not till then will the significance of confirmation and assistance become evident and known, the power of the Kingdom become apparent, and the hosts of the Supreme Concourse run swiftly into the arena of heavenly conquest, to gain victory over the east and west of the hearts, and make the north and south of the spirits of men the flowery regions of the love of God.[152]

It is imperative that all that we do for others and the Faith is done in the spirit of love and sincerity; only then will we see the fruits of our labours.

Justice

O SON OF SPIRIT! The best beloved of all things in My sight is Justice; turn not away therefrom if thou desirest Me, and neglect it not that I may confide in thee. By its aid thou shalt see with thine own eyes and not through the eyes of others, and shalt know of thine own knowledge and not through the knowledge of thy neighbor. Ponder this in thy heart; how it behooveth thee to be. Verily justice is My gift to thee and the sign of My loving-kindness. Set it then before thine eyes.[153]

O people of God! That which traineth the world is Justice, for it is upheld by two pillars, reward and punishment.[154]

The purpose of justice is the appearance of unity among men.[155]

While as Bahá'ís we recognize and rely on the mercy of God, we should also understand that with spiritual maturity nurtured by volumes of Holy Writings we cannot plead ignorance as a justification for our wrong-doings and inadequacies. In addition to being a fountain of love the Faith is not a sentimental liberal movement which tolerates those actions or inactions in our lives for which we have been given clear guidance and repeated warnings.

Forgiveness

> Pray to God day and night and beg forgiveness and pardon. The omnipotence of God shall solve every difficulty.[156]

> Verily, the breezes of forgiveness have been wafted from the direction of your Lord, the God of Mercy; whoso turneth thereunto, shall be cleansed of his sins, and of all pain and sickness. Happy the man that hath turned towards them, and woe betide him that hath turned aside.[157]

We should not feel guilty, because if we feel guilty about what we did or didn't do, then depression sets in. Let's forget that and start a new day and say to ourselves: "This is my new day and I will wait, pray and meditate and receive special blessings, and carry on with the work of God which is to improve my character and to teach the Faith."

Happiness

Being happy is an integral part of being a Bahá'í and if we cannot reflect happiness to all around us, what have we absorbed from the Writings? 'Abdu'l-Bahá says:

This is the day of happiness. In no time of any Manifestation was there the cause for happiness as now. A happy state brings special blessings. When the mind is depressed the blessings are not received.[158]

What most people think of as happiness, 'Abdu'l-Bahá says, does not exist. If we are happy for perhaps a very short time with nice things, a nice person, or nice experiences, it inevitably wears off. Continuous happiness in this world and the next is to love Bahá'u'lláh and to serve His Cause.

Man must so live that he may become beloved in the sight of God, beloved in the estimation of the righteous ones and beloved and praised by the people. When he reaches this station the feast of eternal happiness is spread before him. His heart is serene and composed because he finds himself accepted at the Threshold of His Highness, the One. His soul is in the utmost felicity and bliss even if he be surrounded by mountains of tests and difficulties. He will be like unto a sea on the surface of which one may see huge white waves, but in its deeps it is calm, unruffled and undisturbed. If he trusts his happiness to worldly objects and fluctuating conditions he is doomed to disappointment. Should he gain a fortune and anchor his happiness to that, he may hypnotize himself into a state of so-called joy for a few days, and then that very fortune will become a millstone around his neck, the cause of his worry and melancholy.

But if he lives in accordance with the good pleasure of the Lord he will be favored at the Court of the Almighty. He will be drawn nigh unto the throne of Majesty. He will be respected by all mankind and loved and honored by the believers. This fortune bestows eternal happiness. The tree of this fortune is ever green. The autumnal wind does not sear its leaves nor does the frost of winter rob it of its perennial freshness. This is a happiness which is not followed by any misery but always a source of gratefulness and blessedness. The most great, peerless gift of God to the world of humanity is happiness born of love – they are the twin sisters of the superman; one is the complement of the other. Everything that contributes to the sum total of this human happiness is a gift on the part of God, and that thing which does not add to the aggregate of this ideal felicity must be, little by little, or all at once eliminated.

Therefore, it becomes self-evident that the first bestowal to the world of humanity is happiness, that kind of happiness which is unalterable and ideal. If, by happiness physical enjoyment of material things is meant, then the ferocious wolf is made happy because he kills the innocent lamb and satisfies his hunger for a few hours. This is not happiness. Happiness is a psychological condition created in the brain, mind and heart, the effect of which works out from the centre to the circumference. For example, after many days and night of reflection the philosopher unravels a seemingly unsolvable problem. As a result, a wave of supreme happiness surges through his being. The philanthropist comes to the assistance of thousands of half-starved, half-clothed, afflicted people of a nation. In his deed, he wins much contentment. An engineer spans a large river with a suspension or cantilever bridge, or an architect makes the design of an edifice. Each finds true enjoyment in his work.[159]

Happiness is the ambrosia of the spirit and the nectar of the souls. It confers on man the boon of immortality and the gift of spiritual vision. Happiness is the morning star guiding the wandering to the perennial abode of the blessed. Happiness is the crystalline river flowing from the heavenly mountains through the paradise of the mind and causing to grow upon its banks the imperishable ideals of humanity. Happiness is the cherubim of the Almighty which inspires mankind to perform feats of self-sacrifice and deeds of disinterested philanthropy. Happiness is the melodiously singing nightingale which transforms the darkened world of sorrow into the shining realm of celestial beatitude. Happiness is the surging ocean in the depths of which the diver finds the pearls of resignation and the corals of renunciation. Happiness is the elysium wherein grow the asphodels of goodwill and the amaranths of forgiveness. Happiness is the heaven of God, the blue fields of which are studded with bright rolling orbs of satisfaction and fixed stars of contentment. Happiness is the scintillating crown of humanity the shining gems of which are the teachings of the past prophets and the principles of His Holiness Bahá'u'lláh.

The happiness of man is not dependent upon outward things such as riches, ornaments and clothes. It is, however, dependent upon the susceptibilies of heart and attitude of the mind.[160]

Hope

Far be it from us to despair at any time of the incalculable favours of God, for if it were His wish He could cause a mere atom to be transformed into a sun and a single drop into an ocean. He unlocketh thousands of doors, while man is incapable of conceiving even a single one.[161]

With the promises given to us by Bahá'u'lláh, we have no excuse as Bahá'ís not to be optimistic and view the future for mankind as glorious, even if in the short-term things appear bleak.

Purity

Look at this world. Everything is being beautified. You will say that there are lots of things that are ugly. However, if there were no ugly things, you would not appreciate beauty.

We should look at the Shrines and the Bahá'í Houses of Worship and note how attractive they are. People are initially attracted because of their outside beauty. Once they enter, they discover the inner beauty. In the same way, Bahá'í men, women, and youth must dress in as refined a fashion as they reasonably can, but always with utmost cleanliness. We should be an example to the rich but not an embarrassment to the poor, in our mode of dress.

O Friends of the Pure and Omnipotent God! To be pure and holy in all things is an attribute of the consecrated soul and a necessary characteristic of the unenslaved mind. The best of perfections is immaculacy and the freeing of oneself from every defect. Once the individual is, in every respect, cleansed and purified, then will he become a focal centre reflecting the Manifest Light.

First in a human being's way of life must be purity, then freshness, cleanliness, and independence of spirit. First must the stream bed be cleansed, then may the sweet river waters be led into it. Chaste eyes enjoy the beatific vision of the Lord and know what this encounter meaneth; a pure sense inhaleth the fragrances that blow from the rose gardens of His grace; a burnished heart will mirror forth the comely face of truth.

This is why, in Holy Scriptures, the counsels of heaven are likened to water, even as the Qur'án saith: "And pure water send We down from Heaven,"[25:50] and the Gospel: "Except a man be baptized of water and of the spirit, he cannot enter into the Kingdom of God" [John 3:5]. Thus is it clear that the Teachings which come from God are heavenly outpourings of grace; they are rain-showers of divine mercy, and they cleanse the human heart.

My meaning is this, that in every aspect of life, purity and holiness, cleanliness and refinement, exalt the human condition and further the development of man's inner reality. Even in the physical realm, cleanliness will conduce to spirituality, as the Holy Writings clearly state. And although bodily cleanliness is a physical thing, it hath, nevertheless, a powerful influence on the life of the spirit. It is even as a voice wondrously sweet, or a melody played: although sounds are but vibrations in the air which affect the ear's auditory nerve, and these vibrations are but chance phenomena carried along through the air, even so, see how they move the heart. A wondrous melody is wings for the spirit, and maketh the soul to tremble for joy. The purport is that physical cleanliness doth also exert its effect upon the human soul.

Observe how pleasing is cleanliness in the sight of God, and how specifically it is emphasized in the Holy Books of the Prophets; for the Scriptures forbid the eating or the use of any unclean thing. Some of these prohibitions were absolute, and binding upon all, and whoso transgressed the given law was abhorred of God and anathematized by the believers. Such, for example, were things categorically forbidden, the perpetration of which was accounted a most grievous sin, among them actions so loathsome that it is shameful even to speak their name.

But there are other forbidden things which do not cause immediate harm, and the injurious effects of which are only gradually produced: such acts are also repugnant to the Lord, and blameworthy in His sight, and repellent. The absolute unlawfulness of these, however, hath not been expressly set forth in the Text, but their avoidance is necessary to purity, cleanliness, the preservation of health, and freedom from addiction.

Among these latter is smoking tobacco, which is dirty, smelly, offensive – an evil habit, and one the harmfulness of which gradually becometh apparent to all. Every qualified physician hath ruled – and this hath also been proven by tests – that one of the components of tobacco is a deadly poison, and that the smoker is vulnerable to many and various diseases. This is why smoking hath been plainly set forth as repugnant from the standpoint of hygiene.

The Báb, at the outset of His mission, explicitly prohibited tobacco, and the friends one and all abandoned its use. But since those were times when dissimulation was permitted, and every individual who abstained from smoking was exposed to harassment, abuse and even death – the friends, in order not to advertise their beliefs, would smoke. Later on, the Book of Aqdas was revealed, and since smoking tobacco was not specifically forbidden there, the believers did not give it up. The Blessed Beauty, however, always expressed repugnance for it, and although, in the early days, there were reasons why He would smoke a little tobacco, in time He completely renounced it, and those sanctified souls who followed Him in all things also abandoned its use.

My meaning is that in the sight of God, smoking tobacco is deprecated, abhorrent, filthy in the extreme; and, albeit by degrees, highly injurious to health. It is also a waste of money and time, and maketh the user a prey to a noxious addiction. To those who stand firm in the Covenant, this habit is therefore censured both by reason and experience, and renouncing it will bring relief and peace of mind to all men. Furthermore, this will make it possible to have a fresh mouth and unstained fingers, and hair that is free of a foul and repellent smell. On receipt of this missive, the friends will surely, by whatever means and even over a period of time, forsake this pernicious habit. Such is my hope.

As to opium, it is foul and accursed. God protect us from the punishment He inflicteth on the user. According to the explicit Text of the Most Holy Book, it is forbidden, and its use is utterly condemned. Reason showeth that smoking opium is a kind of insanity, and experience attesteth that the user is completely cut off from the human kingdom. May God protect all against the perpetration of an act so hideous as this, an act which layeth in ruins the very foundation of what it is to be human, and which causeth the user to be dispossessed for ever and ever. For opium fasteneth on the soul, so that the user's conscience dieth, his mind is blotted away, his perceptions are eroded. It turneth the living into the dead. It quencheth the natural heat. No greater harm can be conceived than that which opium inflicteth. Fortunate are they who never even speak the name of it; then think how wretched is the user.

O ye lovers of God! In this, the cycle of Almighty God, violence and force, constraint and oppression, are one and all condemned. It is, however, mandatory that the use of opium be prevented by any means whatsoever, that perchance the human race may be delivered from this most powerful of plagues. And otherwise, woe and misery to whoso falleth short of his duty to his Lord.

O Divine Providence! Bestow Thou in all things purity and cleanliness upon the people of Bahá. Grant that they be freed from all defilement, and released from all addictions. Save them from committing any repugnant act, unbind them from the chains of every evil habit, that they may live pure and free, wholesome and cleanly, worthy to serve at Thy Sacred Threshold and fit to be related to their Lord. Deliver them from intoxicating drinks and tobacco, save them, rescue them, from this opium that bringeth on madness, suffer them to enjoy the sweet savours of holiness, that they may drink deep of the mystic cup of heavenly love and know the rapture of being drawn ever closer unto the Realm of the All-Glorious. For it is even as Thou hast said: "All that thou hast in thy cellar will not appease the thirst of my love – bring me, O cup-bearer, of the wine of the spirit a cup full as the sea!"

O ye, God's loved ones! Experience hath shown

how greatly the renouncing of smoking, of intoxicating drink, and of opium, conduceth to health and vigour, to the expansion and keenness of the mind and to bodily strength. There is today a people who strictly avoid tobacco, intoxicating liquor and opium. This people is far and away superior to the others, for strength and physical courage, for health, beauty and comeliness. A single one of their men can stand up to ten men of another tribe. This hath proved true of the entire people: that is, member for member, each individual of this community is in every respect superior to the individuals of other communities.

Make ye then a mighty effort, that the purity and sanctity which, above all else, are cherished by 'Abdu'l-Bahá, shall distinguish the people of Bahá; that in every kind of excellence the people of God shall surpass all other human beings; that both outwardly and inwardly they shall prove superior to the rest; that for purity, immaculacy, refinement, and the preservation of health, they shall be leaders in the vanguard of those who know. And that by their freedom from enslavement, their knowledge, their self-control, they shall be first among the pure, the free and the wise.[162]

Courtesy, punctuality

It is so important to understand what it means for Bahá'ís to be courteous. It just doesn't mean that it is a tradition or a culture or a habit or a custom. Our graciousness towards others has to be genuine.

We, verily, have chosen courtesy, and made it the true mark of such as are nigh unto Him. Courtesy, is, in truth, a raiment which fitteth all men, whether young or old.[163]

We need to comprehend the subtlety that to be courteous is to be near to God. It brings us near to God. It is like prayer. Prayer takes us near to God. This act takes us near to God. When we are courteous to each other in the sight of God, we are all loved, whatever our age.

O people of God! I admonish you to observe courtesy. For above all else it is the prince of virtues. Well is it with him who is illumined with the light of courtesy and is attired with the vesture of uprightness. Whoso is endued with courtesy hath indeed attained a sublime station.[164]

I don't know why it is, but we Bahá'ís are incurable people as far as keeping time is concerned; we don't seem to be able to shake off our cultures of origin where tardiness is accepted, or we fail to understand that to be late is to be discourteous to those who have turned up on time. I am not saying we are all like that, but why is it we think our meetings should be delayed when we wouldn't expect that of a film or the departure of a plane? When we were on pilgrimage in November 1952, the beloved Guardian would go to the Eastern Pilgrim House every day. The Guardian was always prompt. Every day he would meet us at four. This particular day he said to my husband,

"I'll see you at four."

Naturally, my husband in keeping with his desire for perfection was always on time. He was also, of course, very eager to be with the Guardian every day. That afternoon, for a fraction of a second, his eyes went on his watch to see if the Guardian was on time, which of course he was.

The Guardian apologized two or three times. "I'm sorry if I'm late."

My husband said: "No, my beloved Guardian. You are on the dot. It was just for a fraction of a second that my eyes went to my watch."

But the Guardian insisted: "I'm still very sorry if I'm late." Nevertheless, despite the fact he was on time he was acutely concerned to apologize just in case he had kept my husband waiting, if even for one second. We all know the beloved Guardian didn't have to apologize given his daily work load, particularly as he was on time. For those of you who are too young to know, the beloved Guardian would work from the crack of dawn until one or two a.m. in the morning again. He had so much to contend with and yet, he apologized several times. This should be both an example and a warning to us.

When you are on pilgrimage the Universal House of Justice meets with the pilgrims at a specified time, which currently is four o'clock. The Bahá'ís must be there before the appointed hour, because on the dot the nine members appear and the door is locked. They never fail to be on time. How many more lessons do we want, dear friends? You're never late for your business, you're never late for trains, planes, and doctor's appointments. In the same way, if we are late, we risk losing the spiritual powers which are waiting to assist us. We have to meditate upon this and find a way to be on time. I think it is perhaps easier if we remember that courtesy is a means to being near to God. Let's not deprive ourselves of that blessing.

Obedience

He is come from the invisible heaven, bearing the banner "He doeth whatsoever He willeth" and is accompanied by hosts of power and authority while it is the duty of all besides Him to strictly observe whatever laws and ordinances have been enjoined upon them, and should anyone deviate therefrom, even to the extent of a hair's breadth, his work would be brought to naught.[165]

Thou hast moreover asked Me concerning the ordinances of God. Know thou of a truth that whatsoever hath been prescribed in the Book is indeed the truth, no doubt is there about it, and it is incumbent upon everyone to observe that which hath been sent down by Him Who is the Revealer, the All-Knowing. Were a man to put them away despite his being aware thereof, God would truly be clear of such a one and We too would be clear of him, inasmuch as His ordinances constitute the fruits of the divine Tree and none other than the heedless and the wayward will deviate therefrom.[166]

It is often difficult for us to do things because they are so very different from what we are used to, not because the thing itself is particularly difficult. With you, and indeed most Bahá'ís, who are now, as adults, accepting this glorious Faith, no doubt some of the ordinances, like fasting and daily prayer, are hard to understand and obey at first. But we must always think that these things are given to all men for a thousand years to come. For Bahá'í children who see these things practiced in the home, they will be as natural and necessary a thing as going to church on Sunday was to the more pious generation of Christians. Bahá'u'lláh would not have given us these things if they would not greatly benefit us, and, like children who are sensible enough to realize their father is wise and does what is good for them we must accept to obey these ordinances even though at first we may not see any need for them. As we obey them we will gradually come to see in our-selves the benefits they confer.[167]

I would like to share with you an ancient folk story, emphasizing how people when addressing an issue or problem are keen to have their own way and to display what they believe to be their superior intelligence, an attitude which only leads to argument or futile discus-sion. At the outset I would like to clarify that the sacrifice of a cow in this story is a metaphor for obedience.

The head of a farm was called by God and told, "You people must sacrifice a cow or I'll destroy this town." The farmer goes back into the town and calls together the other tribal leaders and they sit around to discuss God's order. "I have received a message from God that we have to sacrifice a cow or He'll destroy this town."

One man says: "All right, but you didn't ask what age the cow should be."

So the farmer goes back and says: "God, what age should the cow be?"

God answers, "Seven years old."

He returns again to the town and gathers the other tribal leaders and tells them, "God says, seven years old."

Another man speaks up: "You forgot, you didn't ask what colour the cow should be."

So he goes back and says: "God, what colour should the cow be?"

He answers: "Pure white."

"Good," says the man and he goes back and calls the tribesmen back together. "God says it should be seven years old and pure white."

But another one speaks up: "Ah, but you forgot, none of you thought to ask . . ."

Unfortunately, each one is trying to be too clever. "You didn't ask what shape the horns of the cow should be. Should they be straight, sticking out, downward or what?"

So he goes back and asks the same question: "God, what kind of horns should the cow have?"

God says: "Straight, sticking out."

The man comes back and says: "God says that the cow should be seven years old. It should be pure white. It should have straight, sticking out horns."

But then another one speaks up: "But none of you

336

thought to ask what size the tail of the cow should be."

So he goes back and says: "God, what size tail should the cow have?"

God says: "Oh – about half a metre." Now they start looking for a cow like that. They couldn't find one exactly like that in the whole country, and so the town was destroyed.

If they had been obedient and done what God asked initially and obtained just any cow, and sacrificed it and had done with it, they could have saved the whole town, instead of running around and trying to be so clever, with a disastrous outcome. Instant obedience is very important. Clearly, God is not impressed when we try to negotiate with Him!

In considering the effect of obedience to the laws on individual lives, one must remember that the purpose of this life is to prepare the soul for the next. Here in this world one must learn to control and direct one's urges and addictions and not be a slave to them. Life in this world is a succession of tests and achievements, of falling short and of making new spiritual advances. Sometimes the course may seem very hard, but one can witness, again and again, that, as the Universal House of Justice stated in its letter of 6 February 1973 "the soul who steadfastly obeys the laws of Bahá'u'lláh, however hard they may seem, grows spiritually, while the one who compromises with the laws for the sake of his own apparent happiness is seen to have been following a chimera. He does not attain the happiness he sought, he retards his spiritual development and often brings new problems upon himself."

To give one very obvious example: the Bahá'í law requiring consent of parents to marriage. All too often nowadays such consent is withheld by non-Bahá'í parents for reasons of bigotry or racial prejudice; yet we have seen again and again the profound effect on those very parents of the firmness of the children in the Bahá'í law, to the extent that not only is the consent ultimately given in many cases, but the character of the parents can be affected and their relationship with their child greatly strengthened.

> Thus, by upholding Bahá'í law in the face of all diffi-
> culties we not only strengthen our own characters but
> influence those around us.[168]

Capacity: Are we tested more than we can bear?

Trying to assess the individual spiritual capacity of the heart, mind and soul is a pointless exercise, as none of us is capable of achieving an accurate conclusion.

> Prayers are granted through the universal
> Manifestations of God. Nevertheless, where the wish
> is to obtain material things, even where the heedless
> are concerned, if they supplicate humbly, imploring
> God's help, even their prayer hath an effect.
>   . . . Although the reality of the Divinity is sanctified
> and boundless, the aims and needs of the creatures
> are restricted. God's grace is like the rain that cometh
> down from heaven: the water is not bounded by the

limitations of form, yet on whatever place it poureth down, it taketh on limitations – dimension, appearance, shape – according to the characteristics of that place. In a square pool the water, previously unconfined, becometh square; in a six-sided pool it becometh a hexagon . . . and so forth.[169]

We have been given capacity specific to each of us as individuals and it is not for any us to question or judge its measure. If we fulfil our capacity and give back to mankind, then it is accepted by God, however little or how much it may be. If my capacity is a tablespoon-full or a thimble-full or a bucket-full, provided I give of my full amount this will be acceptable in the sight of God. Remember, no other human being has the right to judge another individual, by saying or thinking, "Well, you know, I can give a bucket-full, why can't you?" because he may not have the same capacity. We have no right to question any apparent difference, and what is worse, since you don't know what your capacity is, you too may have fallen short in the eyes of God.

He hath endowed every soul with the capacity to recognize the signs of God. How could He, otherwise, have fulfilled His testimony unto men, if ye be of them that ponder His Cause in their hearts. He will never deal unjustly with any one, neither will He task a soul beyond its power. He, verily, is the Compassionate, the All-Merciful.[170]

Purge your sight, that ye may perceive its glory with your own eyes, and depend not on the sight of anyone except yourself, for God hath never burdened any soul beyond its power.[171]

Naturally there will be periods of distress and difficulty, and even severe tests; but if that person turns firmly toward the Divine Manifestation, studies carefully His Spiritual teachings and receives the blessings of the Holy Spirit, he will find that in reality these tests and difficulties have been the gifts of God to enable him to grow and develop.[172]

Today the greatness of the believers of God depends upon delivering the Cause of God, diffusing the fragrances of God, self-sacrifice in the love of Bahá'u'lláh and attainment to attraction, love, knowledge and wisdom. This door is open before the face of everyone and this arena is spacious for the skill of all. Everyone must think of this alone and know that success and prosperity depend upon it.

Whenever the heart finds attraction, the spirit seeks ecstasy and exultation and turns itself toward the Kingdom, the confirmation of the Holy Spirit will descend. Thou wilt be taught and encouraged; thy tongue will be loosened, uttering clear and decisive explanations. Therefore, when one has attained to spiritual success and prosperity, material advantage will not be of much importance . . .

Rest assured . . . the breaths of the Holy Spirit will aid you provided no doubts obtain in your heart.[173]

Backbiting

Backbiting is another of those activities which should be avoided at all costs and under all conditions. Gossiping about others and their lives is corrosive and is also a very quick route to putting your own life under the spotlight. Social media is a medium which unfortunately directly or indirectly encourages this ugliness in us and we need to be very careful not to succumb, particularly as once it is out there it can never be retrieved.

> . . . backbiting quencheth the light of the heart, and extinguisheth the life of the soul.[174]

> O SON OF BEING! How couldst thou forget thine own faults and busy thyself with the faults of others? Whoso doeth this is accursed of Me.[175]

Envy

The futility of jealousy has long been recognized but perhaps what we fail to understand is that when we harbour jealousy or envy in our hearts it has the effect of contaminating our prayers and making them impotent.

> Envy closes the door of Bounty and jealousy prevents one from ever attaining to the Kingdom of Abhá.[176]

We have to feel happy for everybody, however great their blessings appear, and be content with whatever our own lives have given us. It is this condition of acceptance untarnished by envy which will give our prayers meaning and our spirits comfort. On the other hand, striving to serve as effectively as others is a good objective to long for in our prayers.

> There are some people who make this short span of life miserable for themselves and others because they harbour envy in their hearts. Envy is the most despicable quality in man. Some people are so filled with it that they cannot bear to see any of their friends receive greater privileges and higher promotions in life than themselves. Like poison envy kills all their nobler sentiments. Envy lowers the station of man and makes him a supreme egoist, and self-centered. If man extricates himself from the claws of this ignoble monster he has defeated the powers of Satan. Then he will attain tranquillity and peace of mind.[177]

> O SON OF EARTH! Know, verily, the heart wherein the least remnant of envy yet lingers, shall never attain My everlasting dominion, nor inhale the sweet savours of holiness breathing from My kingdom of sanctity.[178]

You see, dear friends, you may pray, meditate and teach, but if you harbour envy or jealousy and backbite, you are accursed and cannot enter His Kingdom. We must on a daily basis be vigilant about not letting these less obvious failings corrupt our lives and spiritual development. We need to have a pure heart and pray that we may be cleansed of all of these defects.

How noble and excellent is man if he only attain to that state for which he was designed. And how mean and contemptible if he close his eyes to the public weal and spend his precious capacities on personal and selfish ends. The greatest happiness lies in the happiness of others. He who urges the matchless steed of endeavour on the race course of justice and civilization alone is capable of comprehending the wonderful signs of the natural and spiritual world.[179]

WORK IS WORSHIP

There are signs that a culture is developing in many parts of the world wherein young people tend to look on work as a chore and think that if it can be avoided legitimately or otherwise that is their option of choice. There also may be a misconception that because Bahá'u'lláh exalts detachment we should not care for money, and consequently there is no need to earn. No, on the contrary. 'Abdu'l-Bahá quotes the Prophet Muhammad who said:

> Man in this world must be so attentive to his worldly affairs and temporal necessary pursuits, that it may seem as though he thinks he is going to live forever in this world, and he must, at the same time, be so submerged in the love of God and occupied with thought of hereafter, that it may seem as though he is going to die and leave this earth at the very moment.[180]

Detachment is not an excuse for idleness nor should we be looking to others to support us. Begging by Bahá'ís is forbidden and is abhorred by God. We are exhorted to work, and work is clearly given an elevated status of service. It is required of all of us and does not necessarily imply remuneration. Working also gives us self-respect. Every individual who works is in essence worshipping

God. It is irrelevant what our occupation may be or what service we are providing so long as we are doing it to the best of our capacity in the spirit of service to mankind. In the sight of God, every such endeavour is worthy of respect and appreciation.

> O MY SERVANT! The best of men are they that earn a livelihood by their calling and spend upon themselves and upon their kindred for the love of God, the Lord of all worlds.[181]

BECOMING A SPIRITUAL MAGNET

We are probably not aware that our faces may be a mirror of our inner feelings and spiritual being. What we are also not aware of is that if we are spiritually at peace we exude something akin to an aura that is frequently noticeable to others and they are often attracted to it. This is from a Tablet of 'Abdu'l-Bahá:

> O Thou seeker of the Kingdom!
>
> Thou hast forwarded thy photograph and it was considered. In thy face a brilliant light is apparent and that sparkling light is the love of God. All faces are dark except the face which is a mirror of the light of the love of divinity. This light is not accidental – it is eternal. It is not temporal but real. When the heart hath become clear and pure then the face will become illuminated, because the face is the mirror of the heart.[182]

Do not underestimate the impact of a joyous face. I'm sure that many of you must have heard friends say, "Oh, your face is really shining. You look so happy. Your face is so beautiful." And yet, you know that your face is not beautiful as beauty is commonly understood, as defined for example by the film makers in Hollywood. But it is a face that attracts people to you. It is a magnet. That is the love of God and Bahá'u'lláh in you, which becomes like a magnet. It only comes through prayer, reading the Holy Writings and by really putting it into action – meditating, considering how to act and then acting. These things bring about results and then you are confirmed and it shines in your face!

It is necessary, absolutely necessary for us to keep to a daily routine of accessing the Writings, praying and meditating. However, if you want to be a magnet and attract people to the Faith you need to become a channel that has been emptied of everything, and filled with love for Bahá'u'lláh.

This means that we have to so love and respect this glorious Faith of ours that our actions do not tarnish the reputation of the Faith nor diminish us in the eyes of others by not reflecting the teachings in our day-to-day interactions.

> My imprisonment doeth Me no harm, neither the tribulations I suffer, nor the things that have befallen Me at the hands of My oppressors. That which harmeth Me is the conduct of those who, though they bear My name, yet commit that which maketh My heart and My pen to lament.[183]

You have become a Bahá'í of your own free will, so why would you knowingly behave in a way that would sadden the spirit of Bahá'u'lláh? Being mindful of your actions every moment of your day is a continuous demonstration of your love for Bahá'u'lláh. Remember that this is a love which will endure throughout the eternity of your existence, both physical and spiritual. Bahá'u'lláh says in the *Hidden Words*:

> O SON OF BEING! Love Me that I may love thee. If thou lovest Me not, My love can in no wise reach thee. Know this, O servant.[184]

We know, of course, that Bahá'u'lláh and God love all of humankind. The gardener loves his garden, and the farmer loves his orchard and tends to everything. But at the end of the day only the fruits and flowers that are the best are picked and give the most joy, because they have really met the grower's expectations by blossoming and flourishing to perfection.

Your love for your fellow beings and for Bahá'u'lláh is not evidenced by words expressing love. These words are empty unless you back them up with action, thereby becoming a magnet which others are drawn to and in some cases powerless to resist. This is what 'Abdu'l-Bahá has always encouraged us to be. It is not impossible for us to be this magnet which at this stage of the history of the Faith is aiming to attract others in the endeavour of starting the building of a new World Order to last for thousands of years. But as I keep saying, it takes effort on our part now, however far in the future Bahá'u'lláh's vision for the future may seem. Why deprive ourselves of the happiness we have been promised in the next world as acknowledgement of our efforts in this world if we fail to fulfil our contribution to this task?

I'm reminded of a story. At the time when 'Abdu'l-Bahá was in the United States, a young lady went up to Him and said: "Master, give me something to do for the Cause. I'm ready to do whatever you want me to do."

The Master said, "Well, go into the kitchen and wash dishes."

Occasionally 'Abdu'l-Bahá had his own cook and sometimes they would cook Persian food also. The Persian food sticks to the pots, making them very difficult to wash. In those days they didn't have dishwashers, so this poor lady spent the whole time in the kitchen washing dishes, compounded by a constant flow of people coming and going. The lady's name was Grace, but 'Abdu'l-Bahá would call her Grease. She wept, saying: "I'm in grease up to my elbows, and 'Abdu'l-Bahá even calls me Grease. He doesn't even call me Grace!"

After a short period of time, while 'Abdu'l-Bahá was still there, He introduced her to a nice young man and He arranged the marriage, which He performed, and on the day of the wedding He called her Grace.

It's not that 'Abdu'l-Bahá did not know how to pronounce her name, but we all have to work upwards from Grease to Grace. We're not Grace just because we think we are. We're not Bahá'ís just because we think we are and call ourselves Bahá'ís. To be a true Bahá'í we have to do any kind of work in connection with the Faith that helps the progress of the Faith. If we clean the Bahá'í

Centre, stick a label, or stamp envelopes, we may think that it's a menial job, and that it's below us. There's nothing below us! It's an honour. It's a privilege to do any type of work that needs to be done in this Cause, because we are building a new civilization, where humanity for a few thousand years will have peace and happiness. For that, we all have to do whatever we can. Forget thinking about what is my station and what is not. Whatever is to be done, we must roll up our sleeves and do it.

WHAT IS TEACHING?

I would like to clarify what I believe true teaching is. Simply giving the message to someone is proclamation; it's not teaching. Teaching is attracting and encouraging people, with the help of Bahá'u'lláh, into the Faith, deepening them, and preparing them to be another teacher.

There are so many examples of great teachers who were early pioneers during the Ten Year Crusade. Let me give you an example of a lady who went from Bombay to pioneer to another part of India where the word Bahá'í had not yet arrived. She made a few friends and then her mother in Bombay became very sick so she returned to Bombay. It took a long time before she could go back to her pioneering post.

When she finally returned to her house her garden was full of grass which was so high that there were plenty of snakes around. This meant that neither the new Bahá'ís nor her friends would come to the house because they were afraid. She was a widow and no longer young so she couldn't do anything herself about cutting the grass. She had nobody to help and like so many pioneers she didn't have any spare money. She just had enough money to keep body and soul together. She was at a complete loss about what to do but she did pray daily for some inspiration. One day after praying she said: "Bahá'u'lláh, you know I can't cut the grass. Even if I try to get a machete, I don't have the energy and my back hurts. What am I supposed to do?" Nothing happened. No ideas came. No inspiration, but she would always pray at dawn. She prayed again, and again.

One day while she was praying on the veranda where it was cool, she finally made a decision: "Alright Bahá'u'lláh, I have a little money. I will buy a machete and try. All I have to do is try, isn't it?" Her major concern was that by leaving the yard as it was she could have no teaching activities in her home. As she was thinking that she would go and purchase a machete and start cutting from one end of the garden to the other (her eyes had been shut in contemplation), she opened her eyes and there was a man standing there. He said "Excuse me, do you mind if I cut the grass and collect it for my cattle? I'm willing to pay you 200 rupees."

It was neither a coincidence, nor a miracle. It was the confirmation of her prayers and her meditation and her action. Praying alone hadn't worked. She also realized that the meditation had to be put into action. By making the decision that she would do everything in her power to cut the grass and make her home welcoming to others, her sincere motives were confirmed by the unexpected appearance of the man, who came to cut the grass and paid her on top of it!

Her mother was sufficiently better to bring her from Bombay to live with her so that she would not have to leave her pioneering post again. However, her mother was very old and she thought, "My God, if she dies, how and where will I bury her?" She then started to pray again, saying: "Bahá'u'lláh, help me. I don't know what to do. I'm all alone. There are just a few new Bahá'ís here. There is no land, no money and what will I do, and where will I bury her?"

This was her preoccupation for a few days. But there was no way that she could take action. She prayed, she meditated, she knew that this was necessary, but how and what? She was stuck. She then prayed and said: "Bahá'u'lláh, please help me. Show me the way. If you show me the way, I'll act."

Then an old friend of hers came by and said: "You look worried, what's the matter?"

She answered: "I'm concerned that my mother is very old and we Bahá'ís have to be buried, and we don't have any burial grounds here and where could I bury my mother if she dies?"

Her friend said: "Come with me. I have a friend in the government. Perhaps he can help you. He's in charge of municipal land."

She agreed, quickly got dressed and went with him. The official gave her a large acreage of land which was the best plot available for burial. Now, her mother is buried there, as is she. Perhaps you still believe that these events are all coincidences, I am more inclined to believe the rational answer is divine intervention!

All that you are asked to do is believe with all of your heart and soul, and do all that He asks us to do. That's all there is to it. Similar to anything we bring home, your radio or streaming device, or when we board a plane, there is an instruction sheet, and we follow it, and the plane takes off. It is as simple as that. But we have to make sure that everything is functioning and we precisely follow the instruction sheet, which in the case of Bahá'ís is to follow His laws, to pray and to teach. If we do these things, events happen which we could never have believed possible.

We must teach His Cause with love, not as a duty, not as a chore, but as an offering of pure love, to help other people who are suffering. We are so privileged that we have the remedy in our hands, given to us by Bahá'u'lláh and we are duty bound to share it with others with the greatest of love.

Two years ago, in Japan, a Japanese woman walked into a meeting where I was speaking and I asked her: "What's troubling you?"

"Really, I have everything. Nothing is troubling me. But I do want to know one thing. Why was I created?"

As 'Abdu'l-Bahá says, whenever you want an answer to a question, turn to Bahá'u'lláh. Immediately, I internally turned to Him and I was moved to ask Mr Gary Wyckoff, a Bahá'í pioneer, to show her in the Japanese Bahá'í prayer book, the short obligatory prayer which includes the words "Thou hast created me to know Thee and to worship Thee". She read the prayer and said: "I'm a Bahá'í." On a return trip to Japan I asked after her, not only to find she was an active Bahá'í, but that her husband had also become a Bahá'í.

If I had not turned to Bahá'u'lláh, you can guess I would have taken four hours explaining to her why she was created, probably to no good effect. So this is the proof of what Bahá'u'lláh says, to give the teachings in their pure form – that means to give His words.

Another example is of a travel teacher travelling in India. She met a Rajah in one of the small states. The travel teacher talked to him about the Faith and he asked if we have any laws. He said: "Yes, one of the laws is that you must fast."

"Why must I fast?"

"It'll take me four hours to explain."

"Well, I have four hours, so tell me."

After the four-hour explanation, the Rajah asked him: "Who said I must fast?"

The teacher answered: "Bahá'u'lláh."

The Rajah said: "Why didn't you tell me that four hours ago?" He became a Bahá'í and is very active, and has been a member of the National Spiritual Assembly of the Bahá'ís of India.

This goes to show that we could save much time and energy by simply saying Bahá'u'lláh said this, Bahá'u'lláh said that . . . why do we have to put our own opinion in and drag out the conversation, showing we know best? That's why Bahá'u'lláh says that even a five-year-old child can "teach my Cause". Because that five-year-old child has no opinion, and simply recites the words of God.

He suggests that you daily pray to Bahá'u'lláh to let you meet a soul receptive to His Message. The power of prayer is very great, and attracts the Divine confirmations. He, also, will pray for your teaching work there.[185]

Just one mature soul, with spiritual understanding and a profound knowledge of the Faith, can set a whole country ablaze – so great is the power of the Cause to work through a pure and selfless channel![186]

If thou wishest for everlasting joy and happiness, engage thou in delivering (teaching) the Cause of God night and day, for the commemoration of God attracts confirmation and assistance like unto a magnet.[187]

The individual alone must assess its character, consult his conscience, prayerfully consider all its aspects, manfully struggle against the natural inertia that weighs him down in his effort to arise, shed, heroically and irrevocably the trivial and superfluous attachments which hold him back, empty himself of every thought that may tend to obstruct his path, mix, in obedience to the counsels of the Author of his Faith, and in imitation of the One who is its true Exemplar, with men and women, in all walks of life, seek to touch their hearts through the distinction which characterizes his thoughts, his words, and his acts, and win them over, tactfully, lovingly, prayerfully and persistently to the Faith he himself has espoused.[188]

The responsibility of steady progress of the Cause depends upon you! You are the physicians of the sick body of the world of humanity! You must not stay anywhere for a long time. Travel ye from land to land like the Apostles of Christ, and carry with you the glad

tidings of the Kingdom of Abhá to the remotest cor-
ners of the earth![189]

While of course we are very anxious to do the teaching
work, particularly mass teaching, we should remember
the words of our beloved Guardian:

> Without the spirit of real love for Bahá'u'lláh, for His
> Faith and its Institutions, and the believers for each
> other, the Cause can never really bring in large num-
> bers of people. For it is not preaching and rules the
> world wants, but love and action.[190]

Without this, we cannot really bring in very large numbers of seekers. Again, and again, it is dependent upon
our actions. Words, said Bahá'u'lláh, belong to others.
Actions belong to His loved ones.

> O SON OF MY HANDMAID! Guidance hath ever
> been given by words, and now it is given by deeds.
> Everyone must show forth deeds that are pure and
> holy, for words are the property of all alike, whereas
> such deeds as these belong only to Our loved ones.
> Strive then with heart and soul to distinguish your-
> selves by your deeds. In this wise We counsel you in
> this holy and resplendent tablet.[191]

FASTING

The period of the Fast is approximately 2 March through to 20 March depending on the time of the vernal equinox. The *Kitáb-i-Aqdas* states:

> We have commanded you to pray and fast from the beginning of maturity [15 years]; this is ordained by God, your Lord, and the Lord of your forefathers . . . The traveller, the ailing, those who are with child or giving suck, are not bound by the Fast . . . Abstain from food and drink, from sunrise to sundown, and beware lest desire deprive you of this grace that is appointed in the Book.[192]

We may well ask ourselves, what Divine Wisdom is there in fasting?

> The Divine wisdom in fasting is manifold. Among them is this: as during those days (i.e. the period of fasting which the followers afterwards observe) the Manifestation of the Sun of Reality, through Divine inspiration, is engaged in the descent (revealing) of Verses, the instituting of Divine Law and the arrangement of teachings, through excessive occupation and intense attraction there remains no condition or

time for eating and drinking. For example, when His Holiness Moses went to Mount Tur (Sinai) and there engaged in instituting the Law of God, he fasted forty days. For the purpose of awakening and admonishing the people of Israel, fasting was enjoined upon them. Likewise, His Holiness Christ, in the beginning of instituting the Spiritual Law, the systematizing of the teachings and the arrangement of counsels, for forty days abstained from eating and drinking. In the beginning the disciples and Christians fasted. Later the assemblages of the Christians changed fasting into Lenten observances.

Likewise the Qur'án having descended in the month of Ramadán, fasting during that month became a duty. In like manner His Holiness the Supreme (the Báb), in the beginning of the Manifestation, through the excessive effect of descending Verses, passed days in which his nourishment was reduced to tea only.

Likewise, the Blessed Beauty (Bahá'u'lláh), when busy with instituting the Divine Teachings and during the days when the Verses (Word of God) descended continuously, through great effect of the Verses and the throbbing of the heart, took no food except the least amount.

The purpose is this: in order to follow the Divine Manifestations and for the purpose of admonition and the commemoration of their state, it became incumbent upon the people to fast during those days. For every sincere soul who has a beloved, longs to experience that state in which his beloved is. If his beloved is in a state of sorrow he desires sorrow; if in a state of joy, he desires joy; if in a state of rest, he desires rest; if in a state of trouble, he desires trouble.

Now, since in this Millennial Day, His Holiness the Supreme (the Báb) fasted many days, and the Blessed Beauty (Bahá'u'lláh) took but little food or drink, it becomes necessary that the friends should follow that example. For thus saith He in the Tablet of Visitation: "They, the believers, have followed that which they were commanded, for love of Thee." This is one wisdom of fasting.

The second wisdom is this: Fasting is the cause of awakening man. The heart becomes tender and the spirituality of man increases. This is produced by the fact that man's thoughts will be confined to the com-memoration of God, and through this awakening and stimulation surely ideal advancements follow.

Third wisdom: Fasting is of two kinds, material and spiritual. The material fasting is abstaining from food or drink, that is from the appetites of the body. But spiritual, ideal Fasting is this, that man abstain from selfish passions, from negligence and from satanic animal traits. Therefore, material fasting is a token of the spiritual fasting.

That is: "O God! as I am fasting from the appetites of the body and not occupied with eating and drink-ing, even so purify and make holy my heart and my life from aught else save Thy Love, and protect and preserve my soul from self, passions and animal traits. Thus may the spirit associate with the Fragrances of

Holiness and fast from everything else save Thy mention."[193]

Nothing, after prayer, will cause the development of the spirit, save fasting. The "First Point", the Báb, ordained for all the people to fast until they should reach the age of forty-two, but the Blessed Perfection, Bahá'u'lláh, said: "We love fasting! Unless the people become old and weak, they should fast." Thus the limit for fasting was appointed. One should begin to observe the fast from the age of fifteen, and continue the observance of it until the body may become too weak to do so without injury. His Holiness, The Blessed Perfection used to fast throughout the set time every year.

In the *Kitáb-i-Aqdas*, the rules for fasting are as follows: eating and drinking should cease before the rising of the sun and until the setting thereof. The traveller, the sick, pregnant women and nursing mothers are free from obligation.

In Mark 9, 7–29, is related the story of the afflicted child who was brought to Jesus by the disciples after their vain efforts to cast out from him the spirit which tormented him, and of his being healed by Jesus, who said in reply to a question from the disciples that: "This kind can come forth by nothing but by prayer and fasting."

Thus Jesus taught that fasting and praying give strength to the spirit of man, so that it may become enabled to heal the different violent and strong sicknesses which possess him.

The results and fruits of these acts are innumerable, but the few that have been mentioned are the principal ones. We ask the Merciful Lord that this blessed act may become a cause of quenching the fires of lustfulness, animosity and hatred.

"Peace be upon him who follows and carries out the Commands revealed in the Heavenly Books!"[194]

This period of fasting affords us an opportunity to receive inspiration. This cannot happen if our thoughts are all the time on food and drink. Rather, they should be on the Holy Writings because after saying your prayers and meditating upon the Holy Writings, you wait for inspiration and then you should act upon it. Inspiration won't always come and you shouldn't delay action because it isn't there. If you are focused and sincere about teaching the Faith, follow your instincts and be alert to every opportunity, which I am sure will bear fruit.

Don't do what I did as a teenager with one eye on the clock, lying in bed, and just five minutes before the sun rises, dash and have a cup of tea and a slice of toast and then in the evening, with another eye on the clock, dash to grab something to eat at the moment the sun sets. That's not the way to fast. We are often reminded in the Writings that dawn is one of the best times to pray, so since we have to get up before the sun rises, why not use this time wisely and create some peace and space in our minds and hearts to commune with God at our leisure? It is also sensible to approach the day with sufficient sustenance and hydration to sustain you physically so you are able to go about your daily chores and business successfully. My experience has been that this is also not a time to introduce another motive such as losing weight; it rarely works. This is a spiritual period in our year which has only one purpose: to get nearer to God.

We have to approach the Fast sensibly and spiritually, and use it as a time to focus on eliminating our shortcomings. Only each one of us knows our own weaknesses. We must pray and pray and beg Bahá'u'lláh to ask God to help us get rid of our imperfections. The best period for this is during the Fast when we can cultivate a strengthening sense of detachment from material and earthly temptations.

In Japan, when I talked to the Bahá'ís about the Fast and showed them the relevant quotations from the Writings, the Japanese youth could not wait for the first day. They all fasted and were teaching enthusiastically and bringing many people into the Faith, including their families. The same thing happened in Korea.

You see, when we say prayers it should have an effect on ourselves. It's not as though we were an organ or a piano, when the music produced has no influence on the instrument.

One has to first study the prayers word by word, enjoy the words and try to understand the mysteries in them. Then, read the prayers, and you will see how your souls are uplifted. It is very important that we spend time in the morning and in the evening to recite the holy verses. But in between during the lunch break when you won't be eating lunch so will have more time, you can teach the Faith and it will have a tremendous impact. This is really the best time to teach because you are freed from spending time to take in food for your body and you're earning food for your soul, and food for other people's souls, which is the whole purpose of our lives.

Just a note to mention who are exempt from the Fast:

(a) Travellers
   i. Provided the journey exceeds 9 hours.
   ii. Those travelling on foot, provided the journey exceeds 2 hours.
   iii. Those who break their journey for less than 19 days.
   iv. Those who break their journey during the Fast at a place where they are to stay 19 days are exempt from fasting only for the first three days from their arrival.
   v. Those who reach home during the Fast must commence fasting from the day of their arrival.
(b) Those who are ill.
(c) Those who are over seventy.
(d) Women who are with child.
(e) Women who are nursing.
(f) Women in their courses, provided they perform their ablutions and repeat a specifically revealed verse ninety-five times a day.
(g) Those who are engaged in heavy labour, who are advised to show respect for the law by using discretion and restraint when availing themselves of the exemption.

Note: In the *Codification of the Book of the Kitáb-i-Aqdas*, it is mentioned that in Arabic the verb drink also applies to smoking.[195]

There was a young woman who was a lawyer in a large international company and wanted to fast. The matter came to a head because many business meetings continue over lunch. She approached her boss to explain the situation but he said: "No, you cannot fast. It affects the brain and you know what important business we do during lunch time."

She said: "Look, sir. This is my religion and I'm going to fast. At lunch, if I falter or if you feel I am not doing the job properly, then we shall see and we'll talk about it."

He agreed and said: "Fair enough."

As a matter of fact, she sat through many lunches with senior executives from different parts of the world, discussing business and often able to explain why she was not eating which had the added advantage of teaching the Faith. For the entirety of her career she fasted in many destinations around the world and was blessed with professional success and earned the respect of her colleagues.

Lauded by Thy name, O my God! This is the hour when Thou hast unlocked the portals of Thy tender mercy unto all the dwellers of Thine earth.[196]

"This is the hour" means that it is not only for Bahá'ís, but for every human being on this earth.

This is the hour, O my Lord, which Thou hast caused to excel every other hour, and hast related to the choicest among Thy creatures. . . I beseech Thee, O my God, by Thy Self and by them, to ordain in the course of this year what shall exalt Thy loved ones. Do Thou, moreover, decree within this year what will enable the Daystar of Thy power to shine brightly above the horizon of Thy glory, and to illuminate by Thy sovereign might, the whole world.[197]

We have lots of extra time, since we aren't eating or drinking, to go out and teach, meet with the friends and teach the Cause, so that we can become what Bahá'u'lláh wants us to become – exalted! Just read each and every word in this prayer, very carefully, not necessarily as a prayer, but read it to try to understand what He is saying. Here, at the end, it continues:

Render Thy Cause victorious, O my Lord, and abase Thou Thine enemies. Write down, then, for us the good of this life and of the life to come. Thou art the Truth, Who knoweth the secret things. No God is there but Thee, the Ever-Forgiving, the All-Bountiful.[198]

You see, first God showers down all of His bounties on the whole of this world, unlocks the doors of His bounties before the faces of His creatures and opens wide the portals of His tender mercy. Then we need to start teaching, because it is a special hour for His loved ones.

Inspire then my soul, O my God, with Thy wondrous remembrance, that I may glorify Thy name. Number me not with them who read Thy words and fail to find Thy hidden gift which, as decreed by Thee, is contained therein, and which quickeneth the souls of Thy creatures and the hearts of Thy servants. Cause me, O my Lord, to be reckoned among them who have been so stirred up by the sweet savours that have been wafted in Thy days that they have laid down their lives for Thee and hastened to the scene of their death in their longing to gaze on Thy beauty and in their yearning to attain Thy presence. And were anyone to say unto them on their way, "Whither go ye?" they would say, "Unto God, the All-Possessing, the Help in Peril, the Self- Subsisting".[199]

Do Thou, moreover, decree within this year what will enable the Daystar of Thy power to shine brightly above the horizon of Thy glory, and to illuminate by Thy sovereign might, the whole world.[200]

The fasting period of nineteen days is the time we can teach, when we will get more bounties through our efforts, and more victories to illuminate the whole world.

Here's a true story of a Bahá'í who truly understood the importance of the Fast and how to teach. A young man was at boarding school in the United Kingdom. When he reached the age of fifteen and it was the month of March he wanted to carry out his first Fast. On the 1st of March he told his Housemaster: "From tomorrow I have to fast.

I will bring some milk and cornflakes and start my fast at sunrise and I will break it at sunset."

The Headmaster said: "No, no, no – you can't do that in this school. You know you must abide by the regulations."

The youth replied: "Sir, I'm very sorry, but I'm fifteen now and I have to fast."

He insisted so much that the Housemaster sent him to the Headmaster. It's not very easy for a young boy of 15 to go to see the principal of a big boarding school in the UK, but he did. And the principal said: "No, you can't fast."

The youth again responded, "Sir, I am very sorry but these are the laws of my religion, and I have to fast. I will be of no trouble to anyone. I don't want any special arrangements. I'll take milk and cornflakes and I'll be happy with that."

The Headmaster still said: "No."

When the boy answered: "I thought that this was a free country," he realized that this boy was determined, so he said: "Alright, you can fast, but you have to come down and attend all of the meals – that is breakfast, lunch and tea. You must dress up and come and sit there while the other boys eat."

The boy accepted. He would dress up and go and sit at every meal and the boys would tease him, passing around his favourite foods under his nose and making fun of him. But for nineteen days, he held firm and came every day and sat there. At the end of the nineteen days, there were many students who respected him and several of his teachers as well. I am led to believe, that some of them became Bahá'ís. He was not afraid of 400 students or his masters teasing him. He was with Bahá'u'lláh – very firm, very strong. Others looked foolish, and he became a hero. We have to be strong, no matter what age we are. Once we follow the laws of Bahá'u'lláh, no matter what anyone says, we will be successful.

THE FUND

The Bahá'í Fund is the lifeblood of the Faith and it's a privilege and a bounty given exclusively to Bahá'ís to be able to contribute financially to the Faith. Regarding the Fund 'Abdu'l-Bahá tells us:

All the friends of God . . . should contribute to the extent possible, however modest their offering may be. God doth not burden a soul beyond its capacity. Such contributions must come from all centres and all believers . . . O Friends of God! Be ye assured that in place of these contributions, your agriculture, your industry, and your commerce will be blessed by manifold increases, with goodly gifts and bestowals. He who cometh with one goodly deed will receive a tenfold reward. There is no doubt that the living Lord will abundantly confirm those who expend their wealth in His path.

O God, my God! Illumine the brows of Thy true lovers, and support them with angelic hosts of certain triumph. Set firm their feet on Thy straight path, and out of Thine ancient bounty open before them the portals of Thy blessings; for they are expending on Thy pathway what Thou hast bestowed upon them, safeguarding Thy Faith, putting their trust in their remembrance of Thee, offering up their hearts for love of Thee, and withholding not what they possess in adoration for Thy Beauty and in their search for ways to please Thee.

O my Lord! Ordain for them a plenteous share, a destined recompense and sure reward.

Verily, Thou art the Sustainer, the Helper, the Generous, the Bountiful, the Ever-Bestowing.[201]

Study this prayer, dear friends. Then when you say it you will understand when 'Abdu'l-Bahá says: "Be assured that in place of these contributions, your agriculture, your industry, and your commerce will be blessed by manifold increases, with goodly gifts and bestowals." There's no way you can doubt this. Why do you trust banks and insurance companies with your money? Why not trust Bahá'u'lláh with some of your money in His Cause so this world will be a better place to live in? Then we need have no fear that our money or our lives will be wasted. At least we have done something for future generations in building a new world.

There are many stories about people who have sacrificed to give to the Fund. If you remember, when they were building the Mashriqu'l-Adhkár (House of Worship) in the United States, there was this poor elderly widow who had nothing. As she was going toward the future House of Worship, she found a discarded stone in an old building site. She asked if she could take this and put it in a wheelbarrow, and with the help of a seven-year-old boy took it and gave it to 'Abdu'l-Bahá, and he used that as the Foundation Stone, because that was all that she had.

I have known Bahá'ís in India who would give everything they have, and then they would weep. I used to think as a little girl that they were weeping because they were sorry that they had given their all. One man said: "No, I'm sorry that I don't have more to give." This is what the Guardian means when he said that you should give until it hurts

You might be interested to know that most of the money needed to purchase the largest and most expensive plot for the Indian House of Worship was given by a small restaurant owner, a Bahá'í of Zoroastrian background who came from humble origins. Questioned about his gift, he said, "I did not have a penny when I started. All that I accumulated was given to me by God. Now the money was needed for His purposes I am only a temporary trustee." Now blessings will be with him for eternity. What bank would give you that kind of interest? What insurance company would assure you that kind of glory in this world and the next, dear friends? This is something to think about. I'm not telling you to give your life's savings. That's not my place. I'm just telling you about things that wonderful people have done.

During one of my early trips to Japan, I attended a Women's Conference in Kyoto and I talked about the Fund and told some of these stories. There was a young American pioneer living in Japan, who said: "I've always wanted to give a large sum to the Faith. Today I'm here. I've got my return ticket. I don't need anything else."

Everything else he had he put into the fund box. Then he went home. When he arrived he found that lots of bills were awaiting him. He looked at them and said: "O, my God. I got all emotional and look what I've done!" Then he reconsidered and said: "Wait a minute. Let me think." The more he thought the worse it got. He remembered that he had invited all of his friends to come to his house-warming, because he had a new apartment which still needed to be furnished. The more he thought about it the worse his situation seemed. "What have I done?" Then he thought, "Why don't I do the next step – pray and ask for guidance as to what I should do." So he prayed and got guidance that he should go to a second-hand furniture shop. He went there and the shop was closed. So he went to the shopping centre, and found that the prices were sky-high and he had no money. He thought that if he did have money, he still couldn't have afforded that much.

Something told him to go back to the second-hand shop. When he got back there, he found a truck in front of the shop and the woman was putting all kinds of furniture into a truck. He asked her, "What happened?"

"Nothing," she answered, "This building is going to be demolished and I'm taking all of the furniture away."

"Well, where are you taking the furniture?"

"I'm throwing it away."

He asked if he could have some and she said: "By all means" and even helped him fill up his car twice and he got all of the furniture he needed for his own big apartment, plus a garage full of lovely furniture for a future bigger house.

With that, he said: "Thank you, Bahá'u'lláh. That has settled my house. It's all organized and the guests can come. But what about money for food? I have no money. I've given everything away." Then he got a telephone call from an American lady in that area, who was not a Bahá'í, and who had about twelve students in her English classes. She called to ask him to please take over teaching her students for her, because she had to return to the States for good. All of these classes would give him a very nice income. So then he had the money, he had the furniture, and then later on he got more students, so now he has a bigger house and half of it is just like a little private school.

You have to understand these affirmations can come to all of us, no matter what our age or where we are. We all have to try out our faith. Nobody can tell you what to do or what not to do with your money. These are matters left entirely to your own conscience and circumstances. These stories should give us the courage to follow our hearts. No doubt, even after we've contributed the money, doubts may occur but all we need to do is to turn to Bahá'u'lláh and trust in Him.

We often say that we trust in Bahá'u'lláh. But 'Abdu'l-Bahá says that we do not trust in Him, because if we did, we would have no fear. One has to test one's own faith to see the results.

THE NINETEEN DAY FEAST

If a small number of people gather lovingly together, with absolute purity and sanctity, with their hearts free of the world, experiencing the emotions of the Kingdom and the powerful magnetic forces of the Divine, and being at one in their happy fellowship, that gathering will exert its influence over all the earth. The nature of that band of people, the words they speak, the deeds they do, will unleash the bestowals of Heaven, and provide a foretaste of eternal bliss. The hosts of the Company on high will defend them, and the angels of the Abhá Paradise, in continuous succession, will come down to their aid.[202]

O ye loyal servant of the Ancient Beauty! In every cycle and dispensation, the feast hath been favoured and loved, and the spreading of a table for the lovers of God hath been considered a praiseworthy act. This is especially the case today, in this dispensation beyond compare, this most generous of ages, when it is highly acclaimed, for it is truly accounted among such gatherings as are held to worship and glorify God. Here the holy verses, the heavenly odes and laudations are intoned, and the heart is quickened, and carried away from itself.

The primary intent is to kindle these stirrings of the spirit, but at the same time it follows quite naturally that those present should partake of food, so that the world of the body may mirror the spirit's world, and flesh take on the qualities of soul; and just as the spiritual delights are here in profusion, so too the material delights.

Happy are ye, to be observing this rule, with all its mystic meanings, thus keeping the friends of God alert and heedful, and bringing them peace of mind, and joy.[203]

As to the Nineteen Day Feast, it rejoiceth mind and heart. If this feast be held in the proper fashion, the friends will, once in nineteen days, find themselves spiritually restored, and endued with a power that is not of this world.[204]

The story is told of a young man in New York who wanted to go to the local Feast but he lived in an apartment and the way to the hall would take him through an alley. In that particular alley, many people used to get mugged. So he debated with himself, "Shall I go, or shall I not go because the Feast ends quite late, and coming home will be very dangerous and I might get mugged." He knew that 'Abdu'l-Bahá called it the "Last Supper" and that He, 'Abdu'l-Bahá, would be present spiritually. He wanted to participate, so he decided to attend.

When he was coming home, it was already midnight, the alley was dimly lit and empty. As he was walking, he heard some footsteps and saw a man behind him, and he thought "This is it! Yá-Bahá'u'l-Abhá! This is the end of my life!" But the man passed by him and didn't do anything to him. So the young man got home safely and was very happy. When he awoke the next morning, he read in the newspaper that the police precinct nearest his apartment had put a notice in the paper asking if anyone had seen a person between midnight and dawn in that alley, and requesting them to report to that precinct if they had. And so he went, and looked at a line-up of suspects, and was able to identify the man that he had seen in that alley. Then he learned that about twenty minutes after the suspect had passed him in the alley he had murdered a man. This poor young Bahá'í couldn't contain himself, and he was offered the opportunity to approach and ask the man who had passed by him in the alley at midnight: "Why didn't you kill me, and instead murdered the other man?"

The man answered: "It is my policy never to attack if there are two people together."

The young man said: "But I was alone. I was with no one."

But the murderer said: "You were with an oriental man with a white turban, and a long coat, and a long beard. Don't you remember?"

The young man then answered: "Yes, I do remember". That was the description of 'Abdu'l-Bahá who had apparently seen him home safely.

We have no way of understanding or imagining the protection we are granted when we have a deep, deep faith and truly love Bahá'u'lláh, and 'Abdu'l-Bahá.

Important aspects of the preparation of the Feast include the proper selection of readings, the assignment, in advance, of good readers, and a sense of decorum both in the presentation and the reception of the devotional programme. Attention to the environment in which the Feast is to be held, whether indoors or outdoors, greatly influences the experience. Cleanliness, arrangement of the space in practical and decorative ways – all play a significant part. Punctuality is also a measure of good preparation.

To a very large extent, the success of the Feast depends on the quality of the preparation and participation of the individual. The beloved Master offers the following advice: "Give ye great weight to the Nineteen Day gatherings, so that on these occasions the beloved of the Lord and the handmaids of the Merciful may turn their faces toward the Kingdom, chant the communes, beseech God's help, become joyfully enamoured each of the other, and grow in purity and holiness, and in the fear of God, and in resistance to passion and self. Thus will they separate themselves from this elemental world, and immerse themselves in the ardours of the spirit."

In absorbing such advice, it is illuminating indeed to view the Nineteen Day Feast in the context in which it was conceived. It is ordained in the *Kitáb-i-Aqdas* in these words: "It hath been enjoined upon you once a month to offer hospitality, even should ye serve no more than water, for God hath willed to bind your hearts together, though it be through heavenly and earthly means combined." It is clear, then, that the Feast is rooted in hospitality, with all its implications of friendliness, courtesy, service, generosity and conviviality. The very idea of hospitality as the sustaining spirit of so significant an institution introduces a revolutionary new attitude to the conduct of human affairs at all levels, an attitude which is so critical to that world unity which the Central Figures of our Faith laboured so long and suffered so much cruelty to bring into being. It is in this divine festival that the foundation is laid for the realization of so unprecedented a reality.

That you may attain the high mark set for the Feast as a "bringer of joy", the "groundwork of agreement and unity", the "key to affection and fellowship" will remain an object of our ardent supplications at the Holy Threshold.[205]

The following story was recounted by Mr Ramnik Lal Shah, one of the most illustrious Secretaries of the National Spiritual Assembly of India, who served in this position for well over three decades and who passed away in 2007. R. N. Shah was a Bahá'í from a Jain background who had accepted the Faith in Mumbai, or Bombay as it was then called, in the early 1940s. The Bombay community at that time consisted mainly of stalwart Zoroastrian Bahá'ís and the sight of an Indian who had accepted the

Faith was extremely rare. Mr Shah recounts that as soon as he declared he was very eager to attend the Nineteen Day Feast and participate in the affairs of the Bombay community. With great enthusiasm he went to attend his first Feast meeting at the Bahá'í Centre which was located in a building called Krishna Building in Bombay. He says that he entered the hall where the Nineteen Day Feast was being held, enthusiastic and eager, and was immediately confronted by the Chairman of the Local Spiritual Assembly – a crusty old Iranian gentleman – who looked at Mr Shah and promptly asked him to leave the hall saying that the meeting was for Bahá'ís only. Mr Shah protested and tried to explain that he was in fact a Bahá'í. However, the Chairman of the Local Assembly was having none of it and asked him to leave the hall immediately.

Mr Shah says that as he was leaving the hall, feeling embarrassed and humiliated, he swore to himself that once he left that room he would never enter its doors again. As he was leaving, Meherangiz Munsiff came in, looked at him and said "Arrey Ramnik, where are you going?" He explained that he had been asked to leave the hall by the Chairman of the Local Spiritual Assembly since he refused to even listen to Mr Shah's protestations that he was a recently declared Bahá'í. Meherangiz took him by the arm, walked back into the hall with him and gave the Chairman of the Local Spiritual Assembly a piece of her mind.

Mr Shah was to later say that if it were not for Meherangiz Munsiff entering the Bahá'í Centre exactly at the time she did, he might never have returned to the community.

O Ye friends of God! The morn of guidance is radiant and the hearts of the people of faithfulness are like unto a garden. The divine breeze is blowing, the Spirit of God is manifest, the faded hearts are quickened and rejuvenated. Turn your faces toward the rose garden of God, for, verily, the fragrances of the Holy Spirit are passing by. Gaze ye toward the Kingdom of Abhá for his Ancient Bestowal is descending. Look ye up toward the Supreme Horizon for the Sun of Hope is dawning. This bestowal is one of the most particular gifts of this great cycle for from its beginning to its end it is the dawning place of the penetration of the lights of the Ancient Beauty. Therefore appreciate ye the value of these times and let not the opportunity slip by from your hands, for the zephyr of the morn of unity is blowing and the rays of the Sun of Reality are shining from all horizons of the universe with universal force. This century is the beginning of all future generations. The standards of guidance shall wave over all countries, yet in this period the power of confirmation is most perfect and well nigh inexhaustible and the lights of unity are irradiating from the hearts of men. To take one step in this day is equal to one hundred thousand steps in the future and to inhale one breath in this age is compared to one hundred thousand breaths in the future, for this is the beginning of the age of grace, the time of the downpour of rain and the season of the heavenly spring.[206]

Dear, dear friends, the vital purpose and elements of the preceding pages is to encourage you to read, absorb and act upon the words of Bahá'u'lláh, 'Abdu'l-Bahá, the beloved Guardian and the Universal House of Justice. The stories and explanations are simply my way of encouraging you to call upon your love for this glorious Faith of ours and to beg you to trust in God. Your successes will be glorious and your spiritual well-being will be secure through eternity. God bless you.

Appendix 1

A EULOGY

To Mrs Munsiff

So, Munsiff-san, at last the time has come to say good-bye. Was it really so long ago that you first came to us in Japan? You may remember what a difficult time that was for us here in Japan. We were lost and desperate; we didn't know what to do, how to go forward, or what the next step should be for the Faith. We were stuck, and we asked Bahá'u'lláh to send us some help. He sent us you. I almost said, "He sent us you instead." There were moments, believe me, when some of us turned to Bahá'u'lláh and said, "Wait a minute, you know, this is not exactly what we had in mind . . ." But you were exactly what He had in mind – a straight shooter in a country where people have made an art form of never quite saying what they mean. Remember when we first picked you up at the airport in Fukuoka? Picture it, we came in innocently enough, expecting to pick up a sweet harmless little old Bahá'í travelling teacher from India, and we came out feeling as if we'd been run over by a truck. Maybe two or three trucks. Guess it had been a long trip. But we got you home, settled you in, gave you something resembling a hot cup of tea, and found ourselves in the presence of a type of devotion such as we'd only ever read about before.

They told you not to come to Japan. The Japanese were too busy, they didn't believe in God, they were only interested in material things, they had an intense aversion to religion, it would be waste of time, they said. I must admit that even some of the Bahá'ís here thought so, too. As usual you said, "Don't talk rubbish" and came anyway. And instead of expecting a lack of receptivity you treated the Japanese as long-lost friends, as human souls with a natural yearning for spiritual life. And lo and behold, these materialistic money-worshipping atheists began to become Bahá'ís! What a shock! Of course, it was no shock at all to you, but it was indeed a shock to a lot of people. And the way you did it! Instead of apologetically mincing around the concepts of God and religion, you faced the issues head on, you put your cards out on the table, hiding nothing. You'd say, "Without religion in the past, where would civilization have come from? We'd still be swinging from the trees somewhere. Without religion in the future, how can we possibly expect to accomplish the Most Great Peace? Without peace what kind of a life do we have for ourselves or our children? God created you to know Him and to worship Him. And since we can't see God directly, He has sent us Bahá'u'lláh to guide us to Him. And that's good enough for me." And then you'd ask them read something from the Writings of Bahá'u'lláh out loud to see if it touched their hearts. We tried to tell you that the translations were too difficult and the style too archaic to be appreciated by the average Japanese. We suggested that perhaps you might want to explain what the words meant before asking people to read something so difficult. As usual you said, "Don't talk rubbish" and went right ahead. And you were successful. You were successful because you had no prejudices, you had complete confidence that Bahá'u'lláh had prepared many of these souls to recognize Him, and you knew without a doubt that He would help you to reach them.

Year after year you came back to us. Those first few years we couldn't maintain that same intensity after you had left. We felt overwhelmed and depressed. We were a bit ashamed, perhaps. You came back, picked us up and got us going again. You gradually taught us how to maintain our spiritual health. You taught us how to pray. You taught us what it means to meditate, and how to be sensitive to the inspirations that come to us, and you showed us that prayer and meditation mean nothing without action. And what action! You went everywhere, met everyone. Remember that first trip to Okinawa? We went with no plan, knowing no one, and ended up lunching with the Governor's wife and making friends among members of the former royal family. From Okinawa in the south to the Ainu people in Hokkaido in the north. Never stopping, never resting, seldom healthy, usually exhausted, often prostrate with a splitting headache until it was time to leave for the meeting. I'd suggest that we cancel, and you'd say, "Don't talk rubbish", and drag yourself to the car. But when you'd begin to speak the pain would leave and the spirit would flow and we'd all catch a glimpse of something very special and be transported for a few minutes to an entirely different realm.

Let's face it, you were a stubborn woman. And when

you were tired you were cranky, and we worked you so hard that you were nearly always tired. But you refused to rest very much. There was only one thing that brought you joy and made your sacrifices seem worthwhile: to confirm souls in service to Bahá'u'lláh. Here you were in your element, a teacher par excellence. Remember our meetings with the minority caste buraku group? When a radical activist called out saying that they should stand up and fight for their rights, you stood up to him and said that it was about time they stopped whining so much and tried to demonstrate their worthiness not by complaining but by rising up and serving the community so well and so selflessly as to earn by their deeds the true respect of their countrymen. I think I saw a hundred jaws hit the floor that night – no one had ever spoken to them like that before. I was interpreting for you that night. I wanted to add, "And please do remember that I'm just the translator! . . ." You could have heard a pin drop in the hall. And then after a few moments that seemed an eternity the old man who was their leader said, "Well, you know, she may have a point . . ." They accepted what you had to say, and they loved you for it!

I watched you long enough to realize that you had no real teaching method. You had no plan, no pattern, no special technique or method or approach. All you did was pray and rely completely on the inspiration of the Holy Spirit. And it didn't hurt that you had studied the Writings so thoroughly that whenever an illustration was needed you had it ready at hand. I think one of the best examples of the essence of your teaching method, if I may call it that, was in the interaction I witnessed between you and Mrs Y. You had just finished a long fireside. You were exhausted, and I was going to take you back to your hotel to rest before the evening programme. As we were leaving the house, you noticed a Japanese woman talking to one of the American Bahá'ís in an adjoining room as we passed by. She had arrived too late to attend the fireside meeting, and she was now listening somewhat disinterestedly to a long-winded and perhaps intellectual explanation of the Faith. We got to the exit and you paused. You asked me, "Is that woman a Bahá'í?" I told you no, she wasn't. You stopped for a moment. I think you were asking Bahá'u'lláh for permission to go the hotel and sleep. I guess He must have said no, because the next thing I knew you had taken off your coat and were heading back to find her. You sat down next to her took her hand and without preamble said, "Tell me, what's troubling you?" Just like that the woman suddenly burst into tears. "I don't know why I'm alive," she sobbed. Munsiff-san, you didn't say a word. You didn't explain anything or give any sage advice. You simply told me to open the prayer book and have her read the short obligatory prayer out loud. She read, "I bear witness, O my God, that Thou hast created me to know Thee and to worship Thee". When she was finished she turned to you and said, "I see what you mean. I want to be a Bahá'í." So simple, so pure, no gimmicks, no bells, no whistles, no tricks, no embellishments, no personal interpretations, nothing but the unvarnished Truth, straight from the Source.

With your help and by the grace of God we've come a long way here in Japan. You've left a wonderful legacy here. You've touched so many lives: the friends who became Bahá'ís through you, the friends whose lives will forever be enriched by having joined you on one of the several trips to Haifa that you organized, the friends who had a chance to hear directly what it was like to be in the presence of the beloved Guardian. Things were moving so slowly when you first came, but now friends all over the country are attending regular, systematic Institute classes, and the Japanese friends are taking the affairs of the Faith and the teaching work into their own hands.

Munsiff-san, I hope this latest trip hasn't been too bad. You must be glad to be finally travelling without having to pack anything. The joke says that there are no Bahá'ís in heaven because they've all gone travel teaching in hell, but I'm pretty sure that you've been there and done that already, while you were still on this earth. I know how much you hated to travel. It really was hell for you to be away from your home and your family. You derived no joy from sightseeing, or exotic foods or museums, or any of the things that ordinary travellers are supposed to enjoy. I think that you pushed yourself so hard because you wanted to repay the beloved Guardian for the love and the bounties that he showered on you. I'll pray that you attain your heart's desire. I'm pretty sure I know what you're hoping for. Now that your work is done down here I won't mind if you take it easy for a while up there. Enjoy yourself a bit, look up your old friends, have some fun – you deserve it. But I hope you won't forget about those of us left down here, however unworthy we may be. Look in on us from time to time and try to help us stay out of trouble and remain firm and steadfast in the Cause.

Oh God! Please God! I beg Thee to accept from her all that she has done. Anything that was wrong, please make it right. And everything that was right, please make it shine in glory forever and ever.

And finally, if I may, I'd like to offer a suggestion to whoever it is that is fortunate enough to get the job of carrying your bags and helping you to settle in up there – whoever you are, listen up. Remember, she tends to get a bit cranky after a long trip. Don't get upset. Just make her a good hot cup of tea. And then ask her to tell you one of her stories. And then another. And then by and by let her make you laugh. That, my friend, is when you'll really know that you're in Heaven.

Munsiff-san, good-bye for now. Thanks for everything. We love you.

Gary and Susan, Bonnie, Joseph and Daniel, and Shirin
24 June 1999
Kurume, Japan

Appendix 2

Countries and islands visited by Meherangiz Munsiff, 1952–1999

North, Central, South AMERICAS

Canada
United States
Puerto Rico
Mexico
Dominican Republic
Dominica
St. Lucia
St. Vincent
The Grenadines
Grenada
Trinidad
Tobago
Panama
Virgin Islands
St. Martin Is.
Antigua
Guadeloupe
Jamaica
St. Thomas Is.
Barbados
Aruba Is.
Curacao Is.

Bonaire
Bahamas
Virgin Is.
Martinique
St. Croix Is.
Hawaii Is.
Barbuda Is.
Haiti
Venezuela
Guyana
Surinam
French Guiana
Brazil
Paraguay
Uruguay
Peru
Argentina
Chile
Ecuador
Falkland Islands
St. Marten
Bermuda

EUROPE

Is. (Arctic)
Iceland
Norway
Sweden
Denmark
Liberia
Finland
Ireland
Rep. of Eire
Scotland
Wales
England
France
Portugal
Spain
Bornholm Is.
Netherlands
Belgium
Germany
Switzerland
Italy
Liechtenstein

Luxembourg
Austria
Malta
Cyprus
Romania
Bulgaria
Hungary
Yugoslavia
Greece
Corsica Is.
Crete Is.
Sardinia Is.
Turkey
Channel Is.
Orkney Is.
Faroe Is.
Madeira Is
Canary Is.
Azores
Balearic Is.
Czechoslovakia
[Israel]

AFRICA

Egypt
Senegal
Gambia
Sierra Leone
Ivory Coast
Ghana
Togo
Nigeria
French Cameroon
Central African Rep.
Chad

Ethiopia
Zaire
Uganda
Kenya
Tanzania
South Africa
Namibia
Madagascar
Mauritius
Reunion Is.
Benin

ASIA

Iran	South Korea
Aden	Hong Kong
Pakistan	Macau
India	Taiwan
Sri Lanka	Russia
Bangladesh	Georgia
Burma	Armenia
Thailand	Korea
Singapore	Malaysia
Japan	United Arab Emirates

AUSTRALASIA & PACIFIC REGION

Solomon Is.	Western Samoa
Tuvalu I.	Tonga
Fiji	Tahiti
New Caledonia	Cook Is.
Tuamotu Archipelago	Santo Is.
American Samoa	Marquesas Is

Note: These are the countries known to have been visited by Meherangiz. Many countries were visited more than once or twice.

Pioneer posts – Madagascar and French Cameroon (Knight of Bahá'u'lláh)

O Thou kind Lord! Sanctify my heart from all attachment, and gladden my soul with tidings of joy. Free me from attachment to friend and stranger alike, and captivate me with Thy love, that I may become wholly devoted to Thee and be filled with fervid rapture; that I may desire naught but Thee, seek no one except Thyself, tread no other path besides Thine, and commune only with Thee; that I may, even as a nightingale, be spellbound by Thy love and, by day and night, sigh and wail and weep and cry out, "Yá Bahá'u'l-Abhá!"

BIBLIOGRAPHY

Quotations from letters to Meherangiz Munsiff from Shoghi Effendi, Rúḥíyyih Khánum, the International Baháʼí Council, the Universal House of Justice and the International Teaching Centre can be found in her personal papers. The originals were received at the Baháʼí World Centre in 1976.

ʻAbdu'l-Bahá. *ʻAbdu'l-Bahá in London* (1912, 1921). London: Baháʼí Publishing Trust, 1982.
— *Foundations of World Unity*. Wilmette, IL: Baháʼí Publishing Trust, 1968.
— *Life Eternal*, Comp. Mary Rumsey Morris. New York: Roycroft, 1937.
— *Paris Talks: Addresses given by ʻAbdu'l-Bahá in 1911* (1912). London: Baháʼí Publishing Trust, 12th ed. 1995.
— *The Promulgation of Universal Peace: Talks Delivered by ʻAbdu'l-Bahá During His Visit to the United States and Canada in 1912* (1922, 1925). Comp. H. MacNutt. Wilmette, IL: Baháʼí Publishing Trust, 2nd ed. 1982.
— *Selections from the Writings of ʻAbdu'l-Bahá*. Comp. Research Department of the Universal House of Justice. Haifa: Baháʼí World Centre, 1978.
— *Tablets of ʻAbdu'l-Bahá* (etext in the Ocean search engine; originally published as *Tablets of Abdul-Baha Abbas*. 3 vols. Chicago: Baháʼí Publishing Society, 1909–1916). Wilmette, IL: National Spiritual Assembly of the Baháʼís of the United States, 1980.

The Báb. *Selections from the Writings of the Báb*. Comp. Research Department of the Universal House of Justice. Haifa: Baháʼí World Centre, 1976.

Bahá'í Canada. Periodical. Thornhill, Ontario: National Spiritual Assembly of the Bahá'ís of Canada.

Bahá'í News. Periodical. Wilmette, IL: National Spiritual Assembly of the Bahá'ís of the United States.

Bahá'í Prayers: A Selection of Prayers Revealed by Bahá'u'lláh, The Báb, and 'Abdu'l-Bahá. Wilmette, IL: Bahá'í Publishing Trust, rev. ed. 2002.

Bahai Scriptures: Selections from the Utterances of Baha'u'llah and Abdul Baha. Ed. Horace Holley. New York: Brentano's, 1923.

The Bahá'í World: An International Record. Vol. XII (1950–1954). Wilmette, IL: Bahá'í Publishing Trust.

Bahá'í World Faith: Selected Writings of Bahá'u'lláh and 'Abdu'l-Bahá. Wilmette, IL: Bahá'í Publishing Trust, rev. ed. 1956.

Bahá'u'lláh. *Epistle to the Son of the Wolf.* Trans. Shoghi Effendi. Wilmette, IL: Bahá'í Publishing Trust, rev. ed. 1976.
— *The Call of the Divine Beloved: Selected Mystical Works of Bahá'u'lláh.* Haifa: Bahá'í World Centre, 2018.
— *Gleanings from the Writings of Bahá'u'lláh.* Trans. Shoghi Effendi. Wilmette, IL: Bahá'í Publishing Trust, 2nd ed. 1976.
— *The Hidden Words of Bahá'u'lláh.* Trans. Shoghi Effendi. Wilmette, IL: Bahá'í Publishing Trust, 1970; New Delhi: Bahá'í Publishing Trust, 1987.
— *The Kitáb-i-Aqdas: The Most Holy Book.* Haifa: Bahá'í World Centre, 1992.
— *Prayers and Meditations by Bahá'u'lláh.* Trans. Shoghi Effendi. Wilmette,IL: Bahá'í Publishing Trust, 1938, 1987.
— *The Summons of the Lord of Hosts: Tablets of Bahá'u'lláh.* Haifa: Bahá'í World Centre, 2002.
— *Tablets of Bahá'u'lláh Revealed after the Kitáb-i-Aqdas.* Comp. Research Department of the Universal House of Justice. Haifa: Bahá'í World Centre, 1978.

Esslemont, J. E. *Bahá'u'lláh and the New Era.* Wilmette IL: Bahá'í Publishing Trust, 1980.

The Gift of Teaching. Comp. The Universal House of Justice. Oakham, England: Bahá'í Publishing Trust, 1977.

Grundy, Julia M. *Ten Days in the Light of 'Akká* (1907). Wilmette, IL: Bahá'í Publishing Trust, 1979.

The Importance of Obligatory Prayer and Fasting. Comp. Research Department of the Universal House of Justice. Bahá'í Publications Australia, 2000.

The Individual and Teaching. Comp. Research Department of the Universal House of Justice. Wilmette IL: Bahá'í Publishing Trust, 1977.

Lights of Guidance: A Bahá'í Reference File. Comp. H. Hornby. New Delhi: Bahá'í Publishing Trust, 5th ed. 1997.

Living the Life. Comp. UK Bahá'í Publishing Trust, 1974.

The Power of Divine Assistance. Comp. Research Department of the Universal House of Justice. The National Spiritual Assembly of Canada, 1982.

Prayer, Meditation, and the Devotional Attitude. Comp. The Universal House of Justice. National Spiritual Assembly of the Bahá'ís of Australia, 1980.

Shoghi Effendi. *The Advent of Divine Justice* (1939). Wilmette, IL: Bahá'í Publishing Trust, 1984.
— *Bahá'í Administration: Selected Messages 1922–1932.* Wilmette: Bahá'í Publishing Trust, 1980.
— *Citadel of Faith: Messages to America, 1947–1957.* Wilmette, IL: Bahá'í Publishing Trust, 1965.
— *Directives from the Guardian.* Comp. Gertrude Garrida. New Delhi: Bahá'í Publishing Trust, 1973.
— *Principles of Bahá'í Administration.* London: Bahá'í Publishing Trust, 1950.

— *Unfolding Destiny: The Messages from the Guardian of the Bahá'í Faith to the Bahá'í Community of the British Isles.* London: Bahá'í Publishing Trust, 1981.

— *The World Order of Bahá'u'lláh: Selected Letters by Shoghi Effendi* (1938). Wilmette, IL: Bahá'í Publishing Trust, 2nd rev. ed. 1974.

Star of the West: The Bahá'í Magazine. Periodical, 25 vols. 1910–1935. Vols. 1–14 RP Oxford: George Ronald, 1978. Complete CD-ROM version: Talisman Educational Software/Special Ideas, 2001.

Stirring of the Spirit. Comp. The Universal House of Justice. The National Spiritual Assembly of Canada 1990.

The Universal House of Justice. *Messages from the Universal House of Justice 1963–1986: The Third Epoch of the Formative Age.* Comp. Geoffry W. Marks. Wilmette, IL: Bahá'í Publishing Trust, 1996.

— *Messages from the Universal House of Justice 1968–1973.* Wilmette, IL: Bahá'í Publishing Trust, 1976.

— Riḍván Message to the Bahá'ís of the World. 2008, Available at: http://www.bahai.org/library/authoritative texts/the-universal-house-of-justice/messages/.

— *A Synopsis and Codification of the Kitáb-i-Aqdas.* Haifa: Bahá'í World Centre, 1973.

— *Wellspring of Guidance: Messages from the Universal House of Justice 1963–1968.* Wilmette, IL: Bahá'í Publishing Trust, 1976.

REFERENCES

Part I

1. Shoghi Effendi, *The Bahá'í World*, Vol. XIII, p. 289.
2. Bahá'u'lláh, *Gleanings from the Writings of Bahá'u'lláh*, no. CLXI.
3. Letter written on behalf of Shoghi Effendi to Meherangiz Munsiff, 10 August 1953.
4. Letter written on behalf of Shoghi Effendi to Meherangiz Munsiff, 26 March 1964.
5. Letter from the National Spiritual Assembly of the British Isles to Meherangiz Munsiff dated 2 June 1959.
6. Letter written on behalf of Shoghi Effendi to Meherangiz Munsiff, 9 December 1955.
7. Elizabeth Asbury, the United Kingdom Bahá'í Histories Project.
8. Earl Cameron, ibid.

Part II

1. Bahá'u'lláh, *Tablets of Bahá'u'lláh*, p. 161.
2. Bahá'u'lláh, *Hidden Words*, Persian, no. 40.
3. Bahá'u'lláh, *Tablets of Bahá'u'lláh*, p. 108.
4. 'Abdu'l-Bahá, cited in *'Abdu'l-Bahá in London*, p. 87.
5. Bahá'u'lláh, *Tablets of Bahá'u'lláh*, p. 265.
6. The Universal House of Justice, *Wellspring of Guidance*, p. 124.
7. Bahá'u'lláh, *Gleanings from the Writings of Bahá'u'lláh*, no. XLV.
8. Bahá'u'lláh, *Epistle to the Son of the Wolf*, pp. 58–59.
9. 'Abdu'l-Bahá, *The Promulgation of Universal Peace*, p. 186.
10. The Báb, in *Bahá'í Prayers*, p. 22.

11. Bahá'u'lláh, *Prayers and Meditations*, no. 162.
12. 'Abdu'l-Bahá, cited in *Star of the West*, Vol. VII, no. 16, p. 154.
13. Shoghi Effendi, cited in *Bahá'í News*, August 1956, no. 102, p. 2.
14. 'Abdu'l-Bahá, cited in Grundy, *Ten Days in the Light of 'Akká*, pp. 23–24.
15. 'Abdu'l-Bahá, *The Promulgation of Universal Peace*, p. 303.
16. 'Abdu'l-Bahá, *Life Eternal*, p. 86.
17. Bahá'u'lláh, *Tablets of Bahá'u'lláh*, p. 188.
18. 'Abdu'l-Bahá, cited in *Star of the West*, Vol. VII, no. 17, p. 168.
19. 'Abdu'l-Bahá, cited in *Star of the West*, Vol. XVI, no. 4, p. 487.
20. Bahá'u'lláh, *Prayers and Meditations*, no. 46.
21. 'Abdu'l-Bahá, cited in *Star of the West*, Vol. XIII, no. 5, p. 104.
22. Bahá'u'lláh, *Epistle to the Son of the Wolf*, p. 132.
23. Bahá'u'lláh, *The Call of the Divine Beloved*, p. 44.
24. Shoghi Effendi, *Directives from the Guardian*, no. 223, p. 86.
25. Shoghi Effendi, from a letter dated 15 May 1944 to an individual believer, cited in *Prayer, Meditation and the Devotional Attitude*, p. 18.
26. 'Abdu'l-Bahá, *Tablets of 'Abdu'l-Bahá*, Vol. 2, pp. 390–391.
27. ibid. Vol. 1, p. 105.
28. 'Abdu'l-Bahá, cited in *Star of the West*, Vol. VII, no. 16, p. 151.
29. 'Abdu'l-Bahá, cited in *Star of the West*, Vol. IX, no. 14, p. 161.
30. 'Abdu'l-Bahá, cited in *Star of the West*, Vol. VIII, no. 4, p. 41.
31. 'Abdu'l-Bahá, ibid.
32. 'Abdu'l-Bahá, cited in *Star of the West*, Vol. VI, no. 18, p. 303.
33. Shoghi Effendi, from a letter dated 14 October 1937 to an individual believer, cited in *Prayer, Meditation and the Devotional Attitude*, p. 16.
34. Bahá'u'lláh, *Prayers and Meditations*, no. 161.

35. Bahá'u'lláh, cited in Esslemont, *Bahá'u'lláh and the New Era*, pp. 85 and 88.
36. From a letter dated 22 August 1957 written on behalf of Shoghi Effendi to an individual believer, cited in *The Gift of Teaching*, p. 35.
37. Bahá'u'lláh, *Prayers and Meditations*, no. 161.
38. From *Messages from the Universal House of Justice 1968–1973*, pp. 105–106.
39. 'Abdu'l-Bahá, cited in *Star of the West*, Vol. VII, no. 17, p. 168.
40. 'Abdu'l-Bahá, cited in *Star of the West*, Vol. XV, no. 8, p. 229.
41. Bahá'u'lláh, cited in Shoghi Effendi, *The Advent of Divine Justice*, p. 68.
42. Bahá'u'lláh, cited in Shoghi Effendi, *The World Order of Bahá'u'lláh*, p. 106.
43. Bahá'u'lláh, *Tablets of Bahá'u'lláh*, p. 156.
44. Bahá'u'lláh, cited in Shoghi Effendi, *The Advent of Divine Justice*, p. 64.
45. Bahá'u'lláh, cited ibid. pp. 67–68.
46. 'Abdu'l-Bahá, *Selections from the Writings of 'Abdu'l-Bahá*, no. 111, pp. 136–137.
47. Bahá'u'lláh, *Hidden Words*, Arabic, no. 5.
48. Shoghi Effendi, *Principles of Bahá'í Administration*, p. 90.
49. From a letter dated 12 July 1952 written on behalf of Shoghi Effendi to an individual believer, cited in *Living the Life*, p. 34.
50. 'Abdu'l-Bahá, *Tablets of 'Abdu'l-Bahá*, Vol. 1, p. 208.
51. 'Abdu'l-Bahá, cited in *Star of the West*, Vol. VIII, no. 4, p. 47.
52. 'Abdu'l-Bahá, ibid.
53. 'Abdu'l-Bahá, *Selections from the Writings of 'Abdu'l-Bahá*, no. 58, p. 94.
54. The Universal House of Justice, Riḍván Message 2008.
55. 'Abdu'l-Bahá, cited in *The Bahá'í World*, Vol. XII, p. 895.
56. The Universal House of Justice, *Synopsis and Codification of the Kitáb-i-Aqdas*, p. 36.
57. Bahá'u'lláh, *The Kitáb-i-Aqdas*, "Questions and Answers", no. 93, p. 134.

58. Bahá'u'lláh, cited in *The Importance of Obligatory Prayer and Fasting*, no. X, p. 5.

59. Bahá'u'lláh, *The Kitáb-i-Aqdas*, para. 76, p. 47.

60. Shoghi Effendi, from a letter dated 4 January 1936 to an individual believer, cited in *Prayer, Meditation and the Devotional Attitude*, p. 15.

61. Shoghi Effendi, from a letter dated 23 February 1939 to an individual believer, cited in *Prayer, Meditation and the Devotional Attitude*, p. 17.

62. Shoghi Effendi, from a letter dated 24 June, 1939 to an individual believer, cited in *Prayer, Meditation and the Devotional Attitude*, pp. 19–20.

63. From *Messages from the Universal House of Justice 1963–1986*, p. 589.

64. 'Abdu'l-Bahá, *Tablets of 'Abdu'l-Bahá*, p. 622.

65. From a letter dated 1 April 1982 written on behalf of the Universal House of Justice to an individual believer, cited in *Lights of Guidance*, no. 1536.

66. 'Abdu'l-Bahá, *Tablets of 'Abdu'l-Bahá*, Vol. 1, p. 85; also cited in *Prayer, Meditation and the Devotional Attitude*, p. 10.

67. 'Abdu'l-Bahá, cited in *Prayer, Meditation and the Devotional Attitude*, p. 12.

68. From Esslemont, *Bahá'u'lláh and the New Era*, pp. 85–86.

69. 'Abdu'l-Bahá, in *Bahá'í Prayers*, pp. 332–333.

70. Bahá'u'lláh, in *Bahá'í Prayers*, p. 310.

71. Bahá'u'lláh, ibid. p. 307.

72. Bahá'u'lláh, ibid. p. 309.

73. Bahá'u'lláh, ibid. p. 310.

74. Bahá'u'lláh, ibid.

75. Bahá'u'lláh, ibid. p. 318.

76. From a letter dated 6 March 1937 written on behalf of Shoghi Effendi to an individual believer, cited in *Lights of Guidance*, no. 1517.

77. The Universal House of Justice, from a letter dated 24 November 1971 to the National Spiritual Assembly of Upper West Africa.

78. 'Abdu'l-Bahá, *Selections from the Writings of 'Abdu'l-Bahá*, no. 59, p. 95.

79. 'Abdu'l-Bahá, *Selections from the Writings of 'Abdu'l-Bahá*, no. 46, p. 89.
80. From *Messages from the Universal House of Justice 1963–1986*, p. 722.
81. 'Abdu'l-Bahá, *Bahá'í Prayers*, p. 61.
82. 'Abdu'l-Bahá, *Tablets of 'Abdu'l-Bahá*, Vol 1, p. 85; also cited in *Prayer, Meditation and the Devotional Attitude*, pp. 9–10.
83. 'Abdu'l-Bahá, *Selections from the Writings of 'Abdu'l-Bahá*, no. 139, pp. 161–162.
84. The Báb, *Selections from the Writings of the Báb*, p. 94.
85. Bahá'u'lláh, *Tablets of Bahá'u'lláh*, p. 24.
86. Bahá'u'lláh, *The Kitáb-i-Aqdas*, para. 149, p. 73.
87. ibid. pp. 73–74.
88. Bahá'u'lláh, *Gleanings from the Writings of Bahá'u'lláh*, no. CXXXVI.
89. From a letter dated 6 October 1954 written on behalf of Shoghi Effendi to an individual believer, cited in *Living the Life*, pp. 35–36.
90. 'Abdu'l-Bahá, *Selections from the Writings of 'Abdu'l-Bahá*, no. 12, p. 27.
91. 'Abdu'l-Bahá, ibid.
92. 'Abdu'l-Bahá, *Foundations of World Unity*, p. 63.
93. From a letter dated 27 January 1952 written on behalf of Shoghi Effendi to an individual believer, cited in *Prayer, Meditation and the Devotional Attitude*, p. 20.
94. 'Abdu'l-Bahá, *Tablets of 'Abdu'l-Bahá*, Vol. 3, p. 631.
95. 'Abdu'l-Bahá, in *Bahá'í World Faith*, p. 393.
96. 'Abdu'l-Bahá, *Paris Talks*, pp. 96–97.
97. ibid. pp. 174–176.
98. 'Abdu'l-Bahá, cited in *Star of the West*, Vol. VII, no. 11, pp. 107–108.
99. 'Abdu'l-Bahá, *Tablets of 'Abdu'l-Bahá*, Vol. 1, p. 195.
100. ibid. Vol. 2, p. 300.
101. From a letter dated 27 January 1952 written on behalf of Shoghi Effendi to an individual believer, cited in *Prayer, Meditation and the Devotional Attitude*, p. 20.
102. 'Abdu'l-Bahá, *Tablets of 'Abdu'l-Bahá*, Vol 3, p. 706.
103. Shoghi Effendi, from a letter dated 25 January 1943 to an

individual believer, cited in *Prayer, Meditation and the Devotional Attitude*, p. 17.

104. From a letter dated 9 July 1956 written on behalf of Shoghi Effendi to the National Spiritual Assembly of the United States, cited in *The Individual and Teaching*, p. 37.

105. 'Abdu'l-Bahá, cited in *Star of the West*, Vol. VII, no. 10, p. 99.

106. 'Abdu'l-Bahá, *Tablets of 'Abdu'l-Bahá,* Vol. 3, p. 607.

107. The National Spiritual Assembly of Canada to all Local Spiritual Assemblies, 20 August 1973.

108. Shoghi Effendi, cited in a letter dated 6 February 1975 from the Universal House of Justice to an individual believer, in *Lights of Guidance* no. 1503.

109. *Canadian Bahá'í News*, October 1959, no. 117:3.

110. 'Abdu'l-Bahá, cited in *Lights of Guidance*, no. 892.

111. Bahá'u'lláh, *Tablets of Bahá'u'lláh*, pp. 200–201.

112. 'Abdu'l-Bahá, *Tablets of 'Abdu'l-Bahá*, Vol. 3, p. 729.

113. Shoghi Effendi, from a letter dated 22 September 1936, cited in *The Power of Divine Assistance*, p. 230.

114. Bahá'u'lláh, *Tablets of Bahá'u'lláh*, pp. 49–50.

115. 'Abdu'l-Bahá, *Selections from the Writings of 'Abdu'l-Bahá*, no. 39, p. 81.

116. Shoghi Effendi, from a letter dated 22 November 1941 to an individual believer, cited in *Prayer, Meditation and the Devotional Attitude*, p. 17.

117. Bahá'u'lláh, *Tablets of Bahá'u'lláh*, p. 138.

118. Shoghi Effendi, from a letter dated 27 January 1945 to an individual believer, cited in *Unfolding Destiny*, p. 442.

119. Shoghi Effendi, *Bahá'í Administration*, p. 66.

120. 'Abdu'l-Bahá, cited in *Star of the West*, Vol. XIII, no. 6, p. 152.

121. Bahá'u'lláh, *Hidden Words*, Persian, no. 8.

122. The Báb, *Selections from the Writings of the Báb*, p. 123.

123. 'Abdu'l-Bahá, cited in Grundy, *Ten Days in the Light of 'Akká*, p. 59.

124. 'Abdu'l-Bahá, cited in *Star of the West*, Vol. IV, no. 18, p. 299.

125. Esslemont, *Bahá'u'lláh and the New Era*, pp. 82–83.

126. 'Abdu'l-Bahá, cited in *Star of the West*, Vol. VII, no. 12, p. 116.

127. Bahá'u'lláh, *Hidden Words*, Persian, no. 21.
128. 'Abdu'l-Bahá, *Tablets of 'Abdu'l-Bahá*, Vol. 1, p. 68.
129. Bahá'u'lláh, *Hidden Words*, Arabic, ibid. no. 3.
130. ibid. no. 6.
131. ibid. no. 7.
132. 'Abdu'l-Bahá, *Selections from the Writings of 'Abdu'l-Bahá*, no. 174, p. 202.
133. 'Abdu'l-Bahá, cited in *Bahá'í Scriptures*, no. 953, p. 494.
134. Bahá'u'lláh, *Gleanings from the Writings of Bahá'u'lláh*, no. V.
135. Shoghi Effendi, *Principles of Bahá'í Administration*, pp. 44–45.
136. 'Abdu'l-Bahá, *Selections from the Writings of 'Abdu'l-Bahá*, no. 217, p. 270.
137. 'Abdu'l-Bahá, *The Promulgation of Universal Peace*, p. 236.
138. Esslemont, *Bahá'u'lláh and the New Era*, p. 87.
139. Bahá'u'lláh, *The Summons of the Lord of Hosts*, p. 53.
140. Bahá'u'lláh, *Hidden Words*, Arabic, no. 7.
141. 'Abdu'l-Bahá, cited in *Star of the West*, Vol. IX, no. 11, p. 123.
142. Shoghi Effendi, *The World Order of Bahá'u'lláh*, p. 123.
143. 'Abdu'l-Bahá, cited in *Star of the West*, Vol. VIII, no. 4, p. 48.
144. 'Abdu'l-Bahá, cited in *Star of the West*, Vol. VII, no. 13, p. 122.
145. 'Abdu'l-Bahá, cited in *Star of the West*, Vol. VII, no. 10, p. 99.
146. 'Abdu'l-Bahá, cited in *Star of the West*, Vol. VII, no. 2, p. 15.
147. Bahá'u'lláh, *Gleanings from the Writings of Bahá'u'lláh*, no. XLVI.
148. 'Abdu'l-Bahá, *Selections from the Writings of 'Abdu'l-Bahá*, no. 36, p. 76.
149. 'Abdu'l-Bahá, *Paris Talks*, p. 83.
150. ibid. p. 108.
151. Bahá'u'lláh, *Gleanings from the Writings of Bahá'u'lláh*, no. X.
152. 'Abdu'l-Bahá, cited in *Star of the West*, Vol. VII, no. 10, p. 98.

153. Bahá'u'lláh, *Hidden Words*, Arabic, no. 2.
154. Bahá'u'lláh, *Tablets of Bahá'u'lláh*, p. 27.
155. ibid. p. 67.
156. 'Abdu'l-Bahá, *Selections from the Writings of 'Abdu'l-Bahá*, no. 82, p. 116.
157. Bahá'u'lláh, *Epistle to the Son of the Wolf*, p. 46.
158. 'Abdu'l-Bahá, cited in *Star of the West*, Vol. XIII, no. 5, p. 102.
159. ibid. p. 103.
160. 'Abdu'l-Bahá, cited in *Star of the West*, Vol. XIII, no. 6, p. 153.
161. Bahá'u'lláh, *Tablets of Bahá'u'lláh*, p. 176.
162. 'Abdu'l-Bahá, *Selections from the Writings of 'Abdu'l-Bahá*, no. 129, pp. 146–150.
163. Bahá'u'lláh, *Epistle to the Son of the Wolf*, p. 50.
164. Bahá'u'lláh, *Tablets of Bahá'u'lláh*, p. 88.
165. ibid. p. 108.
166. ibid. pp. 188–189.
167. From a letter dated 16 March 1949 written on behalf of Shoghi Effendi to an individual believer, cited in *Living the Life*, p. 29.
168. *Messages from the Universal House of Justice 1968–1973*, p. 107.
169. 'Abdu'l-Bahá, *Selections from the Writings of 'Abdu'l-Bahá*, no. 139, p. 161.
170. Bahá'u'lláh, *Gleanings from the Writings of Bahá'u'lláh*, no. LII.
171. ibid.
172. From a letter dated 6 October 1954 written on behalf of Shoghi Effendi to an individual believer, cited in *Living the Life*, pp. 35–36.
173. 'Abdu'l-Bahá, cited in *Star of the West*, Vol. VII, no. 10, pp. 98–99.
174. Bahá'u'lláh, *Gleanings from the Writings of Bahá'u'lláh*, no. CXXV.
175. Bahá'u'lláh, *Hidden Words*, Arabic, no. 26.
176. 'Abdu'l-Bahá, cited in *Star of the West*, Vol. VI, no. 6, p. 44.
177. 'Abdu'l-Bahá, cited in *Star of the West*, Vol. VII, no. 18, p. 185.

178. Bahá'u'lláh, *Hidden Words*, Persian, no. 6.
179. 'Abdu'l-Bahá, cited in *Star of the West*, Vol. VII, no. 15, p. 133.
180. 'Abdu'l-Bahá, cited in *Star of the West*, Vol. VII, no. 2, p. 15.
181. Bahá'u'lláh, *Hidden Words*, Persian, no. 82.
182. 'Abdu'l-Bahá, *Tablets of 'Abdu'l-Bahá*, Vol. 2, p. 244.
183. Bahá'u'lláh, *Epistle to the Son of the Wolf*, p. 23.
184. Bahá'u'lláh, *Hidden Words,* Arabic, no. 5.
185. From a letter dated 30 September 1951 written on behalf of Shoghi Effendi to an individual believer, cited in *Prayer, Meditation and the Devotional Attitude*, p. 20.
186. From a letter dated 6 November 1949 written on behalf of Shoghi Effendi to an individual believer, cited in *The Individual and Teaching*, no. 75, p. 29.
187. 'Abdu'l-Bahá, *Tablets of Abdu'l-Bahá*, VI, p. 186.
188. Shoghi Effendi, from a letter dated 19 July 1956 to the National Spiritual Assembly of the United States, cited in *Citadel of Faith*, p. 148.
189. 'Abdu'l-Bahá, cited in *Star of the West*, Vol. V, no. 1, p. 6.
190. Shoghi Effendi, *Directives from the Guardian,* no. 190, p. 72.
191. Bahá'u'lláh, *Hidden Words*, Persian, no. 76.
192. Bahá'u'lláh, *The Kitáb-i-Aqdas*, paras. 10, 16, 17, pp. 22–25.
193. 'Abdu'l-Bahá, cited in *Star of the West*, Vol. IV, no. 18, p. 305.
194. 'Abdu'l-Bahá, cited in *Star of the West*, Vol VI, no. 18, p. 303.
195. The Universal House of Justice, *Synopsis and Codification of the Kitáb-i-Aqdas,* pp. 38–39.
196. Bahá'u'lláh, *Prayers and Meditations*, no. 85.
197. ibid.
198. ibid.
199. ibid. no. 56.
200. ibid. no. 85.
201. 'Abdu'l-Bahá, *Bahá'í Prayers*, pp. 84–85.
202. 'Abdu'l-Bahá, *Selections from the Writings of 'Abdu'l-Bahá*, no. 39, p. 81.

203. ibid. no. 48, p. 90.
204. ibid. no. 51, p. 91.
205. The Universal House of Justice, from a letter dated 27 August 1989 to the Followers of Bahá'u'lláh, cited in *Stirring of the Spirit*, pp. 3–4.
206. 'Abdu'l-Bahá, cited in *Star of the West*, Vol. XIII, no. 7, p. 186.

CPSIA information can be obtained
at www.ICGtesting.com
Printed in the USA
BVHW090801171122
652109BV00006B/347

9 780853 986584